Claiming Citizenship:
Rights, Participation and Accountability

Series Editor: John Gaventa

Around the world, a growing crisis of legitimacy characterizes the relationship between citizens and the institutions that affect their lives. In both North and South, citizens speak of mounting disillusionment with government, based on concerns about corruption, lack of responsiveness to the needs of the poor and the absence of a sense of connection with elected representatives and bureaucrats. Conventional forms of expertise and representation are being questioned. The rights and responsibilities of corporations and other global actors are being challenged, as global inequalities persist and deepen.

In response, this series argues, increased attention must be paid to re-examining contemporary understandings of rights and citizenship in different contexts, and their implications for related issues of participation and accountability. Challenging liberal understandings in which citizenship is understood as a set of rights and responsibilities bestowed by the state, the series looks at how citizenship is claimed and rights are realized through the agency and actions of people themselves.

Growing out of the work of an international network of researchers and practitioners from both South and North, the volumes in this series explore a variety of themes, including locally rooted struggles for more inclusive forms of citizenship, the links between citizenship, science and globalization, the politics and dynamics of participation in new democratic arenas, and the relationships between claiming rights and ensuring accountability. Drawing from concrete case studies which focus on how people understand their citizenship and claim their rights, the volumes contribute new, empirically grounded perspectives to current debates related to deepening democracy, realizing rights-based development, and making institutions more responsive to the needs and voices of poor people.

About the Editors

Andrea Cornwall is a fellow of the Institute of Development Studies at the University of Sussex. Her research interests include the ethnography of democracy and the politics of citizen engagement in governance. She is author of *Beneficiary, Consumer, Citizen: Perspectives on Participation for Poverty Reduction* (Sida Studies, 2000), co-editor of *Realizing Rights: Transforming Approaches to Sexual and Reproductive Wellbeing* (with Alice Welbourn, Zed Books, 2002) and *Pathways to Participation* (with Garett Pratt, IT Publications, 2003).

Vera Schattan P. Coelho is a political scientist. She is a researcher and project coordinator at the Brazilian Center of Analysis and Planning (CEBRAP) in São Paulo, Brazil. Her interests centre on new forms of citizen participation, deliberation, and consultation to improve social policies and democracy. She is the author of numerous articles on health policy, pension reform and participatory governance and is editor of *Pension Reform in Latin America* (FGV, 2003) and *Participation and Deliberation in Contemporary Brazil* (with Marcos Nobre, 34 Letras, 2004).

Spaces for Change?

The Politics of Citizen Participation in New Democratic Arenas

Edited by Andrea Cornwall
& Vera Schattan P. Coelho

VOLUME 4 OF CLAIMING CITIZENSHIP
SERIES EDITOR JOHN GAVENTA

ZED BOOKS
London & New York

Spaces for Change was published in 2007 by Zed Books Ltd, 7 Cynthia Street, London N1 9JF, UK, and Room 400, 175 Fifth Avenue, New York, NY 10010, USA

www.zedbooks.co.uk

Editorial copyright © Andrea Cornwall and Vera Schattan P. Coelho 2007
Individual chapters © individual contributors 2007

Designed and typeset in Monotype Bembo
by illuminati, Grosmont, www.illuminatibooks.co.uk
Cover designed by Andrew Corbett
Printed and bound in Malta by Gutenberg Press Ltd

Distributed in the USA exclusively by Palgrave Macmillan, a division of St Martin's Press, LLC, 175 Fifth Avenue, New York, NY 10010

A catalogue record for this book is available from the British Library
Library of Congress Cataloging-in-Publication Data available
Library and Archives Canada Cataloguing in Publication Data available

ISBN 1 84277 552 9 Hb
ISBN 1 84277 553 7 Pb
ISBN 978 1 84277 552 3 Hb
ISBN 978 1 84277 553 0 Pb

Contents

Acknowledgements

This book represents the outcome of a process of collaboration developed over the course of the last five years, under the auspices of the DFID-funded Development Research Centre on Citizenship, Participation and Accountability. We owe a huge debt to John Gaventa, DRC Director, for being such a source of inspiration and moral and intellectual support. We're grateful to fellow members of the DRC 'Spaces for Change' working group, Carlos Cortez, Peter Houtzager, Adrián Lavalle, Bettina von Lieres, Simeen Mahmud, Ranjita Mohanty, Alex Shankland and John Williams, for all the stimulating discussions and exchanges that shaped our collective thinking, and to Marian Barnes and David Kahane, who joined the group as discussants and remained with us as contributors to this volume. We owe special thanks to David Kahane, who reviewed the entire book and made major editorial contributions to a number of papers in it. Kirsty Milward not only lent us her expertise as a copy-editor, but also managed the process of getting the manuscript together from India. Joanna Wheeler and the DRC Coordination Team played a vital behind-the-scenes role in providing support for the group. Lastly, we'd like to thank our funders, the British government's Department of International Development (DFID), for making the research on which this book is based and its publication possible.

Andrea Cornwall
Vera Schattan P. Coelho

List of Acronyms

ACA	Association of Water Committees (Angola)
ARV	Anti-Retroviral
CBO	Community Based Organization
CG	Community Group
CM	Comissões de Moradores (residents' committees, Angola)
COSATU	Congress of South African Trade Unions
CPA	Communal Property Association (South Africa)
CPRN	Canadian Policy Research Network
CSO	Civil Society Organization
CTA	Central de Trabajadores Argentinos (Argentinean Workers' Central)
DFID	Department for International Development (UK)
EPAL	Provincial Water Company (Angola)
FAS	Fundo de Apoio Social (social fund, Angola)
FNLA	Frente Nacional para a Libertação de Angola (Liberation movement, Angola)
HC	Health Committee
HFB	Health Facilities Board (South Africa)
HLC	Healthy Living Centre (UK)
HPSP	Health and Population Sector Programme (Bangladesh)
HS	Health Secretariat
HWC	Health Watch Committee (Bangladesh)
IBGE	Brazilian Institute of Geography and Statistics
ICDS	Integrated Child Development Scheme (India)

KKDF	Kilamba Kiaxi Development Forum (Angola)
LHC	Local Health Council
LPM	Landless People's Movement (South Africa)
LUPP	Luanda Urban Poverty Programme
MHC	Municipal Health Council
MoHFW	Ministry of Health and Family Welfare (Bangladesh)
MPLA	Movimento Popular de Libertação de Angola (ruling party in Angola, former liberation movement)
MSF	Médecins Sans Frontières
NAHO	National Aboriginal Health Organization (Canada)
NHS	National Health Service (UK)
NK	Nijera Kori (Bangladesh)
NLC	National Land Committee (South Africa)
ODA	Organizações para o Desenvolvimento das Áreas (Area-Based Development Organizations, Angola)
PB	Participatory Budgeting
PCG	Primary Care Group
PHM	Popular Health Movement (Brazil)
PMTCT	Prevention of Mother-to-Child Transmission
PT	Workers' Party (Brazil)
RDI	Rural Development Initiative (South Africa)
RDSN	Rural Development Services Network (South Africa)
SACP	South African Communist Party
SAMWU	South African Municipal Services Workers' Union
SC	Scheduled Caste (India)
SCUK	Save the Children UK
SRB	Single Regeneration Budget (UK)
ST	Scheduled Tribe (India)
SUS	Unified Health System (Brazil)
TAC	Treatment Action Campaign (South Africa)
TLP	Treatment Literacy Practitioners
TU	Transformation Unit (South Africa)
UDF	United Democratic Front (South Africa)
UNITA	União Nacional para a Independencia Total de Angola (opposition party in Angola, former guerrilla movement)
UP	Union Parishad (Bangladesh)

Foreword

John Gaventa

Around the world, the forms and meanings of democratic participation are under contestation. In Iraq, Fallujah is bombed in the name of making the country ready for democracy; in Indonesia, Ukraine and the United States, voters and observers are gripped in debates and protests about electoral democracy; in Cancún and other global fora, streets are occupied by those demanding more democracy in global processes; in small villages and neighbourhoods, grassroots groups are claiming their places in local democratic spaces. Democracy is at once the language of military power, neoliberal market forces, political parties, social movements, donor agencies and NGOs. What is going on?

In the midst of such contestation and debate, this book provides rich and compelling empirical case studies of the dynamics of democratic participation, especially in relation to 'new democratic arenas' at the local level. In so doing, the book adds significantly to a rapidly emerging literature on the challenge of 'deepening democracy' – that is, the contemporary project of developing and sustaining more substantive and empowered citizen participation in the political process than what is normally found in liberal representative democracy alone. While much has been written – both normatively and conceptually – about these more participatory, inclusive and deliberative forms of democracy, this book is one of the first to examine what these ideas mean in practice, especially across such a diverse range of case studies, which span experiences from five continents. Building on a long literature on citizen participation and democracy, these cases provide fresh insights into a number of next-generation questions, asking not only how and whether ordinary citizens should engage directly in the governance of public affairs but also what the dynamics and outcomes are when they do.

Across much of the vast literature on democracy, we are confronted with a paradox. On the one hand, there is the somewhat triumphalist view that democracy has spread as never before.[1] By the year 2000, we are told, there were ostensibly 120 electoral democracies in place (out of 192 existing countries), of which some 85 were thought to be 'full' democracies, in the sense that they provided respect for the rule of law, civil and political rights, leading the US-based Freedom House observers to declare the last century the 'democratic century'.

On the other hand, despite the acknowledged spread of democratic institutions and practices, others warn that the quality of democracy is in crisis, faced by a series of democratic deficits which are calling its vitality and very meaning into question. In the Northern more 'mature' democracies, for instance, a large literature discusses declining patterns of political participation, the 'hollowing out' of politics and the growing power of special interests. There is a concern with the dangers of 'diminishing democracy', and conversely with a search for ways in which it can be revitalized – often through new forms of citizen engagement.[3]

Similar concerns emerge in the literature on 'emerging democracies', often countries which have shaken off years of autocratic rule and are now struggling to make democratic institutions work and to provide new opportunities for citizen engagement. Here the concerns are less ones of democratic decline than of whether the forms of democracy inherited from – and often imposed by – the more established democracies are appropriate to differing historic conditions, and whether democracy itself will deliver on solving problems of extreme poverty, growing inequality and social justice. In Latin America, for instance, while the institutions of democracy have taken hold in every country but Cuba, a report in 2004 by UNDP found increasing frustration with how these democracies were functioning. Indeed, scarcely 53 per cent of the population reported that they supported democracy, and only 28 per cent were satisfied with its performance.[4] In Africa, others write of the creation of what might be called 'exclusionary' democracies, in which the institutions and trappings of democratic process are created, but in a situation in which they cannot respond to the needs of the majority in any meaningful way because larger decisions are made by powerful, external actors.[5]

For the triumphalists, democracy-building is about spreading a largely standardized recipe of institutional designs around the world – one that focuses on universal elections, rule of law, and protection of a minimum level of civil and political rights. For those concerned with its deficits, democracy is not only about spread, it is also about deepening its quality and meanings in ways appropriate to the settings in which it is found. Indeed, both perspectives may be important: while the institutional forms and procedures of democracy increasingly are found in many places, the critical challenge is how to deepen their inclusiveness and substance, especially in terms of how citizens engage within new democratic spaces, and how such participation delivers on meeting basic developmental and social needs.

In response to the perceived crisis of democracy, we see a number of competing approaches to reform, each of which has substantially differing views about the role of citizens in the governance of their own affairs. A neoliberal market approach argues for the continued weakening of the state through a combination of decentralization and privatization. In such a formulation, citizens are often reduced to consumers, who express preferences through market choices, and perhaps through co-provisioning of services at the local level, but who exercise little real democratic power over state policies. A second dominant view grows out of the liberal representative model, which puts a great deal of stress on getting the institutions and procedures of democracy right, especially as measured through competitive, multiparty electoral processes. In this view, the role of citizens is somewhat passive. Citizens participate through elections, and enjoy certain rights, but these are primarily the individual rights of freedom from interference by states in matters of private property, expression and political association.

The liberal representative view is extended by a third view, which grows out of long traditions of participatory democracy and which is increasingly referred to as the 'deepening democracy' approach. In this view, democracy is not only a set of rules, procedures and institutional design, and participation cannot be reduced to engagement in electoral processes. Rather it is a process through which citizens exercise ever-deepening control over decisions which affect their lives through a number of forms and in a variety of arenas. In some formulations, especially those emerging from Latin America, this view also is about the extension of rights. Full democratic citizenship is attained not only through the exercise of political and civic rights, but also through social rights, which in turn may be gained through participatory processes, and it is also about the 'right to create rights' through struggles and demands from below.[6] As such, the meanings and forms of democracy are constantly under construction.

In this view, then, the way to deal with the crisis of democracy, or the democratic deficit, is to extend democracy itself – that is, to go beyond traditional understandings of representative democracy, through creating and supporting more participatory mechanisms of citizen engagement, which in turn are built upon, and support, more robust views of the rights and responsibilities of citizenship. A consequence of this view is the creation of many new democratic spaces or opportunities for participation – some based on the extension of rights to participate, others based on invitations for consultation. It is the dynamics of these new democratic arenas – and whether they can fulfil their potential for democratic revitalization and development – which this book on *Spaces for Change?* explores and interrogates.

Even among those theorists and practitioners who support the deepening democracy project, there are competing views of how best more substantive and participatory forms of democracy are to be achieved, especially in a way that improves the lives of people living in the face of poverty, relative powerlessness and inequality.

One approach – widely promoted by donors in the development field through their democracy-building programmes – has been to argue that the biases towards elitism or a lack of public accountability found in traditional institutional design approaches can be offset by investing in a vibrant civil society, as well as in political institutions and electoral politics. Based on long-standing ideas of the importance of 'associationalism' in democracy, a robust civil society can serve as an additional check and balance on government behaviour, through mobilizing claims, advocating for special interests, playing a watchdog role, and generally exercising countervailing power against the state. The case studies in this book, however, raise fundamental challenges for this approach, questioning the assumption that is often made about the inherently democratizing potential of civil society, and also questioning whether civil and political societies can be so clearly separated one from another in everyday practice.

While the civil society approach focuses on building civil society's role as an autonomous, countervailing power against the state, other views focus on deepening democratic engagement through the participation of citizens in the processes of governance with the state, through what has come to be referred to as 'co-governance', participatory governance, or even 'empowered participatory governance' approaches.[7] In practice, participatory forms of governance seek to supplement the roles of citizens as voters or as watchdogs through more direct forms of involvement. These may be seen at many levels – ranging from new forms of citizen engagement in national policymaking to new constitutional or legal mandates for citizen participation in local governance, often associated with the wave of democratic decentralization that occurred during the 1990s in many developing countries, including India, Bangladesh, South Africa and Brazil, as illustrated in this volume.

While the co-governance approach emphasizes the importance of inclusion through participation in democratic processes, a related strand of democratic participation focuses more on the nature and quality of deliberation that occurs when citizens do come together for discussion and debates in public spaces. Such a view builds upon the philosophical work of Habermas, as well other theorists such as Cohen and Dryzek, and argues for 'a more deliberative democracy in which citizens address public problems by reasoning together about how best to solve them.... The ambitious aim of deliberative democracy, in short, is to shift from bargaining, interest aggregation, and power to the common reason of equal citizens as a dominant force in democratic life'[8] The focus here is often more on the 'quality of public talk', less on 'who' participates in the process of public engagement.[9] Like approaches to participatory governance, concepts of deliberative democracy have spawned a huge and interesting array of innovations in practice, such as deliberative polling, large-scale deliberative meetings, or citizens' juries – many of which seek to gain participation through some form of representative sampling of citizens, who then deliberate together to propose new – and arguably more reasoned – solutions to public issues. Again, we see examples in this volume, such as the case study of a large-scale deliberation on health policy in Canada, or in other more local spaces, such as the health councils in Brazil or participatory budget practices in Argentina.

This volume on *Spaces for Change?* goes beyond previous work in several important ways. First, it extends the study of democratic innovation from the somewhat celebrated examples of Porto Alegre, Brazil, or Kerala, India, to a host of other lesser-known, and perhaps more ordinary, settings drawn from a broader variety of political, social and cultural contexts. Second, the book adds to the institutional perspective a more bottom-up approach and multidisciplinary lens to how institutions intersect with everyday practices and cultures of participation.

Looking across these case studies from Angola, Argentina, Bangladesh, Brazil, India, South Africa, Britain and Canada, the book argues that the impulses and innovations for more 'participatory', 'deliberative' and 'empowered' approaches to democracy have contributed to a fundamental change in the relation of civil society and the state, creating in many settings a new 'participatory sphere' that is becoming a crucible for 'a new politics of public policy'. Such a participatory sphere has great *potential* for revitalizing democracy, creating new forms of citizenship and contributing to tangible developmental outcomes.

Yet, the book reminds us, we cannot assume that the institutional design of 'new democratic spaces' will in fact mean that these will automatically become 'spaces for change', especially in ways that normative democratic theory often assumes. Through these empirically rich case studies about how institutional forms actually work, the book reminds us time and again that reforms that are designed as potential 'spaces for change' may interact with different histories, cultures and forms of power to produce radically different outcomes across various settings. By insisting on an interdisciplinary, bottom-up approach to the study of actual democratic practice, the cases illustrate time and again how the micropolitics of engagement can subvert the best intentions of institutional design.

By thus critically studying and engaging with what actually happens within these new democratic spaces, the book also begins to raise a number of next-generation questions about the politics of participatory and deliberative governance: what forms of representation exist even within participatory processes? How do the norms of deliberation translate across different political cultures and settings? How do participatory processes overlay and interact with existing political structures? What are the tangible outcomes – both in democracy-building and developmental terms – of engagement in this new participatory sphere, and how can they be seen in everyday life?

In so doing, the essays in this book also raise many important challenges to scholars and practitioners of democracy alike, illustrating the lesson that – just as in other formations of democracy – the rapid spread of new democratic forms should not be confused with the quality and nature of their performance. In few of the examples studied do new democratic arenas translate easily to either the democracy-deepening or developmental gains for which proponents of participation might hope.

Yet, at the same time, the contributors to this volume do not give up on the *potential* of the participatory sphere. As we must remember, many of these innovations are still in their early days, and their success must be measured over decades, not in a few short years, just as previous extensions of democratic practice in both North and South have taken long periods, often involving contestation and struggle, to take hold. Moreover, the cases give us clues to how the potential of these spaces can be realized. Indeed, when well-crafted institutional spaces for participation come together with champions for change on the inside, and well-organized, mobilized social groups on the outside, positive changes for previously excluded groups may be seen. Where such enabling conditions do not exist, new opportunities for participation can become 'schools for citizenship', create new, unexpected forms of action, and plant seeds for further change in the future.

Reflective perhaps of the themes it has studied, this book has also come out of a process of deliberation and engagement. The researchers whose work is found here have on the whole been associated with the Development Research Centre on Citizenship, Participation and Accountability, an international research network hosted at the Institute of Development Studies, University of Sussex. Contributors to this volume have been associated with one of the working groups of this network, which over several years began to interrogate the ways in which 'new democratic spaces' were unfolding in their own countries. Meeting regularly in various locations, the group used an iterative approach through which it developed initial questions, began the process of study, came together to critique and debate each others' work, refined and sharpened questions and approaches, re-engaged in study and then came together towards the end for further synthesis and discussion. The working group was highly diverse – with participants from eight countries, some from universities, some from NGOs, and spanning a range of disciplines, including anthropology, sociology, demography, urban planning, geography and philosophy. The participatory, deliberative process, as well as the diversity across culture, setting and discipline, made for rich discussions and debates and also brought insights from case material not often found in more narrowly constructed, single-discipline comparative projects.

This volume represents the fourth in the Zed Books series on *Claiming Citizenship*. Earlier volumes, listed at the front of the book, have focused on the meanings of rights and citizenship, the links between science and citizenship and how citizens claim rights and accountability, especially around natural resources. Drawing from concrete case studies – often in examples and cases previously undocumented for international audiences – these volumes contribute fresh insights from South and North to current debates on the meanings and practices of democracy, on struggles for more inclusive and substantive citizenship, and on creating more responsive forms of governance that will contribute to greater social equity and social justice.

It has been my privilege, as series editor, to accompany and participate in this process. My thanks to the co-editors, Andrea Cornwall and Vera Schattan P. Coelho, who have worked together across the distance that separates Brazil and the UK, anthropology and political science, South and North, and have insisted throughout the process that others in the group reach across similar boundaries. Thanks also to the working group participants, who always engaged one another critically, but with respect, and who in so doing created the kind of inclusive and deliberative space which we often seek, yet which, the case studies confirm, is rare to find.

John Gaventa, Director, Development Research Centre
on Citizenship, Participation and Accountability,
Institute of Development Studies, May 2006

Notes

1. This foreword draws on my longer paper, 'Triumph, deficit or contestation? Deepening the "deepening democracy" debate', IDS Working Paper No. 264.

2. Freedom House, *Democracy's Century: A Survey of Global Political Change in the 20th Century*, Washington DC: Freedom House, 1999.

3. See, for instance, Theda Skocpol, *Diminished Democracy: From Membership to Management in American Civic Life*, Norman: University of Oklahoma Press, 2003.

4. UNDP, *Ideas and Contributions: Democracy in Latin America – Towards a Citizens' Democracy*, Report, New York: United Nations Development Programme, 2004, Appendix A.

5. See, for instance, Rita Abrahamsen, *Disciplining Democracy: Development Discourse and Good Governance in Africa*, London: Zed Books, 2000.

6. See, for instance, Evelina Dagnino, '"We all have rights, but..." Contesting concepts of citizenship in Brazil', in Naila Kabeer, ed., *Inclusive Citizenship*, London: Zed Books, 2005.

7. See, for instance, John Ackerman, 'Co-governance for accountability: beyond "exit" and "voice"', *World Development* 32(3) (2004): 447–63; John Gaventa, 'Towards participatory governance: assessing the transformative possibilities', in Samuel Hickey and Giles Mohan (eds), *Participation: From Tyranny to Transformation?*, London: Zed Books, 2004; Archon Fung and Eric Olin Wright, *Deepening Democracy: Institutional Innovations in Empowered Participatory Governance*, London: Verso, 2003.

8. Joshua Cohen and Archon Fung, 'Radical democracy', *Swiss Political Science Review* 10(4) (2004): 24.

9. Martha McCoy and Patrick Scully, 'Deliberative dialogue to expand civic engagement: what kind of talk does democracy need?', *National Civic Review* 91(2) (2002): 117–35.

I

Spaces for Change?
The Politics of Participation
in New Democratic Arenas

Andrea Cornwall and Vera Schattan P. Coelho

The challenge of building democratic polities where all can realize their rights and claim their citizenship is one of the greatest of our age. Reforms in governance have generated a profusion of new spaces for citizen engagement. In some settings, older institutions with legacies in colonial rule have been remodelled to suit contemporary governance agendas; in others, constitutional and governance reforms have given rise to entirely new structures. These hybrid 'new democratic spaces' (Cornwall and Coelho 2004) are intermediate, situated as they are at the interface between the state and society; they are also, in many respects, intermediary spaces, conduits for negotiation, information and exchange. They may be provided and provided for by the state, backed in some settings by legal or constitutional guarantees and regarded by state actors as *their* space into which citizens and their representatives are invited. Yet they may also be seen as spaces conquered by civil society demands for inclusion.[1] Some are fleeting, one-off consultative events; others are regularized institutions with a more durable presence on the governance landscape.

In contrast to analyses that situate such institutions within the public sphere, such as Avritzer's (2002) powerful account of Brazil's participatory governance institutions, or within the ambit of the state, as in Fung and Wright's (2003) 'empowered participatory governance', we suggest that they constitute a distinct arena at the interface of state and society: what we term here the 'participatory sphere'. The institutions of this sphere have a semi-autonomous existence, outside and apart from the institutions of formal politics, bureaucracy and everyday associational life, although they are often threaded through with preoccupations and positions formed in them. As arenas in which the boundaries of the technical and the political come to be negotiated, they serve as an entirely different kind of interface with policy processes than other avenues through which citizens can articulate their demands – such as protest, petitioning, lobbying and direct action – or indeed organize to satisfy their own needs (Cornwall and Gaventa 2001; Goetz and Gaventa 2001). These are spaces of contestation as well as collaboration, into which heterogeneous participants bring diverse interpretations of participation and democracy and divergent agendas. As such, they are crucibles for a new politics of public policy.

This book explores the contours of this new politics. It brings together case studies that examine the democratic potential of a diversity of participatory sphere institutions: hospital facility boards in South Africa; a national-level deliberative process in Canada; participatory policy councils and community groups in Brazil, India, Mexico and Bangladesh; participatory budgeting in Argentina; NGO-created participatory fora in Angola and Bangladesh; community fora in the UK; and new intermediary spaces created by social movements in South Africa. Contributors take up the promises offered by advocates of participation – whether enhanced efficiency and effectiveness of public policy, 'deeper' democracy or a more engaged citizenry (Mansbridge 1999; Fung and Wright 2003; Dryzek 2000; Gaventa 2004) – and explore them in a diversity of social, cultural and political contexts.

Together, contributors examine the extent to which the expansion of the participatory sphere serves to further the project of democratization, via the inclusion of diverse interests and the extension of democratizing practices in the state and public sphere, and that of development, via the enhanced efficacy and equity of public policies. A number of studies focus specifically on health, a sector that combines a history of radical promises inspired by the 1978 Alma Ata Declaration, exciting innovations such as the Brazilian health councils and experiments in deliberation in health systems in the global North, with systemic challenges that include entrenched inequalities of knowledge and power. They are complemented by cases that explore a range of other democratic and developmental spaces, from participation in resource allocation and management to neighbourhood-based associations and fora.

Departing from a literature characterized more by success stories in contexts where progressive government is matched with strong, organized civil society and institutional innovation, such as participatory budgeting in Porto Alegre or participatory planning in Kerala (Heller 2001; Fung and Wright 2003), the majority of the cases we consider here are much more 'ordinary'. And the tales our contributors tell – of 'empty spaces' (Mohanty), of absent representatives and voices (Mohanty; Mahmud; Williams; von Lieres and Kahane; von Lieres), of the play of politics within these arenas (Cornwall; Rodgers) and of the multiplicity of claims to legitimacy levered by civil society (Barnes; Castello, Gurza Lavalle and Houtzager; Roque and Shankland) – attest to the complexities of inclusive, participatory governance. We explore the extent to which Northern debates on deliberative democracy and participatory governance travel to contexts where post-authoritarian regimes, fractured and chronically under-resourced state services and pervasive clientelism leave in their wake fractious and distrustful relationships between citizens and the state, alongside two Northern cases that illustrate some of the challenges of inclusion that remain in progressive established democracies.

The expansion of participatory arenas has, in some contexts, facilitated the creation of new political actors and political subjectivities (Baocchi 2001; Heller 2001; Avritzer 2002). Yet for all the institutional innovation of recent years, there remains a gap between the legal and technical apparatus that has been created to institutionalize participation and the reality of the effective exclusion of poorer and more marginalized citizens. It is with this gap, and the challenges of inclusion, representation and voice that arise in seeking to bridge it, that this book is primarily concerned. It is organized in two sections to reflect a central concern with, on the one hand, substantive inclusion and, on the other, the broader democratizing effects of the participatory sphere. That these are interdependent is evident; accordingly, this introduction weaves together themes arising from across the book as a whole.

In what follows, we seek to contextualize themes emerging from the case studies presented in this book with regard to broader debates on the politics of participatory governance. We begin by highlighting some of the promises of participation, and consider some of the complexities of realizing them in practice. We go on to draw on the case studies presented in this book to explore what they have to tell us about the multiple interfaces through which citizens engage with the state and the new configurations of actors and practices of participation that animate the participatory sphere, and what this implies for democratization and development.

Participation, Democracy, Development

Shifting frames for development intervention have brought debates that have absorbed generations of political philosophers to the forefront of contemporary development policy.[2] From local 'co-governance' and 'co-management' institutions promoted by supra-national agencies and institutionalized by national governments (Ackerman 2004; Manor 2004), to the explosion in the use of participatory and deliberative mechanisms, from Citizens Juries to Participatory Poverty Assessments (Fischer 2000; Chambers 1997), the last decade has been one in which the 'voices' of the public, and especially of 'the poor', have increasingly been sought.

A confluence of development and democratization agendas has brought citizen engagement in governance to centre stage. Decentralization policies promoted in the 1990s claimed to bring government closer to 'the people' (Blair 2000; UNDP 2003). Governance and sector reforms, instigated and promoted by lending agencies and bilateral donors, created a profusion of sites in which citizens came to be enlisted in enhancing accountability and state responsiveness (Crook and Sverisson 2003; Manor 2004; Goetz and Jenkins 2004). A decade of experimentation with participatory methodologies and efforts to 'scale up' participation within development bureaucracies (Thompson 1995; Chambers 1997) led to a late-1990s turn to questions of participatory governance (Gaventa 2004). At the same time, the 'deliberative turn' in debates on democracy and the politics of public policy reflects growing interest in the potential of deliberative institutions and practices for democratic renewal in the North (Bohman and Rehg 1996; Dryzek 2000; Hajer and Wagenaar 2003; Fung 2003), and democratization of state–society relations in the South (Heller 2001; Avritzer 2002; Coelho and Nobre 2004).

These distinct strands come together in the belief that involving citizens more directly in processes of governance makes for better citizens, better decisions and better government (Mansbridge 1999;

Cohen and Sabel 1997; Avritzer 2002; Gaventa 2004). Common to all is a conviction that participatory fora that open up more effective channels of communication and negotiation between the state and citizens serve to enhance democracy, create new forms of citizenship and improve the effectiveness and equity of public policy. Enabling citizens to engage directly in local problem-solving activities and to make their demands directly to state bodies is believed to improve understanding, and contribute to improving the quality of definition and implementation of public programmes and policies (Cunill 1997; Cohen and Sabel 1997; Abers 2001; Fung 2003). These policies and programmes are seen, in turn, as contributing to guaranteeing the access of the poorest to social services, thus enhancing prospects for economic and political inclusion, and for development (World Bank 2001; UNDP 2003).

A host of normative assumptions are embedded in accounts of the benefits of participation, which tend to merge descriptive and pre-scriptive elements without clearly defining the boundaries between empirical reference and normative political discourse. Underlying these assumptions is the belief that citizens are ready to participate and share their political agendas with bureaucrats as long as they are offered appropriate opportunities – and that bureaucrats are willing to listen and respond. As the studies in this book demonstrate, the gap between normative expectations and empirical realities presents a number of challenges for the projects of democratization and development. It becomes evident that the participation of the poorer and more marginalized is far from straightforward, and that a number of preconditions exist for entry into participatory institu-tions. Much depends on *who* enters these spaces, on *whose* terms and with *what* 'epistemic authority' (Chandoke 2003).

Evelina Dagnino (2005) highlights a 'perverse confluence' between two versions of participation in contemporary debates on governance. On the one hand, participation is cast as a project constructed around the extension of citizenship and the deepening of democracy. On the other, participation has come to be associated with shrinking state responsibilities and the progressive exemption of the state from the role of guarantor of rights, making the market what Dagnino has called a 'surrogate arena of citizenship' (2005: 159). In this logic, citizens as 'users' become self-providers as well as consumers of services (Cornwall and Gaventa 2001). The paradox, Dagnino observes, is that *both* require an active, indeed proactive, civil society.

One of the themes that runs through this book is an insistence on the need to unpack the category 'civil society', to examine critically who comes to represent citizens in the participatory sphere and the role that civil society organizations might play in enhancing access and democratizing decision-making in this arena. Civil society organizations are commonly believed to possess the democratizing properties that are associated with the public sphere (Cohen and Arato 1992; Acharya et al. 2004; Edwards 2004). Yet 'civil society' is in effect a residual category, in which more progressive politicized elements come to be conflated with apolitical or positively reactionary civic organizations that may have anti-democratic ideals and practices (Dryzek 2000). After all, as Chandoke (2003) reminds us, civil society is only as democratizing as its practitioners.

Accounts of civil society's virtues highlight the role such organizations can play in holding the state to account. Yet the growing part civil society organizations have come to play as providers as well as intermediaries not only blurs the boundaries of the 'state'/'civil society' binary, it also raises questions about their autonomy and indeed accountability (Chandoke 2003; Tvedt 1998). Where civil society actors are able to stimulate new social and political practices that they then carry into the participatory and public spheres, they can make a significant contribution to inclusiveness and deliberation (Avritzer 2002; Cohen and Arato 1992). Yet it is a leap of faith to extend these positive effects to 'civil society' at large, as Acharya et al. (2004) point out. A key question, then, is which kinds of civil society organizations enable inclusive participation, and what are the conditions under which they come to flourish and gain influence.

The reconfiguration of state–society relations that is taking place with the introduction of the kinds of new democratic sites and practices that are the focus for this book also calls for a view of the state that goes beyond constructing it as a monolith. As Iris Marion Young argues:

> it is a misleading reification to conceptualise government institutions as forming a single, uniform, coherent governance system, 'the state'. In fact, at least in most societies in the world today with functioning state institutions, these institutions interlock at different levels, sometimes overlap in jurisdiction, and sometimes work independently or at cross purposes. (2004: 62)

Indeed, state actors in the participatory sphere may share beliefs, ideals, prejudices and social networks with social actors (Heller 2001); and some of these actors are a far cry from the dull or intrusive bureaucrat (du Gay 2000), even if others make an art form of technocratic obstruction. It is, after all, the state that is often the object of mobilization and that remains the guarantor of rights; and state-provided participatory spaces, such as many of those analysed here, not only provide venues for civil society engagement but can actively stimulate the creation of new political collectivities (Baocchi 2001; Young 2000).

What this discussion underscores is the need to understand both 'the state' and 'civil society' as heterogenous and mutually constitutive terrains of contestation (Houtzager 2003; Skocpol and Fiorina 1999; Chandoke 2003). This calls for a view of participation as 'a contingent outcome, produced as collective actors (civil society, state and other) negotiate relations in a pre-existing terrain that constrains and facilitates particular kinds of action' (Acharya et al. 2004: 41). Democratization comes with this to extend beyond the introduction of standard packages associated with liberal democratic reform programmes. As John Dryzek argues:

> Democratization … is not the spread of liberal democracy to ever more corners of the world, but rather extensions along any one of three dimensions … The first is franchise, expansion of the number of people capable of participating effectively in collective decision. The second is scope, bringing more issues and areas of life potentially under democratic control … The third is the authenticity of the control … : to be real rather than symbolic, involving the effective participation of autonomous and competent actors. (2000: 29)

Participatory sphere institutions potentially contribute along all three of these dimensions, multiplying spaces in which growing numbers of people come to take part in political life, giving rise to new political subjectivities and opening up ever more areas of decision-making to public engagement. It is, however, with the third of Dryzek's dimensions that this book is primarily concerned. And it is in relation to the question of the authenticity and the quality of citizen participation that our work intersects with vibrant debates in political theory on issues of representation and deliberation, as we go on to explore in more depth later in this chapter (Fraser 1992; Young 2000; Mansbridge 2000; Dryzek 2000; Fung 2003).

Towards Substantive Participation

What does it take for marginalized and otherwise excluded actors to participate meaningfully in institutionalized participatory fora and for their participation to result in actual shifts in policy and practice? Institutionalists have argued that the key to enhancing participation is to be found in better institutional designs: in rules and decision-making processes that encourage actors to participate (Immergut 1992; Fung 2003). Social movement theorists have argued that the key lies in social mobilization that pushes for fairer distribution of available resources (Tarrow 1994; Alvarez, Dagnino and Escobar 1998). The studies in this book point to a more complex set of interactions between getting design principles right and stimulating participation 'from below'. If participatory sphere institutions are to be genuinely inclusive and 'have teeth' – that is, if they are to be more than therapeutic or rubber-stamping exercises (see Arnstein 1971) – a number of critical issues need to be addressed.

First, expanding democratic engagement calls for more than invitations to participate (Cornwall 2004). For people to be able to exercise their political agency, they need first to recognize themselves as citizens rather than see themselves as beneficiaries or clients. Acquiring the means to participate equally demands processes of popular education and mobilization that can enhance the skills and confidence of marginalized and excluded groups, enabling them to enter and engage in participatory arenas. The studies in this book by von Lieres, Williams, von Lieres and Kahane, Mahmud, and Mohanty point to the significance of societal spaces beyond the participatory arena in building the capacity of marginalized groups to participate (see Fraser 1992; Kohn 2000). Yet participatory sphere institutions are also spaces for *creating* citizenship, where through learning to participate citizens cut their political teeth and acquire skills that can be transferred to other spheres – whether those of formal politics or neighbourhood action – as Roque and Shankland's, Barnes's, and Cornwall's chapters suggest.

Second, questions of inclusion imply questions of representation. If these institutions are to represent 'the community', 'users', 'civil society' or indeed 'citizens', on what basis do people enter them – and what are their claims to legitimacy to speak for others? What mechanisms, if any, exist to facilitate the representation of marginalized groups, and what do. these amount to in practice? And what else might be needed to create the basis for broader-based representation? Across our cases, there is a significant contrast between settings in which highly organized and articulate social movements participate as collective actors as in Brazil and Argentina (Castello et al., Coelho; Cornwall; Rodgers), and those like Bangladesh, India and South Africa in which individuals take up places made available to them as an extension of family responsibilities, or by virtue of their sex or race, rather than the constituencies they represent (Mahmud; Mohanty; Williams). These questions of representation draw attention to the different kinds of politics and prospects for democracy that emerge in and across different cultural and political contexts.

Third, simply putting structures of participation in place is not enough to create viable political institutions. Much comes to depend on the motivations of those who enter them, and what 'participation' means to them. Is participation promoted so that bureaucrats can listen to people's experiences and understand their concerns, so as to make better policies? Or so that citizens come to play an active part in crafting and monitoring policies? Or, indeed, so that these publics can challenge bureaucrats to be more accountable? Our studies demonstrate not only the polyvalence of the concept of participation (Mahmud; von Lieres; Mohanty) but also the coexistence within any single setting of plural – and competing – understandings of what can be gained that are in constant negotiation (Cornwall; Rodgers; Roque and Shankland).

Fourth, no one wants to just talk and talk and not see anything change. What, then, does it take for participation to be *effective* as well as inclusive (Warren 2000)? Coelho (2004 and here) suggests that the conjunction of three factors is critical: involvement by a wide spectrum of popular movements and civil associations, committed bureaucrats, and inclusive institutional designs that address exclusionary practices and embedded bias. In contexts with highly asymmetrical resource distribution among participants, there is a very real danger of elite capture (Mahmud; Mohanty). Equally, the path-dependency of policy choices can constrain deliberation to issues of implementation, offering little real scope for rethinking policies.[3] Certain institutional designs are, Fung (2003) argues, more or less inclined to promote the legitimacy, justice or effectiveness of decisions taken in these spaces. These dimensions do not converge, Fung points out: it is hard to privilege one without sacrificing others. Where institutions are implanted without attention to design features that help mediate conflict, secure particular configurations of roles and forms of representation, and address the tensions and trade-offs between inclusiveness and effectiveness, it is easy enough for 'old ways' and forms of exclusion and domination to persist in 'new spaces' (Cornwall 2002).

Lastly, what effects do participatory spheres have on citizenship and on political engagement more generally? While some writers are optimistic about their potential to stimulate further participation and democratization from below (Baocchi 2001; Avritzer 2002), others point to the ambivalent effects of institutionalized participation on social and political energy and thus on further democratization (Piven and Cloward 1971; Dryzek 1996; Taylor 1998). Negative effects such as disillusionment and a gradual fizzling out of energy and commitment emerge most clearly in Barnes's chapter. But other chapters point to other, unanticipated, democratizing effects, as institutions that began with a relatively restricted remit gave rise to forms of engagement that spilled beyond their boundaries, or where social actors seized opportunities to repoliticize these spaces (Rodgers; Roque and Shankland). These cases drive home the point that participation is a process over time, animated by actors with their own social and political projects. Most of all, they emphasize the importance of contextualizing participatory sphere institutions with regard to other political institutions and situating them on the social, cultural and historical landscapes of which they form part (Heller 2001; Cornwall 2004).

In the sections that follow, we explore issues arising from these points in more depth. We begin by considering what the studies in this volume have to tell us about the micropolitics of participation in institutionalized participatory arenas. We go on to address questions of difference, and the issues of representation and the politics of inclusion that arise. Finally, we turn to consider the democratizing effects and dimensions of the participatory sphere, with a focus both on engagement with the state and on substantive prospects for democratizing democracy.

Spaces of Power: The Micropolitics of Participation

From the discursive framing that shapes what can be deliberated, to the deployment of technical language and claims to authority that reinstitutionalize existing cleavages in society, to the way the use of labels such as 'users' or 'community members' circumscribes the political agency of participants, power courses through every dimension of the participatory sphere. As 'invited spaces',[4] the institutions of the participatory sphere are framed by those who create them, and infused with power relations and cultures of interaction carried into them from other spaces (Cornwall 2002). These are spaces of power, in which forms of overt or tacit domination silence certain actors or keep them from entering at all (Gaventa 2005). Yet these are also spaces of possibility, in which power takes a more productive and positive form: whether in enabling citizens to transgress positions as passive recipients and assert their rights or in contestations over 'governmentality' (Foucault 1991).

Viewing participation as a contingent, contested process highlights the micropolitics of encounters in participatory arenas. The studies in this book situate this micropolitics in sites with very different histories of state–citizen interaction, configurations of political institutions, and political cultures. From post-conflict Angola to New Labour's Britain, from rural Bangladesh to urban Brazil, the studies in this volume range across contexts with distinctively different histories and cultures. While persistent inequalities and forms of embedded exclusion exist in all, their dimensions and dynamics differ, as do notions of citizenship, and the degree and kinds of social mobilization and state-supported efforts to redress systemic discrimination, whether on the basis of gender, race, caste or class (Kabeer 2005).

Chaudhuri and Heller (2002) argue that a critical shortcoming of the debate on deepening democracy has been its assumption that individuals are equally able to form associations and engage in political activity. This, they argue, ignores fundamental differences in power between social groups:

> If this is problematic in any less-than-perfect democracy (and there are no perfect democracies) it is especially problematic in developing democracies where basic rights of association are circumscribed and distorted by pervasive vertical dependencies (clientelistic relationships), routine forms of social exclusion (e.g. the caste system, purdah), the unevenness and at times complete failure of public legality, and the persistence of pre-democratic forms of authority. (2002: 2)

Williams's account of health facilities boards in South Africa reveals the tenacious hold of older practices of paternalism in these new spaces, reproducing patterns of interaction inherited from the racist past. He argues that the very culture and design of South African health facilities boards serve to perpetuate the dominance of whites, and sustain existing hierarchies of power and privilege. Internalization of norms valuing certain knowledges and forms of discourse can lead to people silencing themselves. Williams quotes a young Black businesswoman: 'Black people do not participate because they feel inferior to white people. Participation requires special knowledge and Black people do not have the necessary knowledge to engage white people on matters such as health.'

Simply creating spaces does little to rid them of the dispositions participants may bring into them (see Bourdieu 1977). Professionals valued for their expertise in one context may be unwilling to countenance the validity or value of alternative knowledges and practices in another; and citizens who have been on the receiving end of paternalism or prejudice in everyday encounters with state institutions may bring these expectations with them into the participatory sphere. Mahmud's study of Bangladeshi Community Groups (CGs), which were created as part of health sector reforms as ways of engaging 'community participation' in the governance of health services, reveals some of these dynamics. She shows how existing social cleavages are mapped onto participatory institutions, reducing poorer men and women to silence. Mahmud cites a landless woman CG member, who commented: 'I am poor and ignorant, what will I say? Those who are more knowledgeable speak more.' Yet she also reveals a reversal of these power dynamics when it comes to other forms of engagement, in which those silenced in participatory spaces regain their agency and voice. She cites a female grassroots Community Group member: 'the educated and well-off members can debate or discuss a point in an organized way but when it comes to protesting they are usually silent and try to stay out of the scene.'

Mohanty's chapter highlights precisely this kind of contrast in the context of rural India: between 'empty spaces' of local governance and watershed management in which women's participation is marginal or absent, and women-only health groups in which they are active. She shows how available opportunities to participate are circumscribed by essentialized stereotypes of women's concerns and capabilities, leaving little scope for women to participate as *citizens* rather than as wards or mothers. In a context where women have scant opportunity to learn the skills needed to engage effectively in the participatory sphere, and where social sanctions work to ostracize those who do assert themselves, there are potent barriers to inclusion. Some women do manage to break with normative expectations and begin to claim their rights to voice. But this may invite other forms of exclusion. She cites Nirmala, a women's health worker:

> Few women here have the awareness about their rights. Some of us who are educated and are aware about our rights, we are seen as a 'nuisance' and a constant threat within the village. Hence, while women who are silent and docile will be called to meetings, we will be deliberately kept outside.

For people living in poverty, subject to discrimination and exclusion from mainstream society, the experience of entering a participatory space can be extremely intimidating. How they talk and what they talk about may be perceived by professionals as scarcely coherent or relevant; their participation may be viewed by the powerful as chaotic, disruptive and unproductive. Iris Marion Young argues that 'norms of deliberation are culturally specific and often operate as forms of power that silence or devalue the speech of some people' (1996: 123). A potent challenge for substantive inclusion is, then, overcoming the embedded inequalities in status, technical knowledge and power that persistently undermine what Chandoke terms the 'linguistic and epistemic authority' (2003: 186) of subaltern actors.

Bridging these inequalities through mediation, training or coaching offers the promise of enhancing the possibilities of deliberation. But there are also risks. As we go on to suggest, strategies to amplify the voice of marginalized groups may complicate efforts to foster deliberation. Barnes describes, for example, how young people in the UK were coached by youth workers to present 'acceptable' versions of concerns that might have been devalued if they were expressed in young peoples' own language. Strategic interpretation on the part of well-meaning intermediaries may, as Chandoke (2003) argues, overshadow authentic communication and leave the subaltern no less silenced than before. Mobilization may bring marginalized actors into participatory spaces, but not necessarily equip them with the skills to communicate effectively with the others that they meet there. And activists with experience in social movements, political parties or unions may bring with them more confrontational and directly partisan styles of politics that depart from the consensus-seeking and 'rational' modes of argumentation of deliberative democracy, as Cornwall's Brazilian case study shows.

Yet these very power dynamics can also imbue participatory spaces with their dynamism. Spaces for participation may be created with one purpose in mind, but can come to be used by social actors to renegotiate their boundaries. Discourses of participation are, after all, not a singular, coherent, set of ideas or prescriptions, but configurations of strategies and practices that are played out on constantly shifting ground (Foucault 1991). In Mahmud's account of the activist NGO Nijera Kori's work with health watch committees in Bangladesh, the transformation of management spaces into *political* spaces redefined their possibilities. Roque and Shankland's account of the 'mutation' of donor-introduced institutions in Angola reveals how participants' other projects refashioned and reconfigured their scope, generating new leadership and democratizing effects. Rodgers's chapter provides a particularly rich account of these dynamics. He shows how the Participatory Budgeting process in Buenos Aires overlaid existing sociopolitical practices and relations to provide 'spaces of autonomy' within the process, which allowed the 'subverting of the subversion' of politicization. These studies reveal the vitality of the participatory sphere and its transformatory potential; they also underscore the point that much depends on *who* comes to participate within its institutions, to which we now turn.

Questions of Representation

Distinctive to the participatory sphere are new, plural and markedly different forms of representation and accountability from those conventionally associated with the institutions of liberal democracy (Houtzager et al. 2004). These encode different logics and norms of democracy, construing different understandings about who *ought to* participate. 'Civil society' comes to be represented in a variety of ways: by individuals speaking about and for themselves, by nominated representatives from non-governmental organizations, by elected representatives from neighbourhood associations, by members of collective actors such as unions or movements, and other variants besides. There is evidence of tension resulting from the different sources of legitimacy that underpin claims to speak and act as representatives; inclusionary aspirations or objectives may conflict with claims based on the legitimacy afforded by evidence of committed action on the part of marginalized groups (chapters by Barnes, and Castello et al.).

The extensive literature on representation offers a range of perspectives on how best to ensure the inclusion of less organized and vocal groups. There is a current that argues for a more direct democratic approach: participatory sphere institutions should be open to everyone who wants to participate. Some point out the risk self-selection poses for favouring those with most resources, and propose methods of random selection that seek to mirror the makeup of the population (Fishkin and Luskin 1999). Others focus less on the methods of selection and more on incentives, concentrating the focus of fora on questions of particular interest to poorer citizens (Fung 2003). This current is counterposed to arguments that the very process of creating a basis for representation for marginalized social groups is only possible if there is a parallel process of mobilization and definition of collective identities and agendas.

Across our cases, there is a diversity of forms of representation that speak to both these perspectives. Mahmud describes how in Community Groups managing village-level health services in Bangladesh individuals speaking as 'community representatives' are generally elites – professionals, teachers, wealthy farmers and their wives – appointed by the chairman. In Williams's account of South African health facilities boards (HFBs), those who speak for patients' interests are more likely to be working for community health than representing particular social groups. Castello et al.'s chapter offers a different perspective, from a context that is markedly different: Brazil's largest city, São Paulo, where 'citizen participation' generally refers to the engagement of registered civil society organizations, of which there are many hundreds. Their findings shed further light on questions of representation in the participatory sphere. Less than 5 per cent of the organizations surveyed represented themselves as descriptive representatives; and a similarly small number saw themselves in classic electoral terms. For almost half, the vast majority, representation was about *mediation*. Such organizations saw themselves as about advocating for the rights of others, and providing a bridge between poorly or under-represented segments of the population and the state.

The experiences brought together in this book point to trade-offs that need to be taken into account when examining the capacity of the participatory sphere to promote the inclusion of sectors of society that have traditionally been marginalized. To what extent, for example, would a preference for forums where the public come to be represented by methods of random selection open the doors of these institutions for those who may otherwise find it difficult to enter (see Fishkin and Luskin 1999)? And to what extent would this reproduce the highly asymmetrical distribution of social, symbolic, political and economic resources that exist in society at large, unmediated by practices of organizing that can lend more marginalized actors the skills to participate effectively? It is one thing for citizens to enter participatory fora to inform themselves and generate opinions from reasoned discussion, and another again for these discussions to consist of debates among politicized collective actors with strongly polarized positions. The challenge associated with the first situation is how to foment processes in which poorer and more marginalized citizens can find their voice; that of the second is the risk of contributing to the radicalization and amplification of the power of veto of groups who feel themselves to be on the margins politically, which can substantially restrict the democratic potential of these arenas.

Deliberative democrats would argue that providing participants with sufficient information and access to expertise, and seeking to encourage them to form positions during discussions rather than to bring pre-prepared positions and agendas with them, can instil new norms of conduct (Fung 2003). Good facilitation can play a hugely important role. Techniques that are explicitly oriented to amplifying the voices of the least vocal enhance the possibilities of deliberation, allowing positions to be openly debated rather than defensively asserted. And the introduction of innovative interactive practices can begin to change the culture of interaction in the participatory sphere, countering the reproduction of old hierarchies and exclusions, and enabling a greater diversity of voices to be heard.

Yet, at the same time, it is evident that *some* actors inevitably arrive at the table with ideas, impressions and knowledge that no amount of facilitation or deliberation can budge; to expect any less is to depoliticize profoundly the process of deliberation, as well as to shunt out of the frame preferences, beliefs and alliances that are by their very nature political. Those who have some resources – for example, links with the party political system or powerful patrons – stand better placed to expand their chances of access to these fora to advance their own agendas. Affiliation to other societally produced means of organizing collective interests, whether mass-based popular movements or formal political parties, are never simply left at the door when people come to deliberate, as Cornwall's, Rodgers's, and Barnes's studies show. Understanding the politics of these spaces requires closer attention to political networks that span the state, participatory and public spheres, and to the implications of the articulations they make possible.

Von Lieres and Kahane's study of a national-level deliberative process in Canada raises a further question: to what extent are the rules of the game adopted to facilitate inclusive deliberation cultural artefacts – and how do they implicitly exclude other culturally defined ways of thinking about representation? The Romanow Commission's review of Canada's healthcare system failed, they contend, to take seriously enough how marginalization may be perpetuated in deliberative spaces. By enlisting citizens as individuals, the dialogue failed to give Aboriginal people sufficient opportunity for voice, precisely because the individualistic premisses of the method used clashed with indigenous forms of group-based representation that works through affiliation. Their analysis highlights the significance of responsiveness to culturally located forms of organization, representation and deliberation, as well as the importance of the creation of spaces for what they call 'affiliated' marginalized citizens.

Jane Mansbridge suggests that in 'communicative settings of distrust, uncrystallised interests and historically denigrated status' (2000: 99), descriptive representation – the representation of a social group by those from that social group who speak *as*, as well as *for*, that group – is necessary if substantive attention is to be given to the issues that affect this group. It is precisely this kind of setting that Williams's account addresses, and he highlights a series of factors that conspire to exclude black participants from being able to engage in a 'politics of presence': a lack of associations that can put forward black interests, a mismatch between mechanisms for enlistment and forms of communication that would reach black citizens, historical domination of similar institutions by middle-class whites – often of the do-gooder variety, whose concern for 'poor black people' eclipses black citizens' capacity to represent their own interests and needs – and internalized disprivilege, with entailments in terms of self-confidence and capacity to associate and voice demands. As Phillips (1995) argues, a 'politics of presence' offers both the symbolic value of visibility and the possibility of more vigorous advocacy of the interests of otherwise excluded groups. In this setting, Williams contends, it is precisely this that is needed.

In a critique of Habermas's (1984) notion of the public sphere, Fraser argues that marginalized groups may find greater opportunities for exercising voice through creating their *own* spaces, which she terms 'subaltern counterpublics'. She suggests that these spaces have 'a dual character. On the one hand, they function as spaces of withdrawal and regroupment; on the other hand, they also function as bases and training groups for agitational activities directed toward wider publics' (1992: 124). Mansbridge (2000) highlights another dimension of such spaces: as 'laboratories of self-interest' they can enable historically marginalized groups to build positions, construct a politics of engagement and gain greater legitimacy to voice demands within participatory sphere institutions. Such spaces can come to serve a politics of transformation by giving previously excluded groups the time and opportunity to construct their political preferences and express their concerns for themselves. They can also provide an arena for making demands and concerns legible to the state.

Mobilization creates not only a shared language but also opportunities for political apprenticeship and the conditions under which new leaders can emerge. In many of our cases it is activist NGOs that have taken the lead in creating these spaces. But, as Mohanty, Barnes and Cornwall emphasize, the state has a crucial role to play in redressing societal discrimination and actively supporting inclusion of marginalized groups in political arenas of all kinds (Young 2000). As Heller (2001) argues, closer attention needs to be paid to synergies between social movements and state-supported political projects in fostering the substantive participation of subaltern actors.

Engaging the State

Greater attention has been given in work on participatory sphere institutions to social actors than to the state actors whose committed involvement is so decisive for their success (Abers 2001; Fox 1996; Heller 2001). Mahmud's case study of citizen mobilization in the absence of engaged state actors shows critical limitations to achieving changes in health delivery if those who plan and deliver services are not part of the discussion, and the significance of recognition and institutional support by the state for the viability of participatory institutions. Coelho highlights the significance of public officials' commitment as a co-factor in producing successful and inclusive participatory fora. Barnes details what such actors contribute to making participation meaningful. But surprisingly little is known about what drives these actors to defend social participation as a political project. What is it that motivates state officials to participate and to follow through decisions arrived at in these spaces? What makes bureaucrats amenable to what can end up being long and convoluted deliberative processes, rather than resorting to quicker and more authoritarian decision-making processes? What incentives motivate them to invest in creating a more enabling environment and act in the interests of poorer and more marginalized citizens? And what do *they* get out of participating in the participatory sphere?

The commitment of politicians and bureaucrats to participatory governance needs to be analysed against a backdrop of a complex conjunction of variables. These include the values and party political affiliations of these actors, attempts to influence and gain information about public opinion, and the structure of opportunities defined by the political system (Skocpol and Fiorina 1999). Where preferences are unstable, it may be expedient for politicians to seek means of securing opportunities to influence as well as respond to the concerns of the electorate. Participatory sphere institutions may offer such an opportunity if they are well grounded in relationships with broader constituencies and communities; it may well be in politicians' interests to seek to enhance their viability (Heller 2001; Mansbridge 2003). As such, they form one way of discovering what influences electoral preferences – alongside instruments such as opinion polls or focus groups.

Yet an ostensible commitment to participatory governance can in itself also pay political dividends. Politicians and senior bureaucrats can adopt the mantle of participation to give themselves distinctive public identities as champions for the cause of open and accountable government. In Brazil, for example, claims to be promoting popular participation appear on many a municipal government logo, and have been the leftist Workers' Party's badge of respectability as well as, arguably, a factor in their electoral success in the past. Politicians may seek new allies in participatory arenas, whether against other politicians or to control the bureaucracy; in turn, participatory bureaucrats may seek similar kinds of alliances, whether against elitist politicians and bureaucrats or to gain support and legitimacy. Participation as a political project can be seen, then, as a strategy that seeks to cultivate allies, strengthen networks and gain votes.

'Champions of change' within bureaucracies play a crucial role in creating and resourcing spaces for change, and as such become allies for social movements and civil society (Fox 1996). Indeed, state support and recognition are needed if these spaces are to function at all, as Mahmud points out. Infrastructural support, funding for public events, and for training and transport to carry out consultations or inspect facilities are tangible measures of commitment; they are also essential for the very viability of these institutions. But there are other dimensions to constructive state engagement. As Barnes suggests, this may be as much about redressing disciplinary tendencies, valuing diverse forms of dialogue and expression, and modifying the official norms and rules that often come to dominate participatory sphere institutions as about offering citizens opportunities to participate. The personal and political commitment of state officials to the participatory project not only makes this support and engagement possible, it also contributes to their willingness and capacity to be responsive. Cornwall shows how a complex mesh of ideology, party-political affiliations and personal and professional biases appear in Brazilian bureaucrats' and health workers' accounts of their role in a municipal health council. She argues that to see these spaces purely in terms of their citizen participants is to miss an important dimension of their democratizing effects.

The politics of inclusion by the state invites further complexities. Von Lieres argues, for South Africa, that in a political context that features prevailing expectations of the non-bindingness of public deliberation, a history of distrust and manipulation, a lack of viable social mobilization to articulate demands, and residual authoritarian and paternalist tendencies in the conduct of state officials, participatory arenas may simply reinforce relations of power patterned by experiences in other institutional spaces, rather than create viable arenas for democratization. It may well be that it is in these other spaces – such as those of oppositional social movements and popular protest – that those who are silent find their political agency, develop their skills and nourish their passion for engagement (see Mouffe 2002). Yet in bridging these arenas and those of the participatory sphere, there may be much at stake. Dryzek (1996) argues that the price of inclusion may be high for groups whose agendas diverge so significantly from state priorities that entry risks co-option and demoralization. For some groups, and for some issues, investment in engagement with the state may fail to pay off as energies are diverted into backwaters that detract from larger political struggles (Taylor 1998). Barnes's analysis of the transformation of an institution initiated by citizens in the UK into a government-sponsored forum demonstrates one of the most evident consequences: a loss of social energy as seeping bureaucratization kills off spontaneity and creativity, leaving such an institution a pale shell of its former self.

Von Lieres's account of the South African Treatment Action Campaign (TAC) shows how engagement at multiple interfaces with the state – from the courts and the streets to the clinic – may offer greater prospects for extending the boundaries of the political (Melucci 1996). It is, she argues, in their capacity to *intermediate*, to work across arenas with a politics of identification that brings together a diverse spectrum of interest groups, that their efficacy lies. As the TAC case shows, strategic participation may come to depend on the exercise of agency outside the participatory arena, to lever pressure for change (Cortez 2004). Barnes's account highlights the significance of the construction and mobilization of an 'oppositional consciousness' as a means of animating participation (see Mouffe 2002). But, as she points out, this in itself poses new challenges for state actors, including the need for skills for creative conflict management to work constructively with oppositional positions without dousing their passion, and for acknowledging a plurality of discursive styles, rather than trying to manage voices into 'acceptable' versions. Intermediation is required *within* as well as across sites for engagement if participation is to produce better mutual understanding between the diversity of actors within the participatory sphere.

Conclusion

The normative expectations of deliberative and participatory democracy find weak support in the findings of the studies of everyday experiences of participatory governance in this book. But, despite considerable shortcomings, the cases presented here give some cause for optimism. Their very ordinariness tells other stories: of incremental change, of a growing sense of entitlement to participate, of slow but real shifts in political agency. They reveal glimpses of how opening up previously inaccessible decision-making processes to public engagement can stimulate the creation of new political subjects as well as new subjectivities and, with it, deepen democracy along all three of Dryzek's axes.

What does it take for participation in the participatory sphere to offer real prospects for change in the status quo for historically marginalized social groups? Coelho shows here how it is the *conjunction* of enabling policies and legal frameworks, committed and responsive bureaucrats, well-coordinated, articulate social actors and inclusive institutional designs that produces greater diversity among representatives, thus expanding access if not the influence of historically marginalized groups. Yet these co-factors do not add up to a one-size-fits-all recipe. Context matters. In many of the cases in this book, a number of these factors are striking in their absence. In contexts such as Bangladesh and Angola, ineffective, under-resourced and corrupt state structures fracture the possibilities for responsiveness. In contexts like the UK, India, South Africa and Brazil where the state is relatively strong, a fear of letting go of control, high levels of bureaucratization and embedded aspects of political culture provide potent obstacles to the participation of traditionally excluded citizens.

These contrasts urge that more attention be paid to the contingencies of political culture. They underline the need for any analysis of participation to be set within the histories of state–society relations that have shaped the configurations and contestations of the present. Political histories and cultures – of struggle as of subjugation, of authoritarian rule as of political apathy – may embed dispositions in state and societal actors that are carried into spaces for participation. These may make alliances with state actors or forms of collaboration difficult to realize, especially for groups whose right to participate at all has been persistently denied in the past. Changing political culture calls for changes 'on both sides of the equation' (Gaventa 2004).

Gaventa's equation highlights the mutually constitutive relationship between state responsiveness and citizen mobilization. Contextual factors modify the possibilities of this relationship. Where state capacity is attenuated by under-resourcing, corruption or plain ineffectiveness, citizens may mobilize to provide for themselves; where cultures of paternalism, patrimonialism or authoritarianism persist, some citizens may gear themselves up for a fight but others may never enter the fray. What a number of the cases in this book show is that in such contexts, the introduction of new political practices, new spaces for the articulation of concerns and interests, and new opportunities for political apprenticeship can begin a process of change that may have broader ripple effects. They point to shifts that have begun to reconfigure democratic engagement.

The routinization of discussion about public policies in the partici-patory sphere has successfully served to broaden debate beyond more closed technical and political spaces, as Coelho, von Lieres and Kahane, Roque and Shankland, Barnes, and Rodgers show. Certain conditions amplify possibilities for change: mobilized collective actors (Castello et al.; von Lieres; Rodgers; Cornwall); state actors interested in building longer-term alliances with civil society (Coelho; Barnes; Cornwall); institutional design characteristics that contribute to reducing asym-metric distribution of resources among participants (Coelho; von Lieres and Kahane); and opportunities to influence resource allocation as well as the shape of public policies (Rodgers; Barnes). Our cases also show that other, more contingent, factors can alter the balance of power. These may be unintended consequences, such as the 'mutations' described by Roque and Shankland or the processes of politicization that accompany resource negotiations analysed by Rodgers, whose net effects are 'unexpected democratization'. Or they may be the subtle shifts that new discourses of rights, social justice and citizenship create as they circulate through networks that support different social actors and expand their interpretive and political horizons.

Participatory sphere institutions can become 'schools for citizen-ship' — in the words of a Brazilian activist cited by Cornwall — in which those who participate learn new meanings and practices of citizenship by working together. The sheer diversity of actors and positions within this sphere offer opportunities for developing an 'expanded understanding' (Arendt 1958) that allows people to see beyond their own immediate problems or professional biases. As Rodgers, Barnes and Cornwall observe, participants in these spaces bring commitment to them and talk of getting an enormous amount of personal fulfilment out of their engagement. Interactions in this sphere can help change dispositions among bureaucrats as well as citizens, instilling greater respect, and enhancing their propensity to listen and commitment to respond. Yet much depends on the openness and capacity of the state. Where entrenched inequalities and the postures and practices of state officials mute marginal voices, and where little willingness or capacity exists to redress these inequali-ties and address the specific concerns of these groups, other spaces outside these arenas become especially critical: as sites both in which to gain confidence and consolidate positions and from which to act on other parts of the state through other forms of political action, including strategic non-participation (Cortez 2004).

Our studies show that pervasive inequalities in power and knowledge and embedded political cultures pose considerable challenges for creating inclusive deliberative fora. They suggest that even in cases where there is considerable political will to ensure the viability of these institutions, inequalities of power and knowledge and embedded technocracy affect their democratizing prospects. What do they tell us about how these inequalities can be addressed and how marginalized groups can become more meaningfully involved? The first step is to guarantee a place at the table for such groups, through rules of engagement as well as of selection that seek to broaden participation beyond established interest groups. This, in turn, requires processes that can build the capabilities of more marginalized actors to use their voices and that extend capacity building efforts to state officials, as much to unlearn attitudes as to acquire the capacity to listen to citizens and recognize their rights.

The challenge for expanding democracy through the participatory sphere may be less the extent to which democratic institutions can bring about change than *which* changes in *whom* and in *whose* interests. An ever-present dilemma is how to insulate these spaces from capture by non-democratic elements, including administrations that simply use them for therapeutic or rubber-stamping purposes (Arnstein 1971). Another is how to guarantee their political efficacy and viability, and address some of the very real tensions that arise between short-term and long-term solutions, between inclusiveness and effectiveness, between struggle and negotiation. The very newness of many of these institutions, the weakness of their institutional designs and the limited purposes for which some of them were originally created have tended to create fragile connections, if any, with the formal architecture of governance. This creates a number of problems, including the difficulty of ensuring the democratic legitimacy of decisions made in fora that bypass electoral and parliamentary mechanisms of representation (Dryzek 2001; de Vita 2004). Ultimately, the extent that the participatory sphere is able to promote legitimate representation and distributional justice may depend not merely on how each space within it performs, but on relationships with other institutions within the public sphere and the state.

Amplifying the democratic potential and enhancing the democratic legitimacy of the participatory sphere, the cases presented here suggest, need to take place on three fronts: catalysing and supporting processes of social mobilization through which marginalized groups can nurture new leaders, enhance their political agency and seek representation in these arenas as well as efficacy outside them; instituting measures to address exclusionary elements within the institutional structure of the participatory sphere, from rules of representation to strategies that foster more inclusive deliberation, such as the use of facilitation; and articulating participatory sphere institutions more effectively with other governance institutions, providing them with resources as well as with political 'teeth'. It is with addressing these challenges – for theory, as well as for practice – that future directions for participatory governance lie.

Notes

We would like to thank the 'Spaces for Change' working group of the Development Research Centre on Citizenship, Participation and Account-ability, and John Gaventa, DRC Director, for all their contributions to the ideas presented in this chapter. Our analysis benefited from the comments of John Gaventa, Peter Houtzager, David Kahane, Ranjita Mohanty and Ian Scoones, to whom we are very grateful.

1. We are grateful to Marcus Melo for this point.
2. The genealogy of writing on participatory democracy can be traced back to Aristotle, and has its more recent roots in the work of Pateman (1970) and MacPherson (1973).
3. Indeed, as Dryzek points out, public policy is not indeterminate and there are 'certain imperatives that all states simply must meet' (2000: 93).
4. The term 'invited spaces' originates in joint work with Karen Brock and John Gaventa (Brock, Cornwall and Gaventa 2001; Cornwall 2002; Gaventa 2004).

References

Abers, R. (2001) *Inventing Local Democracy: Grassroots Politics in Brazil*, Boulder CO: Westview Press.

Acharya, A., P. Houtzager and A. Gurza Lavalle (2004) 'Civil society representation in the participatory budget and deliberative councils of São Paulo, Brazil', *IDS Bulletin* 35(2): 40–48.

Ackerman, J. (2004) 'Co-governance for accountability: beyond "exit" and "voice"', *World Development* 32(3): 447–63.

Arendt, H. (1958) *The Human Condition*, Chicago: University of Chicago Press.

Arnstein, S.R. (1971) 'A ladder of participation in the USA', *Journal of the Royal Town Planning Institute*, April: 176–82.

Alvarez, S., E. Dagnino and A. Escobar, eds (1998) *Cultures of Politics/Politics of Cultures: Revisioning Latin American Social Movements*, Boulder CO: Westview Press.

Avritzer, L. (2002) *Democracy and the Public Space in Latin America*, Princeton: Princeton University Press.

Baocchi, G. (2001) 'Participation, activism, and politics: the Porto Alegre experiment and deliberative democratic theory', *Politics and Society* 29(1): 43–72.

Blair, H. (2000) 'Participation and accountability at the periphery', *World Development* 28(1): 21–39.

Brock, K., A. Cornwall and J. Gaventa (2001) 'Power, knowledge and political spaces in the framing of poverty policy', IDS Working Paper No. 143, Institute of Development Studies, University of Sussex, Falmer.

Bourdieu, P. (1977) *Outline of a Theory of Practice*, Cambridge: Cambridge University Press.

Bohman, J., and W. Rehg, eds (1997) *Deliberative Democracy: Essays on Reason and Politics*, Cambridge MA: MIT Press.

Chambers, R. (1997) *Whose Reality Counts: Putting the First Last*, London: Intermediate Technology Publications.

Chandoke, N. (2003) *The Conceits of Civil Society*, Delhi: Oxford University Press.

Chaudhuri, S., and P. Heller (2002) 'The plasticity of participation: evidence from a participatory governance experiment', Department of Economics, Columbia University, mimeo.

Coelho, V.S. (2004), 'Brazil's health councils: the challenge of building participatory political institutions', *IDS Bulletin* 35(2): 33–9.

Coelho, V.S., and M. Nobre, eds (2004) *Participação e Deliberação: Teoria Democrática e Experiências Institucionais no Brasil Contemporâneo* [Participation and deliberation: democratic theory and institutional experiences in contemporary Brazil], São Paulo: 34 Letras.

Cohen, J.L., and A. Arato (1992) *Civil Society and Political Theory*, Cambridge MA: MIT Press.

Cohen, J., and C. Sabel (1997) 'Directly-deliberative polyarchy', *European Law Journal* 3(4): 313–42.

Cornwall, A. (2002) 'Making spaces, changing places: situating participation in development', IDS Working Paper No. 173, Institute of Development Studies, University of Sussex, Falmer.

Cornwall, A., and V.S. Coelho, eds (2004), 'New democratic spaces?', *IDS Bulletin* 35(2).

Cortez, C.R. (2004) 'Social strategies and public policies in an indigenous zone in Chiapas, Mexico', *IDS Bulletin* 35(2): 76–83.

Crook, R., and A. Sverisson (2003) 'Does decentralization contribute to poverty reduction? Surveying the evidence,' in P. Houtzager and M. Moore, eds, *Changing Paths: International Development and the Politics of Inclusion*, Ann Arbor: University of Michigan Press.

Cunill, N. (1997) *Repensando lo público a través de la sociedad*, Caracas: Nueva Imagen.

Dagnino, E. (2005) 'We all have rights… but: contesting concepts of citizenship in Brazil', in N. Kabeer, ed., *Inclusive Citizenship: Meanings and Expressions*, London: Zed Books.

de Vita, Á. (2004) 'Democracia deliberativa ou igualdade de oportunidades políticas?', in V.S. Coelho and M. Nobre, *Participação e Deliberação: Teoria Democrática e Experiências Institucionais no Brasil Contemporâneo*, São Paulo: 34 Letras.

Dryzek, J.S. (1996) 'Political inclusion and the dynamics of democratization', *American Political Science Review* 90(3): 475–87.

Dryzek, J.S. (2000) *Deliberative Democracy and Beyond: Liberals, Critics, Contestations*, Oxford: Oxford University Press.

Dryzek, J.S. (2001). 'Legitimacy and economy in deliberative democracy', *Political Theory*, October: 651–69.

Edwards, M. (2004) *Civil Society*, Cambridge: Polity Press.

Fischer, F. (2000) *Citizens, Experts, and the Environment: The Politics of Local Knowledge*, Durham NC: Duke University Press.

Fishkin, J., and R. Luskin (1999) 'The quest for deliberative democracy', *The Good Society* 9(1): 1–9.

Foucault, M. (1991) 'Governmentality', in G. Burchell, C. Gordon and P. Miller, eds, *The Foucault Effect: Studies in Governmentality*, Chicago: University of Chicago Press.

Fox, J. (1996) 'How does civil society thicken? The political construction of social capital in Mexico', *World Development* 24: 1089–103.

Fraser, N. (1992) 'Rethinking the public sphere: a contribution to the critique of actually existing democracy', in C. Calhoun, ed., *Habermas and the Public Sphere*, Cambridge, MA: MIT Press.

Fung, A. (2003) 'Survey article: recipes for public spheres: eight institutional design choices and their consequences', *Journal of Philosophy* 11(3): 338–67.

Fung, A., and E.O. Wright, eds (2003) *Deepening Democracy: Institutional Innovation in Empowered Participatory Governance*, London: Verso.

Gaventa, J. (2004) 'Towards participatory governance: assessing the transformative possibilities', in S. Hickey and G. Mohan, eds, *From Tyranny to Transformation*, London: Zed Books.

Gaventa, J. (2005) 'Deepening the deepening democracy debate', Institute of Development Studies, University of Sussex, Falmer, mimeo.

du Gay, Paul (2000) *In Praise of Bureaucracy: Weber, Organization, Ethics*, London: Sage.

Goetz, A.-M., and J. Gaventa (2001), 'Bringing citizen voice and client focus into service delivery', IDS Working Paper No. 138, Institute of Development Studies, University of Sussex, Falmer.

Goetz, A.-M., and R. Jenkins (2004) *Reinventing Accountability: Making Democracy Work for the Poor*, London: Macmillan/Palgrave.

Habermas, J. (1984) *The Theory of Communicative Action*, London: Heinemann.

Hajer, M., and H. Wagenaar, eds (2003) *Deliberative Policy Analysis: Understanding Governance in the Network Society*, Cambridge: Cambridge University Press.

Heller, P. (2001) 'Moving the state: the politics of democratic decentralization in Kerala, South Africa, and Porto Alegre', *Politics & Society* 29(1): 131–63.

Houtzager, P. (2003) 'Introduction: from polycentrism to the polity', in P. Houtzager and M. Moore, eds, *Changing Paths: International Development and the New Politics of Inclusion*, Ann Arbor: Michigan University Press.

Houtzager, P., A. Gurza Lavalle and A. Acharya (2004) 'Atores da sociedade civil e atores políticos – participação nas novas políticas democráticas em São Paulo', in L. Avritzer, ed., *Participação Política em São Paulo*, São Paulo: UNESP.

Immergut, E.M. (1992) *Health Politics: Interest and Institutions in Western Europe*, Cambridge: Cambridge University Press.

Kabeer, N., ed. (2005) *Inclusive Citizenship: Meanings and Expressions*, London: Zed Books.

Kohn, M. (2000) 'Language, power and persuasion: toward a critique of deliberative democracy', *Constellations* 7(3): 408–29.

Lefebvre, H. (1991) *The Production of Space*, Oxford: Blackwell.

Manor, J. (2004) 'User committees: a potentially damaging second wave of decentralization?', *European Journal of Development Research* 14(2).

Mansbridge, J. (1999) 'On the idea that participation makes better citizens', in S. Elkin and K. Soltan, eds, *Citizen Competence and Democratic Institutions*, University Park: Pennsylvania State University Press.

Mansbridge, J. (2000) What does a representative do? Descriptive representation in communicative settings of distrust, uncrystallized interests, and historically denigrated status', *Citizenship in Diverse Societies*, March: 99–124.

Mansbridge, J. (2003) 'Rethinking representation', *American Political Science Review* 97(4) November: 515–28.

MacPherson, C.B. (1973) *Democratic Theory: Essays in Retrieval*, Oxford: Oxford University Press.

Melucci, A. (1996) *Challenging Codes: Collective Action in the Information Age*, Cambridge: Cambridge University Press.

Mouffe, C. (2002) 'Politics and passions: the states of democracy', Centre for the Study of Democracy, London.

Pateman, C. (1970) *Participation and Democratic Theory*, Cambridge: Cambridge University Press.

Phillips, A. (1995) *The Politics of Presence*, Oxford: Oxford University Press.

Piven, F. Fox, and R. Cloward (1971) *Regulating the Poor: The Functions of Public Welfare*, New York: Random House.

Skocpol, T., and M.P. Fiorina (1999) 'Making sense of the civic engagement debate', in T. Skocpol and M.P. Fiorina, eds, *Civic Engagement in American Democracy*, Washington DC: Brookings Institution Press.

Tarrow, S. (1994) *Power in Movement: Social Movements, Collective Action and Politics*, Cambridge: Cambridge University Press.

Taylor, L. (1998) *Citizenship, Participation and Democracy: Changing Dynamics in Chile and Argentina*, London: Macmillan.

Thompson, J. (1995) 'Participatory approaches in government bureaucracies: facilitating the process of institutional change', *World Development* 23(9): 1521–54.

Tvedt, T. (1998), 'NGOs' role at the 'end of history': Norwegian policy and the new paradigm', in F. Hossain and S. Myllylä, eds, *NGOs Under Challenge: Dynamics and Drawbacks in Development*, Helsinki: Ministry for Foreign Affairs of Finland.

UNDP (2003) *Human Development Report*, New York: UNDP.

Warren, M. (2000) *Democracy and Association*, Princeton: Princeton University Press.

World Bank (2001) *World Development Report 2000/2001: Attacking Poverty*, New York: Oxford University Press.

Young, I.M. (1996), 'Communication and the other: beyond deliberative democracy', in Seyla Benhabib, ed., *Democracy and Difference: Contesting the Boundaries of the Political*, Princeton: Princeton University Press.

Young, I.M. (2000) *Inclusion and Democracy*, Oxford: Oxford University Press.

Young, I.M. (2004) 'Reply to Bohman, Drexler and Hames-Garcia', *The Good Society* 13(2): 61–3.

PART I

Inclusion and Representation in the Participatory Sphere

2

Brazilian Health Councils: Including the Excluded?

Vera Schattan P. Coelho

Contemporary debates on experiences of democratic innovation have encompassed heated disagreement about how effective 'new spaces' for citizen participation are in including ordinary citizens, particularly those traditionally marginalized and excluded. This chapter focuses on the Brazilian experience with Health Councils. It reports on research carried out in thirty-one Local Health Councils in the city of São Paulo, which aimed to clarify the relative significance of factors identified as central in establishing the democratic legitimacy of these 'new democratic spaces'.

The idea of making democracy more inclusive is not a new one: it is present, for instance, in the advocacy of proportional representation as a system that creates more opportunities than majority rule for the representation of minorities, as well as in the effort to multiply and strengthen spaces for deliberation within parliaments. It was above all after the mid-1970s, however, that participation and deliberation in 'new spaces' created in the state sphere or in the public sphere at local, national or international level began to be advocated as key ways to make democratic systems more inclusive (Coelho and Nobre 2004). These 'new spaces' are based on the idea that the inability of public policies to promote substantial changes in the status quo results in large part from the non-inclusion of ordinary citizens in the decision-making processes through which such policies are defined. As political institutions become capable of including ordinary citizens in policymaking, policies should become more responsive to their needs. After all, who would know better the problems that affect the population or the quality of services than the population itself? That is a very attractive idea, and it is the basis of the ongoing effort to democratize democracy around the world.

This chapter focuses on Management Councils, which, at least in terms of scale, are the most important participatory mechanism nowadays in Brazil. Over 28,000 of these councils have been established for health policy, education, the environment and other issues. They are organized at all levels of government, from local to federal, and they provide fora in which citizens join service providers and the government in defining public policies and overseeing their implementation. In order to understand better the nature of the participation being fostered in these fora, we conducted a broad survey with the thirty-one Local Health Councils (LHCs) in the city of São Paulo, to answer two main questions: first, is there evidence that a plural representation of civil society is under way, or is representation monopolized by the groups that already have political ties with public managers? Second, assuming that it is possible to recognize distinct patterns – that is, a larger or narrower range of associations included – can we relate these, as suggested by the literature, to certain characteristics of management, institutional design or associational life?

Data collected show that the spectrum of participants in LHCs in São Paulo is quite diverse, including social movements, disabled persons' associations, religious groups, civil rights associations, trade unions and individuals with no associational ties. That spectrum proved to be more comprehensive in areas that simultaneously had public managers committed to participation as a political project and more transparent and inclusive procedures used to select the councillors, and where associativism was strong. We also found that the presence of these conditions was not associated with the socio-economic profile of the areas studied. Our findings suggest that at least the first of the conditions needed to guarantee the basis for social participation – the inclusion of a diverse spectrum of actors – was met in this case.[1]

In the next section we review the literature that discusses the democratic potential of these 'new spaces'. In the following section we review the legal and political context of Municipal Health Councils (MHCs) and LHCs. We then present the associative profile of the participants of the thirty-one LHCs in the city of São Paulo and discuss the importance of political, institutional and social variables in explaining the variation found in the number of associations present in these councils. Next, we discuss how the strategies adopted by civil society and committed public managers play an important part in accounting for the degree of inclusiveness, as they may orient their procedural choices in ways that can significantly expand or constrain the inclusion of non-allies in these 'new spaces'. Finally, we discuss the lessons that can be learnt about how to build more inclusive participatory institutions.

Citizen Participation in Brazil

Given the constitutional reform and political innovations it has witnessed in the last decade, Brazil has been seen as one of the world's most important laboratories of democratic innovation (Gaventa 2004). The 1988 Brazilian Constitution, which established the formal transition to democracy, sanctioned the decentralization of policy-making and established mechanisms for citizens to participate in the formulation, management and monitoring of social policies. Hundreds of thousands of interest groups worked throughout the country as the Constitution was being drafted and collected half a million signatures to demand the creation of participatory democratic mechanisms.

This legal foundation promoted the development of an extensive institutional framework for participation by citizens, which included Management Councils, public hearings, conferences, participatory budgeting, and deliberative mechanisms within regulatory agencies. Of the plethora of participatory mechanisms in Brazil, participatory budgeting and Management Councils gained the greatest momentum in the 1990s. These two participatory mechanisms are linked to the executive branch and emphasize transparency, local control and the redistribution of resources to underserved areas (Coelho, Pozzoni and Cifuentes 2005).

Previous research, however, has raised questions about how effective these councils are at promoting citizen participation. In this view, their democratic promise has been compromised by a lingering authoritarian political culture in the Brazilian state, a fragile associational life, and resistance from both society and state actors (ABRASCO 1993; Andrade 1998; Carneiro 2002; Carvalho 1995). In this context, even when councils are implemented, the poorest remain excluded and continue to lack sufficient resources to articulate their demands, while the costs of participation continue to be lower for those with more resources.

These findings strengthen claims that participatory mechanisms are poor tools to achieve political equality. It has been argued that inequalities pervading the socio-political structure – like access to information, influence over government, and organizational possibilities – entail asymmetries and restrain political participation, which reinforces inequality and so deepens the representation deficit of disadvantaged actors (citizens with low income, low education, and low information access, for instance) (Pozzoni 2002). Participatory processes would therefore generate new forms of societal particularism, and entail risks that include 'the control of decision bodies by more active and established groups' (Jacobi 2000: 107).[2]

An increasing number of studies suggest the opposite: that under certain circumstances these fora might not only include the most disadvantaged segments of society but play a meaningful role in defining public policies. Overall, such analyses stress three determining factors. First, they suggest that certain conditions must be overcome before groups in civil society can effectively mobilize and organize. Second, the success of such fora depends on public authorities' commitment to the participatory project. Third, institutional design is crucial to their success.

With respect to the first factor, Gurza Lavalle et al. (2004) found evidence that new participatory spaces might favour the representation of excluded social groups. According to their study, rich and poor actors in civil society have equal propensities to participate, and the design of the new spaces may favour political initiatives by traditionally under-represented social groups. They argue that 'the participation promoted by the wave of institutional experimentation and innovation in recent years is not merely an exercise of common citizens' political involvement in the design of public policies, but rather includes a diverse range of collective actors' (Gurza Lavalle et al. 2004: 356). This is a crucial point, as collective actors have tendencies and modes of participation that are distinct from those of individual actors, because the former have motivations and organizational resources that lower participation costs.

Data from a survey on 'Associativism in São Paulo' also indicate a wide variation in associative behaviour within the *subprefeituras* (new administrative subdivisions), demonstrating that agents from a broad spectrum of civil society, including residents of the poorest areas of the city, are making a strategic investment in these associations as a way of gaining voice in the political process that decides issues affecting their lives (Avritzer et al. 2004). Popular associativism appears, in the survey, to cover both community associations and those linked to housing, health and education issues, representing 5 per cent of the city's population, and implying that some 500,000 individuals are involved. This means that almost 20 per cent of the overall population linked to associations in São Paulo are affiliated to the so-called popular associativism. Half of this population earns less than twice the minimum wage and has completed basic education only (dropping out of school at age 14), while 60 per cent are women. These data point in the same direction as our data on Health Councils in São Paulo: an important percentage of those who do participate have low levels of education and income. In other words, the poor are participating. Of the other 80 per cent, 51 per cent are concentrated in religious organizations, and it should be noted that an important set of these associations is also active with regard to community, housing and health issues. Yet another aspect underscored by Abers (2001) in her study of Porto Alegre's Participatory Budget is that people's belief that participation will bring them tangible benefits has a mobilizing effect, which balances organizational inequalities between participating groups over time.

As for the second factor – public authorities' commitment to the participatory project – Abers (2001) maintains that a key factor in the success of the participatory budget is investment by public authorities and local public institutions in the 'demonstration effect'. Public policy fora do not attract participants where the relationship of those bodies to people's everyday lives is not clear. However, in the participatory budgeting process studied by Abers, the city government had to make it clear to participants why their presence in assemblies would benefit them, and afterwards it had strictly to fulfil its promises. Abers suggests that a good participatory policy process does not reduce government involvement in decision-making. On the contrary, the state's active commitment is crucial to citizen participation.

Finally, for the third factor mentioned, Cifuentes (2002) and Fung (2003) argue that the ability of participatory fora to contribute to defining an agenda that expresses the interests of the poorest might be favoured by the use of institutional and procedural mechanisms that foster both the inclusion of participants with less technical expertise and fewer communication resources and their ability to take stands. These authors suggest the use of structural incentives,[3] participatory methodologies and deliberative approaches as ways to improve inclusiveness as well as the quality of endogenous processes of preference formation.

This brief overview shows the difficulty of creating conditions to overcome inequalities pervading the socio-political structure. It also shows that there are political and institutional processes that have contributed to changing the profile and scope of civil society's participation in public policies. Nevertheless, it raises an important question about the democratic legitimacy of the processes currently under way: have they been guaranteeing the inclusion of a plurality of civil society's segments? After all, when do public managers or civil society's mobilized segments bring their enemies or competitors into politics? Under what conditions are groups that do not belong to the networks of those managers included?

These are core questions for the debate on social participation. While many studies show that there has indeed been an increase in participation, they also suggest that it has been allowed by networks with strong partisan ties and loyalties (Coelho 2004; Gurza Lavalle et al. 2004; Hayes 2004; Cornwall, this volume). These studies point out that participants already have ties with public officials as political allies or service providers. It seems that sometimes public officials need to ensure civil society's participation and call upon their allies to play this role, and sometimes providers wish to guarantee their contracts with the municipality and use their vote in participatory arenas to bargain. The process might then represent a new mechanism for the exclusion of those outside such socio-political networks.

Data collected during this research show that the new participatory institutions are not inevitably captured by traditional political bodies. We found a diverse profile of council participants, ranging from councils including only one or two categories of associations that have ties with existing political bodies, to councils with a far more diversified composition. The question that remains and that will be tackled in the remaining sections is: how do we explain these differences?

Health Councils in São Paulo

The legal context

The 1988 Constitution defined health as a right of all citizens and a responsibility of the state, and established the Unified Health System (SUS) – the Brazilian public health system – based on the principles of universality and equity of healthcare provision. The SUS introduced the notion of accountability (social control) and popular participation. Health Councils emerged within the legal framework as the institutions responsible for enabling citizen participation in health governance. They were set up from local to state and federal levels, being responsible not only for taking government projects to the population but also for conveying suggestions from the population to the various levels of government.

Health Councils are permanent collective bodies that consist of citizens, health professionals, governmental institutions and health service providers. There are currently more than 5,500 Health Councils involving almost 100,000 citizens and a vast number of associations. Health Councils are political fora in which participants discuss issues and may make alliances to help the Health Secretariat plan and define priorities and policies. The Basic Operational Norms regulating the SUS stipulate that the number of representatives of civil society (citizens) must be equal to that of service providers, health professionals and government institutions taken together.

The strength of the MHCs largely derives from the law granting them veto power over the plans and accounts of the Health Secretariat. If the council rejects the plan and budget that the Health Secretariat is required to present annually, the Health Ministry, which manages 55 per cent of the public health budget, does not transfer funds. MHCs such as the one in São Paulo are of particular importance in health governance because one of the principles of the SUS was decentralization of the health system. Through the process of decentralization, municipal governments took on greater responsibility for both health planning and service provision. This process turned the municipality into a key political space for the definition of health policies, and MHCs into an important arena for participation in policymaking (Coelho et al. 2005).

LHCs were created in a number of Brazilian metropolises to support local administrations as well as Municipal Health Secretariats and councils. They have similar functions to those of the MHC but no veto power, since they lack a constitutional mandate.

Local Health Councils

The city of São Paulo, which has a population of some 10.5 million,[4] is conspicuous for sharp social inequality and unequal access to public services (CEM 2002). Much as in other Latin American mega-cities, the poorest areas are located on the outskirts. Wealthier areas, concentrated in the city centre, receive more public healthcare services and have the largest number of hospital admissions. Poorer areas have the lowest levels of access to healthcare (Coelho and Pedroso 2002). To counter these trends the Workers Party (PT), which governed the city from 2000 until 2004, has prioritized de-centralization and citizen participation. Shortly after rising to power, the PT administration subdivided the city into thirty-one political administrative regions, the so-called *subprefeituras*.[5] The population of these *subprefeituras* varies from 134,204 to 630,202, and their Intra Municipal Human Development Index (IMHDI) varies from 0.65 up to 0.91.[6]

In each *subprefeitura*, an LHC as well as a large number of health unit councils were created. They were set up in two years, involving the mobilization of over 2,500 people to participate in at least one monthly meeting – a significant number, especially considering the limited financial resources available to support the process. The Management Councils of the *subprefeituras* consist of 24 effective and 24 substitute councillors, half of whom represent civil society, and the other half the government, service providers and health workers.[7] The government is represented by officials appointed by the Health Secretariat, by the sub-municipal administrator or by the health co-ordinator of the sub-municipal authority. In the case of users and service providers, the movements, associations and sectors define their candidates and an open meeting is held in which mandates are formalized. Elections are publicized and health system technicians monitor the appointment process. The MHC of São Paulo legally includes representation from popular health movements, social movements, unions and associations of disabled and people with health disorders. LHC rules only specify that 25 per cent represent health workers, 25 per cent represent public and private service providers, and 50 per cent represent civil society.

Despite the importance of understanding how these councils work and whether they have an impact on health policy, this chapter focuses on just one feature: the composition of LHCs, as their democratic potential depends on their capacity to include a diverse and non-biased range of civil society segments.

Selection of Councillors and Composition of Local Councils

In 2001 and 2002, Eduardo Jorge, a historical leader of the 'Sanitarian Movement'[8] – which has existed for over thirty years and mobilizes health professionals around the SUS, especially those in public health – was the Municipal Health Secretary and was responsible for promoting a swift decentralization of municipal health policy. In that process, the first LHCs were created.

In 2001, the Health Secretariat ordered the *subprefeituras* to organize their LHCs – within a very short time and with few resources. We have previously reported the electoral processes during that period in four *subprefeituras* in East São Paulo. In those *subprefeituras*, recruitment for the councils was carried out by public managers within a network of associations with which they had some previous relationship. Other organized groups without the same ties remained apart from the process. In the interviews we conducted with twenty-two leaders of associations that work with health-related issues in the areas studied, but who did not take part in the council, only five were aware of their existence (Coelho and Veríssimo 2004).

In order to see if this dynamic was repeated in subsequent elections, we conducted a survey in 2004–05 on the composition of the thirty-one LHCs, on procedures for selecting councillors and on managers' adhesion to the social participation project.[9] Our first hypothesis was that we would find a broader range of civil society segments represented in councils in *subprefeituras* where managers were more committed to the project and where the council had made efforts to publicize the selection process. To test this hypothesis further we decided to gather information on the different profiles of social mobilization in these *subprefeituras*. Data on associative behaviour were collected and prepared by the survey 'Associativism in São Paulo' conducted in 2002 by Avritzer et al. Analysing these data presented difficulties discussed below, some of them methodological and others relating to the scope of a survey that covered the thirty-one *subprefeituras* in a city as large as São Paulo.

The data gathered on the composition of LHCs in the thirty-one *subprefeituras* show that some include only one or two categories of association, while others include up to seven categories, including non-affiliated representatives. Councillors reported themselves as representatives of: popular health movements; health units; religious associations; neighbourhood associations; unions; civil rights groups; participatory fora; homeless movements; landless peasants movements (MST); community or philanthropic groups; disabled persons' associations; non-affiliated representatives.[10]

Table 2.1 (column 2) shows that in sixteen of thirty-one *subprefeituras* more that three categories are represented. At least three of these categories – community groups, disabled associations and non-affiliated representatives – have no traditional association with the PT. Twelve *subprefeituras* included non-affiliated representatives, and their inclusion is not strongly associated with IMHDI rank. It seems reasonable to argue, then, that the LHCs are opening spaces for representation of the range of associations that make up civil society in the city, and that they have real potential as a space where different groups can negotiate projects and proposals concerning public health.

Nevertheless, the survey also found that twenty-nine of thirty-one *subprefeituras* concentrated recruitment in health units. Six *subprefeituras* included only these. In eastern and southern regions this way of organizing representation is strongly associated with the Popular Health Movement (PHM), which has been highly active in those regions since the 1970s and has strong ties with the PT (Bógus 1998). Other categories historically often related to left-wing parties, such as religious associations, participatory fora and the homeless movement were also more frequently represented (in fifteen, seven and ten *subprefeituras* respectively). Of the fifteen *subprefeituras* representing three categories or less, eleven have a strong presence of associations with ties to the PT.

So does the difference in the number of sectors represented relate to how elections were organized and the degree of managers' commitment to the social participation project?

In order to identify differences between electoral processes that occurred in the various sub-municipal authorities, we determined whether a database of associations and movements in the region had been organized, what means were used to publicize the elections (newspapers, radio, Internet, mail campaigns), whether candidatures were granted both to individuals and to organizations, and whether documentation on the entire election process was available. We also attempted to determine whether or not there were systematic contacts between the council, civil society, the health system and the political system, since we believe that by improving those contacts

Table 2.1 Characteristics of councils by *subprefeituras*, municipality of São Paulo, 2003–05

Subprefeituras	1 IMHDI	2 No. of categories of association represented	3 Score for procedures and contacts	4 Score for management of participation	5 Score for popular associativism	6 No. of above-average scores for 3, 4 and 5
Jd Ângela	0.64	1	4	3	13	1
São Miguel	0.67	1	8	11	6	1
Cidade Ademar	0.69	1	9	8	5	1
Casa Verde	0.73	1	8	9	9	1
Penha	0.73	1	7	9	14	1
Campo Limpo	0.74	1	8	11	3	1
Cidade Tiradentes	0.67	2	4	10	5	0
Freguesia do Ó	0.70	2	10	9	7	1
Itaquera	0.71	2	2	5	8	1
Santo Amaro	0.85	2	7	11	3	1
Tremembé	0.68	3	6	10	5	0
Ermelino	0.73	3	9	14	0	2
Jabaquara	0.73	3	13	13	6	2
Ipiranga	0.76	3				
Santana	0.81	3	9	15	7	2
Parelheiros	0.65	4	6	12	3	1
Socorro	0.67	4	14	12	2	2
Vila Maria	0.73	4	7	12	12	2
Aricanduva	0.76	4	15	15	1	2
Lapa	0.85	4	6	11	6	1
Pinheiros	0.91	4	12	11	13	3
Itaim Paulista	0.67	5	9	8	11	3
São Mateus	0.67	5	7	11	4	1
Vila Prudente	0.69	5	6	11	13	2
Pirituba	0.71	5	7	11	16	2
Guaianazes	0.67	6	10	14	1	2
Mooca	0.80	6	10	11	4	2
Vila Mariana	0.88	6	10	6	7	1
Perus	0.69	7	9	12	2	2
Butantã	0.79	7	9	9	12	2
Sé	0.84	7	9	10	13	2
Average			8.33	10.46	7.03	

councils tend to become better known, increasing the likelihood that elections become more competitive.

Data collected showed that the 2003 and 2004 elections were organized in very different fashions in the distinct *subprefeituras*. In some of them, civil society was in charge of the electoral process and in others it was limited to organizations already known to public managers. There were also cases of active work by those managers in order to contact and involve a wide range of organizations and users. Table 2.1 (column 3) presents information relating to the process of choosing councillors who represent civil society and the intensity of relationships established between the council, civil society and the political and health systems. On the basis of responses to our questions we calculated values (between 1 and 15) for these relationships and procedures: the higher the value, the more relationships that council has and the more inclusive are its adopted procedures. We did not find, however, any significant statistical association between the spectrum of associations represented and the process of choosing councillors or the intensity of relationships established by the council.

As to public managers, we expected that those most committed to the project of social participation would invest in the construction of effective councils, which in turn should contribute to raising society's interest in participating. That is, we expected that the higher a manager's commitment, the more segments would be represented in councils. This commitment was inferred from the replies to questions on the existence of a budget provision; the type of information submitted and the way in which it was made available to councils; the regularity of submission of such information; the presence of the health coordinator within the council; and councillors' ease of access to the authorities and the information they requested. On the basis of responses we calculated values (between 1 and 15), which are presented in column 4: the higher the value, the greater the commitment shown by the public-sector manager to local social participation. We did not find, however, any significant statistical association between the spectrum of categories of civil society represented in the councils and the commitment of public officials to participation as a political project.

These results suggest the need to revisit the stance of those who intend to explain variation in participation by the degree of civil society organization. According to that argument, given that civil associativism is unevenly distributed over the city, it should be pos-

Table 2.2   Number of sectors present in Local Health Councils and characteristics of management of social participation, of associativism, and of the selection procedures, São Paulo, thirty *subprefeituras*, 2003–05

No. of associations	Up to 1 favourable condition	2 or 3 favourable conditions
Up to 3	11 *subprefeituras*	3 *subprefeituras*
More than 3	4 *subprefeituras*	12 *subprefeituras*

Note: Favourable conditions are understood as the presence of committed managers, a high degree of associativism and inclusive procedures. Favourable conditions can range from one, when only one of these conditions is present, to three, when all three are present.

sible to explain the variation in number of categories of associations represented in the councils by the degree of associativism in the distinct *subprefeituras*: that is, we should find more segments represented where the proportion of participants in civil associations is higher. Associative behaviour was evaluated on the basis of the statistical data gathered by the survey on 'Associativism in São Paulo' and refers to the number of individuals from a sample who declared they had taken part in activities linked to popular associativism. Column 5 presents the weighted frequency of participation in activities linked to popular associativism by those who replied. However, we have not found any significant statistical association between the spectrum of segments represented in the councils and the degree of civil associativism present in the *subprefeituras*.

These findings suggest that the inclusion of a wider spectrum of participants cannot be explained only by design (publicizing the elections), political variables (commitment of public officials) or associative variables (percentage of participants in civil associations).[11] So, once again, how do we explain the differences in the range of associations represented on different councils? We next tried an alternative approach aimed at assessing the role of the simultaneous presence of the variables we had analysed. Using the available data, we assigned the councils one point for each variable that was above average (Table 2.1 column 6). Based on that analysis, we found a strong pattern. The data point to a positive association between the simultaneous presence of these variables and a wider spectrum of associations represented in the council.[12] This association is summarized in Table 2.2.

Our analysis suggests that none of the three variables analysed by itself explains the breadth of segments represented in the councils, but the simultaneous presence of these variables in a given sub-municipal authority does favour diversity.[13]

These data are worth closer inspection. The simultaneous presence of the variables in question is associated not only with a greater range of associations but also with the presence of non-affiliated representatives.[14] While we have no means of reconstituting the associational universe of the *subprefeituras*, we know that there are 'non-affiliated citizens' in all of them and that those autonomous citizens are indeed more systematically present in the *subprefeituras'* councils where the variables in question also have a stronger presence. Given that those councils also include a higher number of civil society sectors, we have good reason to believe that this is due to a process of interaction between public managers and civil society sectors that seek to influence health policy, and it is not merely a result of a higher number of sectors in a given *subprefeitura*.

Civil society, managers and procedures in the *subprefeituras*

We are then led to another question: which kind of interaction between public managers, social associations and procedures favours the inclusion of a wider spectrum of civil society segments in the councils? In order to outline an answer we used data gathered in qualitative interviews made with public officials, health managers and councillors.

To understand the context in which these councils were set up, we have to bear in mind that decentralization creates a new field for disputes over resources between and within *subprefeituras*. In a government that has social participation as one of its mottoes, those with the support and endorsement of civil society will be in a better position to negotiate their demands. In that context, it comes as no surprise that a relevant percentage of managers have dedicated their efforts to the project of organizing the councils.[15]

More surprising was that managers established the councils based on alliances and using quite different strategies. While some chose the Health Movement as their prime ally, others sought a wider support network, which included both conservative and progressive movements and associations, as well as autonomous representatives. In the first case, the manager–movement alliance seems related to a more incipient institutionalization of procedures for choosing representatives and to the predominance of the Health Movement presence. In the second case, the manager–society alliance was possible, to a large extent, through active work by the health coordination team towards mobilizing and publicizing the council among a broader public.

Protagonists in the first group are the managers who report a life history strongly entangled with that of the Health Movement – some of whom have even become managers based on their participation in popular movements and organizations or in the Health Movement itself. In those cases, managers and leaders of the movement reported a strong common identity. They share a 'history of struggle' and a common 'political project' rooted in the social movement history that gave birth to part of the PT. That identity explains the delegation of the organization of electoral processes to the movement and the justification given for that delegation. It is a strategy to preserve 'civil society's autonomy', as well as the acknowledgement of that group as the one most qualified to organize the process (Galvanezzi 2004). Therefore, organizing the selection of councillors becomes itself less institutionalized, thus guaranteeing space for the Health Movement within the council. As Hayes has properly pointed out, 'the history of the health movement in the area of São Miguel predicts their presence in the Health Council but their over-representation would appear to be related to their control of the selection process' (Hayes 2004: 36).

In the second case, we find associations that do not have the same ability to organize popular mobilization as the Health Movement, and professionals related more to the hospital and labour union areas, as well as to public health. Those professionals moved areas and clientele due to changing guidelines and programmes of the municipal administration over the last fifteen or twenty years. As a result of this history there exists both a certain ease in establishing contact with movements and associations – since in their careers numerous partnerships were established in order to guarantee the implementation of distinct health programmes – and a certain territorial 'uprooting'. When facing the need to organize the council and to demonstrate that civil society endorsed their demands to both the *subprefeitura* and the Municipal Health Secretariat, those managers did their best to identify possible sources of support, which lead to mobilization of a diverse set of segments, as well as non-affiliated representatives.

So we have one case in which managers and health movements guaranteed their political strength by restricting the process of selection of councillors to a universe of actors with close political ties. In the other case, 'uprooted' managers, as well as movements, associations and autonomous representatives that do not have the same organization and identity as the Health Movement, defined their political strength by establishing a more fluid but also more diverse network of alliances. Those two situations do not exhaust the richness of cases or the specific conditions that characterize the distinct *subprefeituras*, but they allow an initial approximation of the nature of the actors, their interests, and the constraints involved in the process of organizing decentralized and participatory management in the city of São Paulo.

Final remarks

The democratic experiences described in this chapter represent important innovations, building political institutions that seek to promote engagement with the citizenry: a network of councils distributed throughout the municipality, covering both central and peripheral areas, as well as rich and poor ones. These councils fall into two groups: those that include up to three categories of civil society associations, of which many have ties to the PT; and the remaining sixteen councils that include more than four categories of associations, and where there is a strong presence of non-affiliated representatives and also of associations that have no historical ties to the PT. What has our analysis shown about how to build more inclusive participatory institutions?

As discussed above, previous analyses of participatory processes, particularly of Management Councils such as those analysed in this chapter, highlighted variables that restricted the democratic potential of these 'new democratic spaces' in Brazil: the legacies of a lingering political culture and lack of social mobilization, as well as bureaucrats' resistance to power-sharing. Other analyses focusing on the participatory budget process offer more optimistic conclusions, showing how constraints to participation could be overcome with the involvement of committed public officials. More recent work in this field also points to a particular characteristic that seems to amplify the democratic potential of these spaces: the presence of a mobilized civil society.

In previous work we drew attention to the central role that institutional design could play in deepening the democratic potential of these spaces, a role not being addressed in the debate. We argued that improving the process of council member selection and developing appropriate procedures to ensure the inclusion of all participants in discussions and decision-making processes were key elements of this institutional design.

The results presented in this chapter confirm the results described earlier by the more optimistic authors, in that the set of variables previously identified played an important role in explaining the diverse profile of councils established in the city. Drawing on the data presented, we argue that political authorities and civil society help to define procedures regulating the operation of these councils, and that the procedures chosen will significantly expand or restrict the spectrum of civil society involved. Nevertheless, our results go further as they show the significance of the *simultaneous* presence in a given *subprefeitura* of managers committed to the project of social participation; a wide spectrum of popular movements, civil associations and citizens that display interest in participating in the health policy; and a certain know-how about the organization of participatory institutions that leads to a more inclusive range of participants.

The remaining question is a difficult one: why, in certain conditions, do public officials and mobilized groups in civil society open the doors of the councils to a wide spectrum of participants, which may include partisans' competitors and those with antagonistic interests? As we have seen, the answer depends on the strategic choices made by managers and participants about which alliances and procedures they believe will best serve their interests and values. That is to say that the democratic potential of these 'new spaces' emerges neither from the participants' renunciation of struggle for political space, nor from their moral decision to adopt a package of 'best participatory practices,' but from both the perception that they must fight to have power in these spaces and from the strategies they choose.

The democratic experience we have described allows some optimism about broadening the debate and experimenting with questions and practices of constructing more inclusive representation.

Table 2.3 Categories of associations represented in the Local Health Councils of the thirty-one *subprefeituras*, São Paulo 2003–05[16]

Council	HDI-M	Popular Health Movement/Health Unit	Religious Assoc.	Neighbourhood Assoc.	Non-affiliated	Civil Rights Group	Participatory Forum	Homeless Movements	Disabled Person's Assoc.	Community or Philanthropic Group	Landless Peasants (MST)	Unions	No.
Jd Ângela	0.64	•											1
Parelheiros	0.65	•	•	•		•							4
Socorro	0.67	•	•	•						•			4
Itaim Paulista	0.67	•	•	•	•	•							5
Cidade Tiradentes	0.67	•				•							2
Guaianazes	0.67	•	•	•	•			•			•		6
São Mateus	0.67	•	•	•	•			•					5
São Miguel	0.67	•											1
Tremembé	0.68					•		•		•			3
Cidade Ademar	0.69	•											1
Perus	0.69	•	•		•	•	•	•			•		7
Sapopemba	0.69	•	•			•		•	•				5
Freguesia do Ó	0.70	•					•						2
Itaquera	0.71	•		•									2
Pirituba	0.71	•	•	•				•		•			5
Casa Verde	0.73	•											1
Ermelino Matarazzo	0.73	•	•			•							3
Jabaquara	0.73	•	•	•									3
Penha	0.73	•											1
Vila Maria	0.73	•	•	•	•								4
Campo Limpo	0.74	•											1
Aricanduva	0.76	•	•	•						•			4
Ipiranga	0.76	•	•					•					3
Butantã	0.79	•		•	•	•	•	•	•				7
Mooca	0.80	•	•		•		•	•				•	6
Santana	0.81	•					•		•				3
Sé	0.84	•	•	•	•		•	•				•	7
Lapa	0.85	•		•	•	•							4
Santo Amaro	0.85	•							•				2
Vila Mariana	0.88	•	•		•		•		•	•			6
Pinheiros	0.91		•	•	•					•			4
Total		29	15	14	12	9	7	10	6	6	2	2	

It would be particularly instructive to extend investigations into how the capacities for democratic citizenship and participation among poor and marginalized groups can be deepened, as well as which capabilities, mechanisms and government practices have the potential to favour a pluralistic representation of civil society inside the councils. It remains to be seen whether the actors involved in this process will be motivated and able to experiment in this way. The answer will be given in the sphere of politics, but, as ferment around these 'new spaces' is growing, we can speculate that the spectrum of social, state and political actors motivated to take part in the game will broaden.

Notes

This chapter presents the results of the 'Participation and Social Inclusion in Brazil' project, carried out by the Centro Brasileiro de Analise e Planejamento (Brazilian Centre for Analysis and Planning: CEBRAP) with the support of the Development Research Centre on Citizenship, Participation and Accountability, Institute of Development Studies, University of Sussex.

We would like to thank the Advisers on Social Participation of the Health Secretariat of the Municipal Authority of São Paulo, the Municipal Council, the Health Coordination Team and Management Councils of the *subprefeituras* for their support and interviews, as well as John Gaventa, Argelina Figueiredo, Andrea Cornwall, Alex Shankland, Joanna Wheeler, Marian Barnes, Marcus Melo, G. Baiocchi, David Kahane, Adrian Gurza Lavalle, Simeen Mahmud, and the 'Spaces for Change' research group for their valuable comments and suggestions, and José Veríssimo, Tiago Borges, Carolina Galvanezzi and Nílian da Silva for their valuable contributions in collecting and organizing research data.

1. In recent work, Fung (2004) points out that participatory institutions face a trade-off between legitimacy (inclusion), justice (endogenous formation of preferences) and effective governance. Clearly, more inclusion does not necessarily lead to more effective governance. We need more reflection and empirical data to understand these trade-offs better.

2. Observers of participation in political campaigns and voting behaviour in richer countries have shown the powerful effect of income on participation (Verba et al. 1995).

3. These incentives are possible as participatory processes may facilitate access to public goods.

4. This figure refers to the Municipality of São Paulo. The Greater São Paulo area has a population of 17.6 million.

5. In 2000, the city was divided into forty-one health districts corresponding to the forty-one district councils. In mid-2003, the city was divided into

thirty-one *subprefeituras*, with the district councils absorbed by these and being renamed local councils. The term 'local councils' will be used to refer to both periods.

6. The IMHD is calculated for each *subprefeitura* based on data about income and education of the head of the family gathered by the Censo and informed by the Brazilian Institute of Geography and Statistics (IBGE) and infant mortality and longevity rates informed by the State Foundation for Data Analysis (SEADE).

7. In 2001, the law stated that these councils should have a total of 16 representatives, of which 8 should be from civil society. Today, these totals are 24 and 12 respectively.

8. The Health Movement originated in the early 1970s in the eastern part of the city. The Movement militated for a better public health system and was supported by Christian grassroots communities, students and public health workers.

9. We were unable to complete all the questionnaires for the *subprefeitura* of Ipiranga. This *subprefeitura* appears in Table 6.1 as we have information about the associational profile of the councillors, but was not included in the remaining analysis due to the lack of data concerning the other variables.

10. See Table 6.3.

11. We also tested the hypothesis that in *subprefeituras* where HDI-M is higher there would be more segments represented in the councils. That hypothesis corresponds to the classic argument present in literature about participation, according to which in areas with more resources there is more availability and interest in participation. We did not find any association between the two variables.

12. Pearson Correlation = 0.531★★. A correlation of 0.431★ also appears for the simultaneous presence of committed managers and inclusive procedures.

13. However, we found no association between the simultaneous presence of those variables and the HDI-M of *subprefeituras*.

14. Pearson Correlation = 0.473★★.

15. In nineteen out of the thirty *subprefeituras* studied we found managers committed to the project of creating and organizing LHCs.

16. The table only informs whether a given category of association is present in the council and not the number of councillors representing each sector. It is worth noting that the distribution of the number of councillors among these categories of association replicates the same pattern described in the 'total' row. The majority of councillors are linked to health movements/health units and only a few are linked to the MST and unions.

References

Abers, R. (2001) *Inventing Local Democracy: Grassroots Politics in Brazil*, Boulder CO: Westview Press.

ABRASCO (Brazilian Association of Collective Health) (1993) *Relatório final da oficina: incentivo à participação popular e controle social em saúde* [Final report:

Popular participation and social control in health], Série Saúde e Movimento (Health and Movement Series), vol. 1, Brasília: ABRASCO.

Andrade, I. (1998) 'Descentralização e poder municipal no Nordeste' [Decentralization and municipal power in the northeast], in J.A. Soares, ed., *O orçamento dos municípios do Nordeste brasileiro* [The municipal budget in the Brazilian northeast], Brasília: Paralelo15.

Avritzer, L., M. Recamán and G. Venturi (2004) 'Associativismo em São Paulo' [Associativism in São Paulo], in L. Avritzer, *Participação em São Paulo* [Participation in São Paulo], São Paulo: Unesp.

Bógus, C.M. (1998) *Participação Popular em Saúde* [Popular participation in health], São Paulo: Anna Blume.

Carneiro, C.B.L (2002) 'Conselhos: Uma reflexão sobre os condicionantes de sua atuação e os desafios de sua efetivação' [Councils: challenges for their implementation], *Informativo CEPAM* 1(3) March: 62–70, São Paulo: Fundação Prefeito Faria Lima.

Carvalho, I.A. (1995) 'Conselhos de saúde no Brasil' [Health Councils in Brazil], ENSP/FIOCRUZ, Série Estudos, *Política, Planejamento e Gestao em Saúde* 3: 5–41, Rio de Janeiro: Ibam/Fase.

CEM (Centre of Metropolis Studies) (2002) 'Dossiê espaço e política na metrópole' [Dossie Space and politics in the metropolis], *Novos Estudos* 64, November, São Paulo: Editora Brasileira de Ciências.

Cifuentes, M. (2002) 'Political legitimacy of deliberative institutions', Master's thesis, Institute of Development Studies, University of Sussex, Falmer.

Coelho, V.S. (2004) 'Conselhos de saúde enquanto instituições políticas: o que está faltando?', in V. Coelho and M. Nobre, *Participação e Deliberação: teoria democrática e experiências institucionais no Brasil contemporâneo*, São Paulo: 34 Letras.

Coelho, V.S., and M. Nobre (2004) *Participação e Deliberação: teoria democrática e experiências institucionais no Brasil contemporâneo* [Participation and deliberation: democratic theory and institutional experiences in contemporary Brazil], São Paulo: 34 Letras.

Coelho, V.S., and M. Pedroso, (2002) 'Distribuição de serviços públicos de saúde no município de São Paulo', *Novos Estudos* 64; November: 141–52, São Paulo: Editora Brasileira de Ciências.

Coelho, V.S., B. Pozzoni and M. Cifuentes, (2005) 'Participation and public policies in Brazil', in J. Gastil and P. Levine, *The Deliberative Democracy Handbook*, San Francisco: Jossey Bass.

Coelho, V.S., and J. Verissímo (2004) 'Considerações sobre o processo de escolha dos representantes da sociedade civil nos conselhos de saúde em São Paulo' [Considerations about the process of chosing concillors in São Paulo's local health councils], in L. Avritzer, *A Participação em São Paulo*, São Paulo: Unesp.

Fung, A. (2003) 'Recipes for public spheres: eight institutional design choices and their consequences', *Journal of Political Philosophy* 11: 1–30.

Galvanezzi, C. (2004) 'A representação popular nos conselhos de saúde' [Popular representation in health councils], research report, São Paulo: Fapesp.

Gaventa, J. (2004) 'Prefácio', in V. Coelho and M. Nobre, *Participação e Deliberação: teoria democrática e experiências institucionais no Brasil contemporâneo*, São Paulo: 34 Letras.

Gurza Lavalle, A., P. Houtzager and A. Achrya (2004) 'Lugares e atores da democracia: arranjos institucionais participativos e sociedade civil em São Paulo' [Places and actors of democracy], in V. Coelho and M. Nobre, *Participação e Deliberação: teoria democrática e experiências institucionais no Brasil contemporâneo*, São Paulo: 34 Letras.

Hayes, L. (2004) 'Participation and associational activity in Brazil', Master's thesis, Institute of Development Studies, University of Sussex, Falmer.

Jacobi, P. (2000) *Políticas Sociais e a Ampliação da Cidadania* [Social policies and citizenship], São Paulo: Editora da FGV.

Pozzoni, B. (2002) 'Citizen participation and deliberation in Brazil', Master's thesis, Institute of Development Studies, University of Sussex, Falmer.

Verba, S., L.K. Schlozman and H. Brady (1995) *Voice and Equality: Civic Voluntarism in American Politics*, Cambridge MA: Harvard University Press.

3

Spaces for Participation in Health Systems in Rural Bangladesh: The Experience of Stakeholder Community Groups

Simeen Mahmud

In 1998, as part of health sector reforms, the Bangladesh government initiated efforts to enhance community participation in the public health system. This chapter examines two experimental initiatives that sought to bring about more 'people-centred' public health provisioning. It seeks to identify barriers in establishing people's participation, as well as factors and processes that contribute to making participation effective, even if in a very limited fashion. Analysis of this experience finds that the absence of prior mobilization is liable to make these spaces ineffective in realizing the right to health and promoting citizen participation. Additionally, although citizen participation is adopted as a strategy by the state, forms of participation that fail to engage public providers and local state officials may offer little prospect of holding the state to account at the local level. Simply creating spaces will not lead to participation if people are not also sufficiently motivated to engage in them, but participation without engagement with providers may not be adequate to bring about the anticipated change in provider attitudes and behaviour vis-à-vis citizens.

Origins and Experiences of People's Participation in Health in Bangladesh

In the Alma-Ata Declaration of 1978, a 'people-centred' approach to health was put forward as not just involving contributions to support the functioning of local health systems, but also involving people actively in defining health priorities and allocating scarce resources. Community participation, through ownership and implementation of local health services, is now a widely accepted means of ensuring that people have a say in local health systems (Dasgupta et al. 2001; MoHFW 1997). Behind this lies a widely held expectation that participation in decision-making will lead to better health outcomes and reduce inequality in outcomes and access to services. When the link between policymakers and providers is weak and supervisory mechanisms are inadequate, users are often best placed to monitor provider performance (World Bank 2004: 64). Giving people 'voice' in the health system is thought to allow them to translate their knowledge of poor service quality into political power and influence at the local level.

By creating public pressure and generating debate, people's participation also facilitates the democratic process. Informed and more inclusive participation is held to be good not only for the health system but also for promoting citizenship practice and rights claiming. If the government is unable or unwilling to ensure provider accountability, people may have no option but to develop mechanisms for engagement and inclusion in local-level service institutions. This type of citizen action by poor people, whether on their own or in alliance with others, may even make politicians and policymakers respond in ways that compensate for systemic weaknesses. However, while a more engaged, and indeed political, understanding of public involvement informs efforts to bring about accountability through participation, it is more common in practice for people's participation to be seen simply as an additional ingredient in healthcare delivery, valued primarily for its instrumental role in making health services more cost effective (Kahssay and Oakley 1999). The long-term broader objective of enabling poor people to become more active citizens through participation in the management of delivery systems is not usually recognized as an expected outcome.

The health sector in Bangladesh is a combination of both private and public healthcare delivery, but the public policy approach to service delivery and attitude to users dominates both sectors. Apart from a number of targeted vertical services, like the expanded programme of immunization, public healthcare provision is plagued by negligence of duty and unprofessional behaviour by healthcare providers, poor maintenance of physical facilities, illegal user fees and long waiting times. In addition, there is extreme wastage of scarce resources by leakages of medical supplies and provisions. The national government has for some time realized that state provisioning of health services does not meet minimal standards of care quality and service accountability, and that access to services is inequitable. Although internal mechanisms to ensure quality of care and account- ability of service providers have traditionally been in place within the health system, these have been non-functional.

Since the mid-1990s, the Ministry of Health and Family Welfare (MoHFW) undertook massive reforms of the health system through the Health and Population Sector Programme (HPSP), designed to reduce wastage and ensure long-term financial sustainability (Mahmud and Mahmud 2000). Influenced by prevailing thinking within international development agencies, notably the World Bank, these reforms were intended to make health services 'responsive to clients' needs, especially those of children and women and the poor, and achieve quality of care with adequate delivery capacity and financial sustainability' (MoHFW 1997). The HPSP comprised six separate but interwoven components[1] that were to be implemented through a strategy involving direct participation by all stakeholders (health service users at the grassroots level, healthcare professionals and care providers, government, private and volunteer organizations engaged in healthcare planning and provision, and donor agencies providing financial assistance). In addition, there was to be a shift in the approach to service delivery, from separate health and family planning services to a reproductive health approach with integrated services. This coincided well with the donor condition of a shift from project aid to sector-wide programme aid. A number of challenges confronted the implementation of this ambitious strategy in the context of Bangladesh.

Community Participation: Challenges and Prospects

In Bangladesh, most people rely totally on the state to provide and ensure all rights, almost precluding any role for citizen engagement in overseeing state provisioning. The primary responsibility for creating a 'good society' is invariably vested upon the *sarkar* (government), which is expected to provide education, healthcare, jobs and personal security (Mahmud 2004a: 6). Poor people see themselves as having very limited responsibility and even less ability with respect to participation in public processes. Increased reliance on the market because of very low quality public service reduces incentives for participation in the public health system. People lack confidence in questioning government action since their knowledge about state delivery mechanisms is limited and they are unable to assess how the system operates. The realization that participation requires time and effort dampens enthusiasm and propensity for action. It is not surprising that the poor are virtually absent from any kind of public process or space. They engage in informal spaces that are directly and immediately relevant to their livelihood pursuits, like the *shalish* (informal courts), village factions, informal labour and credit markets, informal savings groups and NGO-mobilized groups. Strong dependency relationships hinder individual agency and action in claiming even legitimate and formally recognized rights, because the poor and marginalized are very risk-averse and unlikely to violate common practices of allegiance and submission. Consequently, people do not have a lot of experience in and even fewer expectations from participation in public processes.

The institutional character of service delivery organizations also discourages participation. In the health system, since services are 'free', providers view users as recipients and passive beneficiaries instead of as citizens with rights to claim and dissent. Providers have expert knowledge and believe that they know best what the community needs and how to deliver this. Citizen participation and civic engagement are not only regarded as unnecessary but even viewed with suspicion and hostility. Indeed, public policy has been described as 'managerial paternalism' and as 'disciplining' to create 'good' citizens who are compliant users of public provision (Cornwall et al. 2002). People are not willing to participate if they do not feel that they are able to make a difference, if mechanisms and procedures for participation are unfamiliar or too costly, or if they feel they are not in control (Mahmud 2004b).

Finally, poverty mediates all action. Poverty conditions rationales not only of the powerless poor but also of the powerful non-poor. Poor people can spare little time and effort for actions that do not have direct and immediate relevance for their livelihoods. The costs of participation by the poor can be prohibitive and gains negligible. Poverty also strengthens the hand of the powerful through the real threat of withdrawal of support, and hence limits the spaces in which poor people are able to participate.

What prospects are there in this context for the enhancement of people's participation in health systems? The following sections take a closer look at two experimental institutional mechanisms set up to attempt to implement 'people-centred' healthcare.

Designing Institutions for People's Participation

In 1998, two distinct types of invited institutional spaces for people's participation were initiated experimentally by the Bangladesh government. In one case, village community groups were mobilized for local essential healthcare provision by the elected local government body with support from local public health providers. In the second case, Health Watch Committees (HWCs) were established at Upazila (subdivision) and Union (lower than subdivision) levels with the support of non-state agencies such as NGOs working in the community.

Community groups

Informed by the association of improvements in service quality and access with the direct involvement of the community in constructing, operating and 'owning' health facilities, the MoHFW decided to set up community-owned and managed clinics in every village/ward. These aimed to provide a one-stop service for reproductive and primary health to the most deprived population groups (women, children and the very poor). The expectation was that community participation in their management would make essential health services accessible to such groups (MoHFW 1997). Community ownership would be ensured by building the clinic on land donated by the village and by having the community share the costs of construction and operation of the clinic with the government.

In each locality, a community group (CG) would be mobilized by the Union Parishad (UP) (an elected local administrative body). Selected by the local elected UP chairman, nine village residents were to sit on the committee, which would be composed of local elected representatives, local service providers, local influential residents representing various professions and social classes, and representatives from landless groups and women. This group would be responsible for the operation of the clinic. The CG represented a unique departure from the existing provider-driven service delivery model and centralized, top-down policymaking environment.

The construction of community clinics and health worker salaries were to be financed by government funds. Clinic maintenance (cleaning, security) was supposed to be financed by the community, but, in the event, members were generally unable or unwilling to mobilize funds. Some expressed the opinion that poor villagers could not make donations or even pay a token fee for services, but even well-off villagers and CG members did not make personal donations as originally planned. Clinics were usually in disrepair with leaking roofs and broken tubewells. Although the Upazila health complex was supposed to supply all the medicine required for the clinic, medicine supplies were always inadequate, and the Upazila medical officers were generally unresponsive to requests from the CGs. By 2001, all clinics under the initiative had been closed.

Health Watch Committees

Emerging from a related, but distinct, logic – one in which stakeholder participation is seen as a means to increase accountability and reduce wastage – MoHFW decided to establish stakeholder committees of service users to monitor the performance of public providers at the local level. The strategy in this case was to elicit the active support of non-state agencies to set up citizen's HWCs, composed of local residents. The ministry decided to use NGOs for the purpose, since they had good access to the communities they worked in. It requested that several NGOs attend a meeting to discuss an experimental project to give voice to people's reactions to and problems with the healthcare system. Nijera Kori (NK), a rights-based NGO working in rural areas since the mid-1980s, was asked to arrange a series of workshops to let poor people in rural areas voice their complaints and expectations of such committees. Later, NK and three other NGOs were given the responsibility of forming local-level HWCs with community representatives at the Upazila and Union levels. This was started on an experimental basis in nine Upazilas.[2]

The ministry proposed that the HWCs should consist of members from different professional and social groups. NK slightly modified the suggested structure: they proposed two Union HWCs instead of one and also decided that half the members should be women.

At the Union level the female UP member was chair and the NK worker was secretary. In addition, there were five other members: two from the NGO landless groups (one male and one female), two professionals (lawyer, journalist), one teacher, and one service holder. At the Upazila level, the HWC was to have nine members, including a journalist, a lawyer, a non-government doctor, an NGO representative, a teacher, one woman, one grassroots service holder, a UP member and two representatives from the Union HWCs.

Partnership with NGOs – strong and visible actors on the Bangladesh development and governance landscape – to complement public service provision is not new. The expectation was that monitoring from outside would act as a powerful tool for delivering accountable health services. What is unique and of interest, however, is the reliance upon an NGO that is not the usual service delivery type, but has a long history of mobilization and action around the rights of poor and marginalized people. Unfortunately, the new health policy launched in 2004 no longer has any provision for supporting the HWCs. Except for the HWCs mobilized by NK the others have been dissolved.

Participation, Inclusion and Voice

Comparing and contrasting the two institutions, a number of striking differences emerge. These are significant for assessing the democratic potential of these invited spaces as well as their prospects for improving health service delivery. The analysis that follows explores in more depth questions about who participates, why participants take part, how they participate and in what kinds of decision-making processes.

Who participates?

Processes of recruitment and selection to CGs and HWCs differed significantly. CGs were supposed to be mobilized by the elected UP chairman through broad-based local consultation. In our research sites it was evident that selection was neither transparent nor participatory. Membership was biased towards better-off and professional classes, such as schoolteachers, businessmen and well-off farmers. Selected women members were usually the wives of wealthy villagers. The elite bias limited acceptability within the community. The community clinics were frequently referred to by villagers as the 'personal family hospital' of some influential local elite.

In the HWCs, selection was fairly transparent and more participatory. The HWC was selected by 'popular' voting at an open workshop in the community, attended by people from different social classes and professions, government officials, health administrators, doctors, landless farmers, members of NK landless groups in the village and local NK workers. Names were proposed by local people in the open workshop. Inclusion in HWCs was largely on the basis of pre-existing relationships with NK. Most of the people invited to the workshops to form the committee were familiar with activities of NK. Most of the selected members, whether poor or well-off, were associated with NK in some way or other.

However, although members did not represent the entire community, particularly non-NK members, participation was more inclusive and democratic than in the CG. Representation of landless groups in HWCs was around 50 per cent and even higher in the Union HWCs. The HWCs also managed to have at least 50 per cent women members and most of the Union HWCs were chaired by women. In other words, women's representation was relatively greater in committees that were closer to the community. The Union HWCs were more homogeneous, as most members belonged to NK landless groups and were neighbours, while in the Upazila HWCs other professional members were not necessarily NK members or poor.

While CGs had representation from the medical profession, government providers were excluded from HWCs. Initially doctors posted at the local health facilities were interested in being on the HWCs since they did not want to be accountable to a body in which they had no representation. But at the initial workshops, local people expressed their unwillingness to include doctors because the interests of the committee would be compromised. Instead they proposed that HWCs would invite doctors to the meetings but they could not be a part of the official monitoring mechanism. They felt that if powerful people were involved in the committee, they would lose their hold over it, and they would be dominated. Instead they wanted to understand problems by themselves and wanted to solve these with the cooperation of the doctors. One woman member of Upazila HWC in Dumuria said:

In the first meeting where the committee was formed, the doctors protested violently and said that if such a committee were to be made, then they must be a part of it. But we didn't agree with the doctors and stood firm in our position and from then on we have had a conflictual relationship with them.

Why participate?

Initial motivation for participation in government CGs was not very strong. A third of the members interviewed said they had wanted to be included in the CG; the remainder agreed when asked by the UP chairman. Those who wanted to join thought it was a good cause and might bring some benefit to the community. Some thought there would be some future personal gain from membership, like a job. Few protested their inclusion in the CG, and, once nominated, members appeared enthusiastic about sitting on the committee since it raised their status in the village. Apart from the UP member, none of the other members had any experience of participation in any public decision-making forum.

Awareness among members about the CG's role was poor. Five members (10 per cent) failed to mention any function for the CG at all. Operating and maintaining the clinic was seen as a role for the CG by 60 per cent; monitoring the performance of health workers was seen as a role by half; motivating people to use the clinic was seen as a role by one-third; while fund mobilization was seen as a role by only three members (16 per cent). Actual activities of members consisted primarily of visiting the clinic (50 per cent) and motivation (20 per cent), while one-fifth reported no activity. Only seven members, or less than one-fifth, attended CG meetings. Some felt that they were performing their duty simply by attending meetings.

Women members were less likely to be aware of their roles as CG members and were even less active. In one case, women members complained they had not been informed about their inclusion in the CG and that membership was thrust upon them. In two cases, members did not know they were on the CG and only discovered it at the time of our interview. When asked about his role, one male CG member (the land donor) answered: 'I myself am not aware that I am a member, so I do not know what my responsibility is.' Another male CG member said: 'I know I am a member. Members have no specific work.' One male chairperson of CG said: 'I am the one who launched the clinic. I hear [from others] that it is functioning.'

Among members of HWCs, motivation to participate in the new invited space was strong. At the initial workshop, people on their own suggested mechanisms for their participation and proposed to do this without any compensation like payment or fees. The only return demanded was to be taken seriously, so that when they informed the ministry of problems some action would be taken. Members of NK landless groups have been trained to participate in different kinds of social spaces as part of the goal of NK to establish rights in a systematic and organized manner. HWCs also had better communication as a group since members were relatively more homogenous.[3] NK group members had acquired the skills and capabilities for participation and were trained to overcome communication gaps with more educated and professional people.

Previous experience at an individual level was also a resource for participation in the new space. One woman member of an Upazila HWC who had been an elected UP member for several terms described her participation as follows:

> Whenever anyone in my area has a problem with their health they request me to accompany them to the hospital. We take the emergency patients to the emergency services where the doctor should be present 24 hours but one night I didn't find a single doctor in that department. For half an hour I shouted and then the doctor came and asked me what happened. I threatened him that we will arrange processions and a movement against him the next morning. So he went to Khulna hospital and requested a transfer.

Rules and norms

The ministry provided guidelines for establishing both the CGs and the HWCs, which stipulated a regular monthly meeting and the broader objectives of these institutions. In the CGs we researched, meetings were extremely irregular and were convened by word of mouth. There were no written minutes and attendance was extremely poor. The CG chairman and the health worker who was secretary were the most vocal members at meetings, while women were largely silent. Clinic maintenance and the lack of medicine supplies dominated the discussion at meetings, but fund-raising to meet costs of maintenance or to purchase medicine for free distribution was rarely discussed. There was a lack of effective leadership and proper delineation of authority and responsibility within the CG. Some chairmen of CGs were only seen on paper: they did not even know that they had been selected to chair the CG. Most CG chairmen had very little time to convene and attend meetings, which were basically conducted by the health worker. For all practical purposes the clinic functioned like a satellite clinic of the Upazila health complex, but with even fewer services.

Since rules for deliberation and negotiation were not explicit in the CGs, existing hierarchical social relations of family, kin and community tended to be re-created within these newly opened spaces. These unequal social relationships, such as between rich and poor, young and old, or women and men, caused differential capabilities among members to participate. Professional and higher social status members dominated deliberations at meetings, while poor members and women were silent. Hence, decisions were always by consensus, with almost no dissenting opinions or conflicting views. The minutes of meetings confirm this observation.

HWC meeting minutes showed that meetings were held regularly, past activities were reviewed and duties for the next period were assigned as a matter of routine. These duties included asking doctors to attend hospital on time and enquiring about medicine supplies, which they did even when faced with complaints and resistance from doctors. Meetings were well attended and conducted in a very disciplined way: the agenda was read, each member reported their work progress, and a workplan for the following month with individual duties was finalized. The minutes were written by the secretary in a register but were not circulated among individual members.

Rules for deliberation and participation were more explicit in the HWCs. Participants of the initial workshop, facilitated by NK, established their own set of rules to run the committee. NK gave committee members a basic orientation training, explaining the objectives of the committee and their duties, what activities they would perform, which places they should visit, how they could perform social surveys and find out about prevalent problems in their area. The orientation mentioned how committee members would be accountable to each other and responsible for different assigned jobs; and how differences of opinion between the committee members would be resolved through discussion. There was training for NK landless group members to increase their ability to overcome communication gaps with more educated and professional members.[4]

Inclusion and difference

Differential participation was very common in the CGs. One educated woman CG member felt that being a woman made her inadequate to speak at meetings: 'I have no ability on my own, and besides I am a woman.' A landless woman CG member commented: 'I am poor and ignorant, what will I say? Those who are more knowledgeable speak more.'

The opportunity to speak at HWC meetings was relatively more egalitarian. Some women HWC members felt that everyone had equal opportunity to participate but sometimes members had nothing to say. Women's greater presence in terms of numbers and leadership roles was a factor in their relatively greater activity and voice in the HWCs, but the presence of professional and 'elite' men in the Upazila HWC nevertheless constrained women's voice and activism. Women were more vocal and active in the Union committees, whose membership was more homogenous and less male or elite dominated. The chairman of one Union HWC noted: 'Female members of my committee are quite vocal at the Union Committee meetings. But in the Upazila meeting, they sometimes feel shy to give their opinion because they don't have proper knowledge about some issues discussed such as supply of medicine, health policy etc.'

Case tracking of four women members of Union HWCs showed that women were more active in raising awareness in their locality about the relatively greater health problems faced by women (safe delivery, regular antenatal care, nutrition, hygiene, sanitation, vaccination, family planning and, most importantly, violence against women). They did this through informal discussion in neighbourhood public places or someone's courtyard. The female members were also more active in dealing with health crises, such as working in flood shelters. Elite members and grassroots members appeared to have different strategies for participation in the HCWs. NK staff believed that poor people were more willing to engage in protest than the elites, who did not want to get drawn into conflict and confrontation. A woman member said: 'The educated and well-off members can debate or discuss a point in an organized way but when it comes to protesting they are usually silent and try to stay out of the scene.' A landless farmer said: 'The educated members speak well, which we cannot do, but we can fight to protest, which they cannot.'

Professional members of the HWCs have a perception that non-professional members lack awareness of problems. One HWC member, a diploma-holding doctor, commented:

> At the Union Committee every member is given the floor but everyone does not participate equally because some members, especially women, are less expressive and feel more reserved or do not have issues to raise. But at the Upazila level the committee members are more equally vocal and participate very seriously because every member is an aware member of society. But there is no one who does not participate at all.

Some members felt that Union committees actually functioned better than Upazila HWCs because Union HWC members were more familiar with the poorer villagers, while the educated members of the Upazila HWC were more distant from the community and also frustrated at not being able to bring about much change. Health workers at the Union level also had similar socio-economic backgrounds to the Union HWC members and hence were less likely to be hostile, compared to doctors at the Upazila level.

Leadership and authority

In the CGs, lack of decision-making authority was accompanied by an absence of effective leadership. The CG chairman was usually the UP member, who, being a politician and elected representative, did not have much time for CG work. Lack of commitment by leadership of the CG was evident in the fact that in only two of the seven CGs studied were meetings held regularly, minutes written, or members in regular attendance. Despite being a people's representative, the CG chairman did not have much clout with the Upazila health complex doctors with regard to medicine supplies for the clinic or with the clinic health workers, who continued with their home visits instead of treating patients at the clinic.

Villagers who were aware of the CG did not have much confidence in the ability of the chairman. One woman commented: 'It is no use speaking with the chairman or a member. They say, "Go now. I shall see what I can do." But nothing happens because they don't give us any importance.' Another villager said: 'There is no medicine. I complained to the committee about it, but they don't like to listen to anything.' Another poor woman with a sick son lamented: 'When my son had fever, the chairman told me to take him to the Upazila hospital. You tell me, what use is the clinic then? I can't do anything about it because I am poor.'

In HWCs, the NGO worker who was member secretary played the crucial role of facilitator, and NK local staff provided leadership. NK organized and mobilized the community workshops, motivating local elites and professionals to join the committees. NK was instrumental in the decision to have two instead of one Union HWC and in modifying the structure of the committees. NK also provided training to members in participation and deliberation, and institutional support when faced with hostility from doctors. All the public meetings were arranged through NK's initiative. NK workers convened committee meetings, recorded minutes, produced reports for the ministry and maintained links with ministry administration.

HWCs, however, continued to lack authority in seeing through decisions. The president of one Union HWC commented: 'We only discuss matters and take decisions but cannot execute them, particularly decisions about reforming the hospital administration. We don't have the authority. The meeting resolutions are to be stored in the files only.'

What Difference Has Community Participation Made?

The most striking contrast between the two institutions is in their impact on participants and on service delivery. The CGs studied appear to have had negligible positive impact or outcomes. The HCWs have, however, had some interesting outcomes that are worth exploring in more detail.

NK's leadership built the capacity to participate among members, stimulating awareness and providing a channel for their energies and frustrations with existing service provision. One member said: 'Although there were problems at the health centre people were not so aware of these and they didn't have any intention to get together and protest these...they didn't know who to complain to.'

A woman member said:

> NK helped us to get organized and to let different types of people come together and work together.... I always thought about forming a committee like this but I never managed to do it. But we will be able to continue it. NK will not be there always but we will have to carry on this organization.

Another woman member, when asked whether they would have been able to form the HWC on their own, said:

> No, I think that people would protest about the doctors at some point but it would have taken more time…. NK gave a forum to come together and work together, which is more effective. However, we as a group think that we will now be able to continue without NK.

Participants in the newly created HWC spaces, even when coming from varying socio-economic backgrounds, established their own ways of working together. They worked around communication barriers and concentrated on activities where they had strengths and resources. Despite differential abilities for participation and deliberation in the beginning, the members learned to participate more equally so that all members had the opportunity to express opinions. One Union committee member said:

> Of course not everyone talks equally. Myself and the chairman, the journalist and one of the college teachers tend to talk the most. When the others understand these things then they give their response…. We just discuss these problems informally. The problems are discussed very seriously in the meetings and we plan what to do next. But if it has anything to do with the hospital then the committee generally asks me to go and see what happened.

Another woman member said:

> I think that we always try to participate equally in the meetings but there are differences in education level and status so there is a difference in people's ability to think and talk. However, if a member is remarkably silent then we encourage them to speak up.

The most visible changes have occurred at the community level rather than at the provider level. The communities were more aware about what services were available; the number of people coming to the health complexes for maternal healthcare, immunization and family planning had increased; awareness regarding different superstitions related to diseases, the nutritional value of different foods, and proper hygiene and sanitation had increased. A woman member of Dumuria Upazila Committee said:

> People are now more … conscious about healthcare in general. When people refer to us in the hospital they get better attention. Now they get medicines more often. And when they don't get proper healthcare and complain to me then I go to the hospital and speak to the doctors.

And a male Bandhapara Union Committee member noted:

> At least we have been able to ensure that the doctors come to the hospitals at the right time and stay there until their duty hours end. Today I noticed that some of the hospital staff came to the complex even before their hour for reporting to work.... We have been able to make people conscious about proper healthcare and nutrition requirements. We did several campaigns for pregnant women and now we are campaigning for the nutrition programme and pressing pregnant women to go there and check their prenatal health.

Implications and Lessons

This case study suggests the importance of a number of factors in making institutions for community participation viable and effective:

Enabling language and policy

The language and rhetoric of rights and people's participation among government agents, professionals, bureaucrats and service providers, although having primarily a token value, were used to advantage by some of these new spaces. The HWCs continued asking for accountability from hostile doctors because they knew government agencies were talking about people's right to health. Yet the absence of laws to regulate the performance of public healthcare professionals and the powerful medical association allowed government doctors to ignore the HWCs and even take an openly hostile stance.[5] In one study area, government doctors sat in on meetings to discuss how to prevent the HWC from 'interfering' in their duties, for example by restricting them from levying 'charges' from patients.

Authority over decision-making

The decision at the centre to establish community clinics did not involve any devolution of decision-making or policymaking to villagers. Residents were not consulted about the clinic site or about their healthcare needs, and clinics were usually established on land donated by the elected UP member or a relative, even when villagers found the location inconvenient. These factors hampered motivated participation. While NK was vested with responsibility for organizing the HWCs, the committees were not accorded the authority needed to monitor provider performance. Promises of legal backing were not forthcoming, and the committee's authority declined.

Official and financial support

The role and function of CGs was unique and unfamiliar, and created the possibility of conflict and hostility. Lack of strong and visible official support in the face of this undermined the authority and effectiveness of these new spaces. No funds were allocated for holding CG meetings, and no further support was given to ensure that the CGs functioned, even for basics such as the procurement of medicine. Eventually even the limited institutional support was withdrawn, and the clinics were closed down.

In the HWCs, some small funds were allocated by the ministry for organizing the initial community workshops and to facilitate regular reporting of HWC activity by NK to the Ministry. NK provided logistical support (place for meeting, stationery, postage) for holding committee meetings, but members had to pay for transportation and refreshments themselves. Although funds were earmarked for annual reviews of the committees, these never took place because the ministry said that there was no money available. Members often spoke about the lack of funds, which restricted their ability to assist poor people, who could not even afford the conveyance cost to the health complex.

Official recognition for the HWCs was promised by the Ministry of Health, which assured community members that HWCs would be given a legal basis for their mandate and members would be provided with identity cards. HWC members were enthusiastic in the beginning about visiting health facilities as they felt they had the authority to monitor the doctors and hospital administration. But their authority was undermined when they did not receive official recognition or identity cards. As a result doctors came to ignore the HWC. One member commented: 'We used to visit the hospital regularly at first, and though the doctors opposed us they took us seriously. But now the doctors don't care about us and refuse to talk to us regarding hospital issues.'

The need for grassroots mobilization and awareness-raising

In the case of CGs it was assumed that the UP chairman was best placed to nominate members to represent villagers' interests. In reality, all the non-professional CG members were either related or closely connected to the UP chairman; the women members were housewives from well-off households, having little access to the public domain or interaction with ordinary villagers. Poor community mobilization was indicated by the fact that villagers were largely unaware of the existence of the CG.

For the HWCs, it was assumed that NK would be able to mobilize the community and devise a mechanism to ensure a representative selection procedure, since they had a long history of working with marginalized groups. But, despite NK's experience, community awareness of the existence of the HWC was limited. All the residents interviewed in two locations said they had not heard of a committee where they could go and complain about discrepancies in the health complex. One user, a petty trader, said: 'I don't know where to complain but I really want to complain. If you tell me who I can complain to, I will go and complain to them – if it works.' When asked whether villagers knew about the committee, one NK worker replied: 'People may not know about our committee but they know the members. Members of other NK groups know about this committee but the rest of the people outside NK do not know much about the HWC.'

Conclusion

These experiences of people's participation in rural Bangladesh offer a number of insights into designing viable institutions that can deliver on some of the promises of people's participation in health. First, it is clear from this analysis that resources are needed for people's effective participation in invited spaces, in the form of both official recognition and financial resources. Other resources include sustained institutional support at least until these spaces take an institutional shape and gain community acceptance. Second, the analysis shows that where community mobilization accompanies establishment of new spaces, opportunities are gained for proper representation and community acceptability and to create real pressure behind people's participation. Without such mobilization and without building aware-ness among the population, invited spaces will lack legitimacy as well as efficacy. Third, if people have previous experience of participation in other spaces, this can make participation and deliberation more meaningful. This kind of experience can be built through capacity-building, such as through training. It can also have wider effects, such as contributing to poor and marginalized people's ability to engage in organized public protest.

Participation for voice is only the first step in establishing account-ability, and even strong voice can be meaningless and fail to influence provider performance if policymakers are not interested or do not have the capacity to listen. The exclusion of officials from the invited space creates hostility and conflict and undermines the credibility of people's participation efforts among health professionals. Alliances of community representatives with administrators and managers are likely to be more successful in establishing accountability because this can ensure the support of the higher administration or powerful members of society (like pharmaceuticals companies, police) and be a more direct way of registering complaints and demanding action. There may even be some merit in including providers (doctors) in the beginning to avoid demoralizing and unproductive conflict. The participation by users and service seekers to the exclusion of providers and managers can mean voice is ignored or not heard. But since the poor feel more comfortable with the present structure, the inclusion of administrators and providers can be a way to start to build internal capacity and mutual trust before moving on to more conflictual and difficult areas like monitoring.

The Bangladesh experience with peoples' participation for making healthcare provision more 'people centred' indicates that under certain conditions even efforts that originate from outside can be effective and sustainable. It is important to recognize that there are structural factors (institutional support, prior experience, strong com-munity mobilization, and resources) that can promote and encourage participation in a context where citizen action by the poor and marginalized entails many costs, and where rights claiming is not a part of peoples' livelihood strategies.

Notes

This chapter is based on research with seven community groups located in Upazilas in three geographic regions of the country (Pabna in the north, Madaripur in the centre, and Chittagong in the south), consist-ing of interviews with members of the Community Group (CG), users and non-users resident in the locality, and in some places Union- and

Upazila-level health personnel (see Mahmud 2004b). In all, information was available for 49 (15 women) CG members, 92 users and 61 non-user villagers. For the experience of the Health Watch Committees (HWCs) we rely on case studies of the HWCs established with the support of Nijeri Kori (NK), a rights-based NGO, in four districts, with one Upazila and two Union Committees in each area. Case studies included 53 in-depth interviews with members of the HWC, local NGO workers, NK staff at Dhaka, user and non-user residents, and local public healthcare professionals at the Upazila health complex. Several meetings of Upazila and Union HWCs were also observed.

1. These components were an essential services package, reorganization of service delivery at Upazila level, integrated support services, hospital-level services, sector-wide programme management and policy, and regulatory action.

2. Earlier, a national Stakeholder Committee had already been formed, which had taken a decision to set up grassroots stakeholder watch committees composed of local people and professional groups at the Upazila and Union levels.

3. In the Union HWC of Dhonbari all non-professional members were members of other NK groups. The UP members and village doctor in the Upazila HWC in Dumuria were members of NK as well.

4. Elementary, secondary and higher-level training, and training on land laws, globalization, agriculture, trade, information etc.

5. In fact, doctors are so powerful that the medical association filed a legal case against the government declaring HWCs illegal on the grounds that outsiders monitoring their performance was against the terms of reference of their appointment. The government won the case and HWCs were formed, but doctors' hostility continued.

References

Cornwall, A., M. Leach, I. Scoones, A. Shankland and R. Subrahmanian (2002) 'Sectoral dimensions of participation in policy: a comparative view of educa-tion, health and environment', IDS Workshop (draft), Institute of Development Studies, University of Sussex, Falmer.

Dasgupta, M., H. Grandvoinnet and M. Romani (2001) 'State-community syner-gies in development: laying the basis for collective action', Policy Research Working Paper No. 2439, Washington DC: World Bank.

Kahssay, H.M., and P. Oakley (1999) *Community Involvement in Health Development: A Review of the Concept and Practice*, Geneva: World Health Organization.

Mahmud, S., and W. Mahmud (2000) 'Policies, programs and financing since the International Conference on Population and Development: Bangladesh country study', in S. Forman and R. Ghosh, eds, *Promoting Reproductive Health: Investing in Health for Development*, Boulder CO and London: Lynne Rienner.

Mahmud, S. (2004a) 'Citizen participation in rural Bangladesh: reality and percep-tion', *IDS Bulletin, Spaces for Change* 35(2).

Mahmud, S. (2004b) 'Increasing voice and influence in the health sector in rural Bangladesh: is there a role for community participation?' (draft), Bangladesh Institute of Development Studies, Dhaka.

MoHFW (Ministry of Health and Family Welfare) (1997) *Health and Population Sector Strategy*, Ministry of Health and Family Welfare, Government of Bangladesh, Dhaka.

World Bank (2004) *World Development Report 2004: Making Services Work for the Poor*, Washington DC: World Bank and Oxford University Press.

4

Gendered Subjects, the State and Participatory Spaces: The Politics of Domesticating Participation in Rural India

Ranjita Mohanty

In the last two decades, a variety of institutional spaces have been created by the Indian state at the village level to invite, encourage and enhance the participation of poor, low-caste (*dalit*), and tribal groups and women. Claiming to be based on democratic principles and procedures, such spaces promise to include the excluded people in deliberations and decision-making. The spaces are attractive to people for the sheer logic that they are created by the state, yet there are caveats, problematics and challenges that characterize their participation in these democratic institutions and the processes that take place within them. Often the existence of other spaces created by movements, NGOs or people themselves, where they practise participation, enable them to transfer their learning and skills to state-created spaces and energize them (Mohanty 2004). However, in the absence of other spaces, the state is possibly the only actor that is expected to create conditions for the actualization and animation of the institutional spaces it constructs. If the state fails to do that, the spaces remain largely empty ones, where otherwise excluded groups, such as women, may never gain entry to actualize participation, despite their eagerness.

This chapter examines the presence and absence of women in three institutionalized spaces created by the state to promote development and democracy: sectoral institutions of health and watershed development, and the constitutionally mandated institutions of local government called panchayats. It traces the practices and dynamics of representation, inclusion and voice within these spaces in three villages in Karuali district in the state of Rajasthan: Khubnagar, Akolpura and Bhikampura. The first is the home of the local panchayat headquarters, the second is a revenue village which has basic service institutions, and the third is a hamlet. All three are mostly populated by scheduled castes (SCs) and scheduled tribes (STs)[1] in a context marked by extremes of poverty and exclusion.

My analysis raises questions about how women are represented in these institutions, whether their inclusion leads to substantive participation and voice, and whether these spaces are capable of enhancing the political agency of women, fashioning their political imagination and resulting in their political empowerment. In analysing women's experiences of participation in this setting, I explore the challenges of building genuinely inclusive and substantive representation and voice for marginalized actors.

Visions of the State

Women in Karuali have known the state in many forms: as provider of essential services such as the post office, school, health centre and roads. They have images of the state as it manifests itself in ostentatious election campaigns – cascades of motor cars on the dusty and uneven roads, shining flags, larger-than-life photographs of future leaders, and public meetings where people gather in their millions. They have also known the state as the police, and as the revenue officer, essential in ensuring legal order. The might of the state, despite its non-performance, is a seductive force. The idea of the state as the powerful big brother is also in the post-colonial imagination. A combination of welfarism, developmental and social justice agendas are also associated with the state. Out of both fear and respect, people would like to associate with the state. Hence, despite being a merely formal presence, and notwithstanding all the humiliations that they are subjected to, women may still want to be part of the institutional spaces created by the state.

The contemporary democratic revival, with its emphasis on building and strengthening local institutions, has brought the role of the state into sharp focus. Studies have shown that in many contexts, poor and resourceless people continue to look to the state to intervene and solve their problems when it comes to the fulfilling of basic needs, physical security and conditions of dignified living.

For historical reasons, the state still looms large in the perception of millions of people. Notwithstanding the retreat of the state under a globalized and liberalized economy, in countries like India the state is an everyday presence in the lives of poor and vulnerable sectors such as low castes, women and tribal people. As codified power, ultimate decision-maker and resource mobilizer, the state impinges on the lives of people more than any other force, thereby determining how affairs in society are to be managed.

As Chandhoke puts it, political preferences for the state over other actors are 'the outcome of historical processes...that preference formation takes place in a historical context, that of specific institutions or systems of rules. These shape interest, fix responsibility and guide the formation of expectations' (2005: 1037). To understand participation in state-created developmental spaces, it is important to understand the nature of the post-colonial state and the depth of people's relationships of dependence and patronage with it. It is important to capture how the state features in the imagination of people, since it is their relationship with the state, ranging from disillusionment and despair to seeing it as a patron and a benefit, which is reflected in their relationship with state-created institutions. Despite the failure of the state to erase unequal material and social relationships, it has instilled a sense of political consciousness among the deprived section, though that consciousness is often played out on the basis of groups, which try to compete with each other for social and political dominance. In this competition and negotiation for power, women in general and low-caste and tribal women in particular are left at the margins. It is only with the creation of local institutions and reinforcement of affirmative action through reservations in political, educational and development institutions that their political participation has gained some impetus.

The local institutional spaces that I explore in this chapter have come into existence through different traditions of thought and policy decisions. Sectoral development projects, such as for watershed management and health, are guided by the state's mandate of uplifting the socio-economic conditions of the rural poor. The health institutions are part of the Integrated Child Development Scheme (ICDS) in which women are selected by government functionaries to run *anganwadi*, which are children's schools and health centres for expectant mothers and small children. The watershed project is a time-bound sectoral project. It has a village-level committee in each village to implement the project, to which representation of women and men is sought through nomination; each village committee has a total of ten or eleven members, out of which three or four members are women.

The panchayats, unlike the development committees, were created as units of local governance though the 73rd Constitutional Amendment in 1992. Understood variously as the grassroots units of governance, village republic, and local governance (Sinha and Nandy 2000; Hiremath 1997; Mathew and Nayak 1996; Jain 1996; Rai et al. 2001) the panchayats are part of a three-tier system of governance that begins at the village and ends at the district. Each panchayat consists of several revenue villages and hamlets, and is divided into several wards from which candidates are elected to the panchayat. These members are referred to as ward members/*panch*, and the head of the panchayat is called *sarpanch*. *Gram sabha*, or the village council, which is the general body of all the adult residents in the villages of which the panchayat is constituted, is the body to which the panchayat members are accountable. A third of the seats in each panchayat are reserved for women. Women are expected to stand for the seats that are reserved for them, as well as for the general/open seats. Provisions are also made to reserve seats for SCs and STs in accordance with their numerical presence in a particular panchayat.

The different routes through which these spaces have evolved historically explain some dimensions of the way women's membership is constructed within them. Watershed development projects, which are fixed-duration target-oriented projects, constitute the committee to engage women actively in the project so that they can influence poverty outcomes through effective resource management, decision-making and ensuring an equitable distribution of benefits. The new policy guidelines are based on a process change approach and call for the state to change from a controlling authority to becoming a provider of technical advice and support services in the development of the watershed. To strengthen the local institutions, the policy speaks of developing the institutional, managerial and technical capacity of people so that they can manage natural resources. It calls upon the state to develop a new role based on a spirit of partnership with the users of the natural resources in the village.

The Integrated Child Development Scheme (ICDS) of the Department of Women and Child Development has a thirty-year history, and aims to improve the nutritional and health status of vulnerable groups through a package of services, including supplementary nutrition, preschool education, immunization, health check-ups, referral services, and nutrition and health education. It provides an integrated approach for converging basic services through community-based *anganwadi* workers and helpers, through supportive community structures/women's groups and the *anganwadi* centre, which is a meeting ground for mothers and frontline workers. At the village level, the *anganwadi* centre has become a pivot of basic healthcare activities, contraceptive counselling and supply, nutrition education and supplementation and preschool activities. As part of its thrust on building the community organization of women, the ICDS forms self-help groups of women to engage in saving and credit activities.

Panchayats, in contrast to these two developmental spaces, have a constitutional mandate to encourage political participation of women and engage them in governance so that they can participate as well as ensure democracy at the local level. Evolved as a result of de-centralization of decision-making, panchayats are supposed to engage people in assessing local needs, planning and executing solutions. While development projects have a welfarist approach in providing for women's membership in the committees, membership in panchayats is guided by the principles and legalities of affirmative action emanating from the state's agenda of social justice. Developmental thinking, directed towards changing the socio-economic landscape, engages women as committee members, users and beneficiaries; governance institutions, directed towards involving rural communities in local democracy, engage women as elected representatives in the framework of democracy. In their normative orientation, both institutions have a transformative agenda and women, at least theoretically, come to occupy different categories and are expected to enact roles that make them agents in influencing the developmental and democratic outcomes of the institutions.

Invited spaces as empty spaces

'Invited spaces' are conceptualized by Cornwall (2002) as spaces created by external agencies such as the state into which people are invited to participate. She contrasts invited spaces with the social and associational spaces of everyday life by suggesting that externally created spaces can be sites in which participation is domesticated, and in which the dynamics of power between actors within them offer very different possibilities for exercising voice and agency from those spaces people create for themselves. In the villages where this study is located, women's visibility in public spaces and their participation in state-created local institutions are negligible. Situations of chronic poverty together with rigid caste hierarchies, entrenched patriarchy and an apathetic bureaucracy have given rise to a situation where women have failed to participate in a meaningful way. Hence when we look at these institutional spaces through the lens of gender we find them largely empty and non-functional for women. One way of analysing this is through the conceptual category of *empty spaces*, a subcategory of invited spaces, denoting contexts where a marginalized group fails to populate an official invited space. The procedures and structures are there; also in some cases formal membership of women can be found. Yet all these do not translate into meaningful political participation.

In reality, an empty space is seldom completely empty. Even in the dismal scenario where women are purposely kept outside the boundaries of officially created spaces, in their own ways they try to enter that space. In my earlier research in Uttaranchal, where I could see traces of women's engagement, I argued that institutional spaces such as these can be considered as necessary though not sufficient conditions for participation and democracy (Mohanty 2004). In the context of empty spaces, can we hold the same argument that institutional spaces, despite all their shortcomings, have a normative grounding which *can be* activated to create conditions for women's engagement in development and democracy? What would explain the 'emptiness' of the panchayat and watershed committees as participatory spaces for women? And how can we best understand women's engagement with these spaces – either in seeking entry, or in maintaining their 'emptiness'? What do *they* see as the benefits of engagement, and how do they view the barriers they experience to inclusion and voice?

In what follows I describe my own standpoint in investigating this question, and point to three key elements that explain the failures of these invited spaces to secure the meaningful political participation of women: the control by men of the recruitment of women and of women's representative voices; women's relegation to being beneficiaries and wage earners within invited spaces; and stereotypes of women's public roles that go unchallenged by a putatively neutral state.

Investigating women's roles in participatory spaces

Conducting research, I would like to think, is a different experience for a researcher who is also an activist. At one level it is a deeply satisfying act, to visit the villages, talk to the women, develop a relationship. At another level, it is frustrating to see the poor conditions: to contrast it with the urban centre where I live. I am acutely aware of my personal and professional locations that drive me to Karuali: my academic training in the university in social sciences and my long years of working with NGOs. I try to be a disciplined, systematic scientific researcher; I also try to be empathetic and sensitive. The cognitive and emotive threads run inside me, making research at once a cathartic and a disturbing experience.

I visit the Society for Sustainable Development, an NGO based in the district town of Karuali. I spend long hours talking to them, before I visit the villages. I tell them that I want to visit villages where they are not working, in fact where no NGO has ever gone and worked. I had a mental picture of what the villages would look like. But regrettably the reality is somewhat different. The roads are dusty, dust from stone mines casting a thick veil over our heads. When we step into the first village, I decide almost intuitively that I will just make a round of the village talking to people informally. I do not want to be, at the moment, pressured with the thought that I have a research agenda. The *varanda* where I am sitting is a post office, and I develop a friendship with the person who distributes the mail. I know from my days spent with my grandparents in their village that this is a person whom everybody likes, who knows who lives where and who does what. I am fortunate to have met him. We fall into conversation. I request that he accompany me to the village. He agrees and we start walking. We meet many people on the way and greet them. People are friendly and courteous, inviting us to their homes for tea. I am not constrained by time or research methodology. I sit drinking tea, chatting. Preethi, my colleague, who is still researching her M.Phil., is excited, but thinks I am crazy: 'We have not yet met a single woman – Ranjita, lets try to meet them.'

By now it is obvious that we have to meet the women in their homes; I have gathered some sense of the social positioning of women, which – it is not difficult to make the link – influences their political position in local institutions. But women reveal, during that first meeting, a far deeper fracture in their relationship with the spaces that exist at the local level for their participation:

roji roti mein sari jindagi nikal gayi ham garibon ki, kya pata kameti mein kya hota hai- furshat ho to pata karen ('Poor people like us spend all their time in pursuing their livelihood; if we had the luxury of time, we would find out what happens in the committees').

Jab apne ghar aour samaj ham par pabandi lagata hai to ham use kaise todien ('When our family and our community restrict us, how can we break that?').

Ham kuchh kaehn koi sunta bhi hai ('does anyone listen to what we say?'). *Jab ham aksham hai, jab hamra sajma aisa hai to sarkark ko hi to kosis karna chhiye na? Aour kaun karega* ('When we are poor and not capable of engaging our society, government must act').

Hame bas itna malum hai ki ham kameti ke sadshya hai, uske bad pata nahin ('I only know this much, that I am a member, nothing beyond that').

Ghar ke longon ne kha kin mahil ke liye arkshan hai– tum choonab mein khadi ho jayo, baki uske bad ham smbhal lenge ('Family members said that there is a seat reserved for women; you contest the election, we will manage it after that').

A vivid picture of Uttaranchal comes to my mind, different people, different narratives: women visible in public spaces, eager to do things, have belief in their own agency. I return to my hotel room and start arranging my thoughts. A few things become clear: looked at through women's eyes, the institutional spaces created by the state are largely empty, women trying but are not gaining inclusion; the state, except for creating these spaces, has done nothing to actualize the spaces; women's identities are being manipulated in a manner that restricts their participation in these spaces. These impressions shaped the contextual background and analytical constructs I developed for the study.

I have my own understanding what participation is. I try not to impose, but to find threads of similarities, albeit in different contexts. Does exclusion create similar feelings, does inclusion mean similar struggle? Intuitively we achieve a rapport – the urban educated middle-class researcher and the women in the villages. Despite our belonging to different places, wearing different kinds of clothes, speaking different languages, we begin to talk. I am aware, like many of these women, that there are many differences and barriers between us that cannot be dismantled; yet there is an element of trust that I will understand their stories. They, as much as I, know that there is nothing to offer except an empathetic ear. A comradeship grows – after a few meetings, women open up, pour out their stories. I am aware that when I go back to Delhi, my university colleagues will tease me for turning social science research methods upside down, but I am convinced that there could not have been a better methodology to study participation.

Recruiting Members: Denial of Choice, Imposition of Choice

The genesis of representation in the Indian context has its base in the principles of affirmative action. Special efforts in the form of affirmative action to ensure political participation are meant to rescue excluded groups such as SCs, STs and women from social discrimination. Thus political participation and social participation are meant to reinforce each other – that is, political participation, by bringing excluded identities into the political spaces of decision-making, would bring them political equality that would negate some of the social inequalities they are subjected to, and social equality would equip them to seek inclusion in political spaces of decision-making and achieve political equality. Both are essential for citizenship and participation and both require that women, low castes and tribals as ascribed social categories be recognized by the state.[2]

In practice, however, these norms of representation are dissonant with the realities of the inclusion – and indeed exclusion – of women from local institutional spaces. In the watershed developmental committee, women members are often selected in the village meeting. Selection is an informal process even though it takes place in the formal meeting. At times, the project bureaucracy selects women to be representatives because they are educated, or part of the panchayat system, or family members of 'influential' people in the village who have economic, political and/or social dominance at village level. At times, project bureaucrats ask these influential people to select women members. Women's willingness to be part of the committee is often taken for granted, and they are never asked about their choice as representatives. Representation in the ICDS is of a different nature to that of the watershed committee. Women from the community are recruited to implement the project – that is, they run the health centre-cum-school and provide healthcare assistance to women. Hence there is a professional aspect to ICDS and it is treated as a salaried job. The community worker at village level is called the *anganwadi* worker; as education is a requirement, it is often the most educated woman from the community who is recruited. The project also has provisions to recruit widows and women who are 'deserted' by their husbands, and in such cases education no longer remains the sole criterion.

It is all too obvious that women are recruited to the watershed committee to meet procedural requirements. It seems ironic to talk about 'choice', since most women members are not even aware that they have membership of the committee. Both the project bureaucracy and male members know that women will merely be decorative members, leaving men the prerogative to rule the committee. Thus from the very beginning, the stage is set for keeping women outside and excluded from the committee. Women, too, get this sense; hence during the course of the project when meetings take place in their absence and they are sent papers to sign, endorsing decisions taken by male members, they do not resist.

Even in panchayats where women get elected, who will stand for election is a matter rarely decided by women. The 'politics' of representation in these invited spaces is a combination of local dominance, cultural codes of patriarchy and the working of the local administrative bureaucracy. The study villages are mostly populated by SCs and STs who live together with upper-caste Hindus. Often there is a village hierarchy in which groups who have numerical strength, together with economic and political resources, come to dominate. For example, most women from Bhikampura, which is densely populated by Jatavs, an SC community, are of the opinion that they are not treated very well in the panchayat, where an open seat for the *sarpanch* is occupied by Rajputs, the higher-caste Hindus from Harnagar, which is a panchayat village. Men obviously want their family members to stand for the reserved seats so that the 'power' of panchayat membership remains within the family. Though being elected gives women representatives a political and constitutional legitimacy, in the micro-contexts of the village, these are inconsequential as men determine not only who will be given representation but also 'who will be represented by whom'. We therefore find husbands, brothers and sons conducting all the affairs in the village meeting on behalf of actual members.

When participation is imposed because there is a seat reserved for women, women are subjected to multiple humiliations. Women remain formal members, but men from their families exercise all the power associated with that membership. At the same time other women in the village find the situation difficult to accept. It is of course not a good feeling, even in a patriarchal system, to know that they are being used and domesticated by the very system that is intended to bring them empowerment and emancipation. I heard about Rajana Jatav, a low-caste woman, who contested and won election to the panchayat in the village of Akolpura, but whose husband attends the meetings to represent his wife. He also takes all the decisions which, as a panchayat member, she should be taking.

I wanted to meet Rajana, but she never came to any meeting I organized with women in the village. 'She is shy', they said; 'you must meet her at her home'. I asked if someone could take me to her home. There was a surge of excitement among them as they walked with me towards her house. We reached Rajana's house. She came out into the courtyard to greet us – a young woman, certainly shy, with a long veil. I asked her if she is required keep that on while talking to us. She nods silently, but does not remove the veil. We begin talking; she hardly answers the questions. All she has to say is that she never attends the meetings, adding that her husband is quite active. Why did she contest the election then, I ask. Her voice chokes: 'family members insisted, but you see, it's so humiliating. All these women make fun of me all the time and tell me that I am no more than a peon in the panchayat.' I refrain from hurting her sensibilities further, promising that I will see her when I come to her village next time, and leave quietly.

I am tempted to compare Rajana with Ankuri Jatav, the only woman member who claims to have subverted the male local bureaucracy's agenda of using women only as 'proxy' representatives. A Jatav low-caste woman, Ankuri says that she has the support of her community and therefore could win the election. There probably is some truth in that since the SCs in Bhikampura actively compete with upper-caste Rajputs of Harngar, particularly because the post of the *sarpanch* in Harngar panchayat is an open post occupied by a Rajput. The Jatavas, working as labourers on the farms of Rajput, have found Ankuri an ally in their determination to challenge their Rajput masters politically. However, her own persona has to a certain extent shaped her political aspirations. She says that she is not intimidated by men or local bureaucrats, she goes to meetings and makes her point; she has struggled, but has created a space in which she has won acceptance. 'Why, then, have other women not followed you?' I ask. She responds thoughtfully: 'It is not often easy for women to ignore or even infuriate their family and society.' That simple truth indicates how the choices that women might exercise in fulfilling their political ambition are hijacked by the state and the larger society to keep women confined to what the culture demands of them.

Creating Identities and Assumptions: Reinforcing Stereotypes

Cultural roles of subservience within the family support a dynamic whereby women tend to be relegated to the roles of beneficiaries, wage earners and proxy representatives within the invited spaces under study (Cornwall 2004). Mere formal membership, stripped of the choices and freedoms that might come with representative authority, creates a scenario in which women come across as formal members in development committees, and as beneficiaries and users of the project, which often takes the shape of their being employed by the project as wage workers, and as proxy representatives in the panchayat, who legitimize the use of their position and power by male members of the family.

In the spaces provided by the panchayat, women's inclusion in *gram sabha* meetings merely serves the purpose of including their physical presence. They are neither encouraged nor discouraged to attend meetings. Men do not show overt aggression to women attending meetings or speaking in public, but there is an indifference which women find very humiliating. In watershed committees their role is even further diminished as even women's physical presence is not considered desirable by male members. The head of the institution, together with his allies in the committee and in local administration, sets the agenda for the meeting, and this often determines who will be included or excluded. Women in watershed projects are often found attending meetings when work is to be distributed during implementation, thereby reducing themselves to no more than labourers, ironically in the very context that is designed to give them ownership and participation in the project (Mohanty 2004). While membership of the panchayat, and therefore inclusion, is largely driven by the male members of the family, in the watershed committee membership is required to fulfil formal provisions. Inclusion is therefore never thought about as important, or as something that women may find desirable and on which basis they might make their claim. More than their presence and inclusion, it is their signature on official documents that is valued. 'What stops them refusing to sign such documents?' I ask. 'The fear and risk involved in annoying powerful people in the village and one's own family members', Nirmala, an *anganwadi* worker, argued:

> Few women here have awareness about their rights. Some of us who are educated and are aware about our rights, we are seen as a 'nuisance' and a constant threat within the village. Hence, while women who are silent and docile will be called to meetings, we will be deliberately kept outside.

In Akolpura, one of the women members – wife of the chairperson of the watershed committee – looked embarrassed to talk about her role in the committee. 'I do not need to be there all the time – my husband plays an important role in the committee. We do not have disagreements on issues', she says. In the social relations of power within patriarchy, women often echo what men think appropriate. Earlier on that day, talking to a group of women in the village, I gathered that in their view 'power' is transferred from a man to a woman – if a man is powerful in the public domain, so is his wife. Why, then, must women claim their 'own share of power'?

While women are not encouraged to take part in deliberations in the watershed committee meeting and influence decisions in the project, they are encouraged to step out of their homes to earn extra income for their families. Since most people have very small land holdings and work as wage labourers, women often go out of their houses to work. Hence watershed projects, which create this opportunity for local employment in dam construction, building rain-harvesting structures, maintaining plantations, raising nurseries, and so on, are able to include women only as labourers. Further reduction of their agency takes place in the panchayats, where, except for the rare occasions where they come across as elected members, women behave as good supportive wives and mothers, transferring their position and power in the panchayat to their husbands and sons.

In the case of the ICDS, women are actively included – indeed, it is not difficult to find women in a programme exclusively designed for them. Women have no hesitation in frequenting the *anganwadi* centre. Since the programme reinforces the traditional images and assumptions that families and society have of women as wives and mothers, it is considered safe for women to visit the *anganwadis*. Everyone seems to be happy as long as women are part of a programme that prepares them to be better wives and mothers; it is even better if they can build some savings and credit that the family can fall back upon during times of crisis. No one seems to mind women frequenting a non-threatening space where they interact only with other women. Yet the ICSD has had effects on the agency of women recruited as *anganwadi* workers. We find Nirmala, for instance, very vocal, often raising issues during my meeting with her: 'We have started from scratch – there was nothing available to women in this village to prove that they could excel in education and prove their capabilities. Projects like this have given us this space.' One can appreciate their sense of self-worth being acknowledged by the project. But the 'professional identity' that ICDS constructs for women like her and the sense of professional satisfaction that the work gives to them do not translate into any radical possibilities for the large number of women receiving healthcare in ICDS, who participate only as 'mothers' eulogizing the domesticated conflict-free identity which is so valued by the larger society and their own families.

These identities of beneficiaries, wage earners and proxy representatives are intricately linked with the assumptions that go with them, and these assumptions then begin to govern the local institutions:

> *Auraten ghar mein khus rahti hain* ('Women are happy serving their family').

> *Jo faishla uske pati aur putra kartein hain, bahi uska bhi faishal hota hai* ('She would naturally want to support her husband's and son's decisions').

> *Parivar ki khushali ke liye woh ghar ke bhar bhi kam kar leti hai, lekin rajniti uske bas ki bat nahin, yah woh bhi smmajhti hai* ('She has an obligation to work to fulfil livelihood demands, but she also understands that politics is not her cup of tea').

> *Unhe samaj aur sanskriti ki parvah karni chahiye – unko ijjat usi mein milta hai* ('They are taught to respect society and its culture – that is where they have to gain her respect').

Constructions of Gendered Participation

Stereotyped understandings of women's public roles restrict their
participation in invited spaces, so long as the state – in its role as
space-maker – acts as a putatively neutral facilitator of this participation. The state sides with the dominant social forces, groups and
individuals to avoid conflicts. The process take place in such a manner
that women are excluded from its sphere. A dominant construction
of gendered participation manipulates the state institutions and
shapes participation, and is premissed upon four critical aspects of
participation: wisdom, space, power and voice.

I am talking to a group of women, some of them quiet, some
eager to talk. It is impossible to keep men out of such meetings. They
are curious to know what is going on. The men are trying to assess
my identity and are anxious to be party to the conversation that
is going on. Some of them watch from a distance, some gradually
draw closer. They interrupt the women, give their version of the
issue. The presence of men makes women self-conscious. I ask the
men not to interrupt a woman while she is talking. One of them
is sharp. He says: 'Then you have to talk to us separately after you
finish here.' Then they withdraw; a few more men gather in the
meanwhile and wait at a distance. I finish talking to the women; it
is getting dark, but I will have to talk to these men who have waited
patiently for so long. So I join them. More tea is served. First they
want to know whether or not I am a government officer. It takes
a while to convince them that I am just doing a study. 'What are
you going to do with the study?' one of them asks. 'Let's see', I try
to be evasive, 'maybe some good recommendation for your village
will come up'. We begin talking. Gradually the suspicion gives way
to a kind of temporary camaraderie.

Seen through the lens of these forces, we get a particular picture
of the *wisdom* that women exercise in the pursuit of participation,
the *spaces* where women seek inclusion, the *power* that participation
offers to those who pursue it, and the *voices* that can be raised to
animate participatory spaces.

Wisdom   *Unki samajh mein nahi ayega* ('they will not understand') is
the common refrain from men regarding women's interest in what
goes on in the village meetings. The institutional space is seen by men
as technical in its content, masculine in its manner of deliberation,

and external in its goal, as opposed to the generic discussions women have within the household, which more often than not refer to the feminine pursuits of nurturing and caring for family members.

Space Women's space is never seen as external – it is always space within the four walls of the house where they are expected to participate. If women seek inclusion, it has to be within the family; if they seek deliberation and negotiation, it has to be with family members. The family space is almost sacrosanct, and women seeking inclusion in the external spaces offered by the institutions are looked upon as transgressing the boundaries of their defined spaces.

Power The majority of men feel that the power a woman has is directly proportional to that which her husband wields. If the male is powerful, so is his wife. Making men the reference point for power also gets its impetus from the fear that empowering women can have political consequences. Hence we find men happy with their women so long as they are part of the saving and credit group, which is perceived as non-threatening and non-political, and do not aspire to be watershed committee members or panchayat members, where deliberation and negotiation of a different kind take place.

Voice Male reactions to female voices raised outside of the home are either indifferent, or amused, or simply dismissive. The reactions understandably are directed towards keeping women silent. As *sarpanch* of Harnagar says, *hamri gaon ki aurtaen to bas baat karna janti hai, sauk hai unki* ('Oh they love to talk and talk. That, after all, is their habit!'), implying that women's speech is without much substance. A common reason men cite for keeping women silent is their lack of political language – 'they do not know what to say in a meeting'. Hence the fear is that women may annoy government officials and influential people in the village by uttering something 'useless'.

If participation is all about political negotiation, democratization and empowerment, certainly these conventional patriarchal notions of participation do not offer much possibility to women. But things are worse when these notions get transferred to state institutions created to promote participation. The state, rather than critically looking at the forces that subvert its developmental and democratic agenda, poses as innocent, pretending that everything is alright with the way its institutions function. For instance, it is fairly well under-stood that women are often silent in public spaces because cultural codes do not allow them to speak in front of older men – fathers, fathers-in-law, brothers and uncles. It is considered disrespectful and brings dishonour to families if women are found talking in public meetings. Hence one of the ways to keep women silent is by not bringing any women-related issues to the meeting for discussion.

In institutions where women find representation following specific directives issued by the state, discussion of women's issues, where women might represent a collective interest, has been superseded by discussion of more generic issues. Two women *sarpanch* who won panchayat elections because seats were 'reserved' for women have spent their five years' tenure planning the construction of school buildings and roads, because in popular perceptions that is what village development is all about and the *sarpanch* is expected to develop infrastructure facilities in the village. In ICSD, since it is a health project targeted at children and women, women's issues are understandably represented in meetings. In the watershed committee, which is a forum to implement a highly specialized project, however, discussion invariably centres on issues pertaining to that project. It is seldom that women, as a collective or as individuals, or their issues, are represented in committee spaces. By treating certain issues as 'non-decisionable' and thereby keeping them outside the institutional decision-making process and concentrating on popular 'safe' issues, which will not result in conflict because women will not participate in such deliberations, the institutions help society exercise its power over women (Kabeer 1994). This eventually turns women into absentee members or silent spectators.

It is not only that women speak or do not speak, but the extent to which when they do speak they are comprehensible to men and the local bureaucracy. Women are not encouraged to speak because they do not know the political language of the public space or the language of the state. In the context of distance between the state and people, activists have often worked as interpreters. In our particular context, where a highly negligent state distances itself from poor, *dalit* and tribal women and the activist-interpreter is not present, women's voices are virtually absent from official institutional spaces.

Conclusion

State-created spaces are attractive because they are grounded in the normative principles of equality, justice and empowerment. However, in contexts where these institutions reproduce stereotyped identities, assumptions and expectations for women, women – instead of fashioning their political imagination and democratic aspirations – come to experience multiple doses of humiliation, discrimination and exclusion. As a result, and despite the provision for representation, looked at from rural women's vantage points, these spaces appear largely empty. In such situations, even the normative grounding of these spaces is not enough to create the necessary conditions for participation to take off. Women, incapacitated by poverty and social exclusion, display a sense of resignation, and it seems unlikely that they will organize on their own to negotiate and claim their equitable stake in these local participatory institutions. The state, which is expected to facilitate women's participation, has failed them in many ways.

Let me, at the risk of sounding prescriptive, end this chapter with a small note on what would help in such contexts to mobilize women's substantive representation, inclusion and voice. My earlier research in Uttaranchal shows that women's participation, facilitated by NGOs, movements, and at times even by the state, in 'other supportive spaces', enables them to participate in the invited spaces of development and governance institutions. Their participation receives further impetus when local bureaucrats, particularly those placed at the higher level, encourage, mobilize and create conditions for women's participation by directly intervening at the village and district levels. The coexistence of these two conditions is essential, because the absence of one will result in too much dependency on the other. Too much dependency on the state, as the three villages in Rajasthan indicate, creates a situation where women will unquestioningly accept what the state offers to them. Likewise, too much dependency on women's organizations or NGOs will result in bypassing the state. When these organizations facilitate women's participation, they help in creating a larger supportive environment for women to gain entry to and participate in the official invited spaces. When the state, through its local bureaucracy, accommodates women's genuine interests in the local institutional spaces, it helps in building the participatory character of these spaces to *institutionalize* such interests as women's rightful stake in processes of development and democracy.

94   SPACES FOR CHANGE?

Notes

1. Scheduled Castes (SC) and Scheduled Tribes (ST) are identified in the Constitution of India for special consideration in the form of protective discrimination/affirmative action. Scheduled castes, known as untouchables or *dalits*, occupy the lowest rung in the Hindu caste hierarchy. It needs to be noted that in Indian villages, athough the SCs and STs live together with the upper castes, their habitats are often located on the outskirts of the village. The peripheral physical space they occupy within the village is reflective of the many layers of social and economic inequalities persistent in the Indian countryside.
2. Affirmative action has been a contested issue in India. It is seen both ways: as a transformative tool in liberal democracy, as well as a means to polarize the electorate in a democracy for political gain. Readings that illuminate these aspects include: Gupta 1998; Mahajan 1998; John 2000; Kumar 2001.

References

Chandhoke, N. (2005) 'Seeing the State in India', *Economic and Political Weekly*, 12 March.

Cornwall, A. (2002) 'Making spaces, changing spaces: situating participation in development', IDS Working Paper No. 170, Institute of Development Studies, University of Sussex, Falmer.

Cornwall, A. (2004) 'New democratic spaces? The politics and dynamics of institutionalised participation', *IDS Bulletin* 35(2): 1–10.

Gupta, D. (1998) 'Recasting reservations in the language of rights', in G. Mahajan, ed., *Democracy, Difference and Social Justice*, Delhi: Oxford University Press.

Hiremath, U. (1997) 'Women in grassroots politics', *Social Welfare* 44(2).

Jain, D. (1996) *Panchayati Raj: Women Changing Governance*, New Delhi: UNDP.

John, M.E. (2000) 'Alternative modernities? Reservations and women's movement in 20th century India', *Economic and Political Weekly*, 28 October.

Kabeer, N. (1994) *Reversed Realities: Gender Hierarchies in Development Thought*, New Delhi: Kali for Women.

Kumar, P. (2001) 'Reservations within reservations', *Economic and Political Weekly*, 15 September.

Mahajan, G. (1998) *Identities and Rights: Aspects of Liberal Democracy in India*, Delhi: Oxford University Press.

Mathew, G., and R. Nayak (1996) 'Panchayat at work: what it means for the oppressed?' *Economic and Political Weekly*, 6 July.

Mohanty, B. (1995) 'Panchayati Raj, 73rd Amendment and women', *Economic and Political Weekly*, 30 December.

Mohanty, R. (2004) 'Institutional dynamics and participatory spaces: the making and unmaking of participation in local forest management in India', *IDS Bulletin* 35(2).

Rai, M., M. Nambiar, S. Paul, S. Singh and S. Sahni (2001) *The State of Panchayats: A Participatory Perspective*, New Delhi: Samskriti.

Sinha, D., and Nandy, B. (2000) 'From spectators to participation: panchayat as public domain for dispute settlement', *Journal of the Anthropological Survey of India*, Kolkata.

5

Social Change and Community Participation: The Case of Health Facilities Boards in the Western Cape of South Africa

John J. Williams

This chapter investigates whether South Africa's post-apartheid legislation has had any significant impact on how Health Facilities Boards (HFBs) respond to the constitutional right of ordinary people, especially Black[1] people, to participate in the provision of healthcare services in their communities. It investigates community participation in HFBs by focusing on the historical context of participation in South Africa; the ideals of participation in the post-apartheid regime; the practices of participation; and the tensions that inform it. Analysis of two HFBs in the Western Cape suggests three possible reasons for the racially skewed nature of HFBs and why Black people in general do not participate in them. First, historically, whites have dominated institutions of governance in South Africa, including hospitals and their related structures. Second, procedures for the election of HFBs seem to favour literate and influential members of a community at the expense of poorer, largely illiterate members. Third, the culture of deference to professional authority undermines substantive dialogue and the empowerment of Black communities. Drawing on evidence from surveys of hospital users and interviews with hospital managers and members of HFBs, this chapter seeks to unravel some of the dynamics of exclusion from these invited spaces and explore some of the steps that might be taken to amplify the representation of hitherto excluded actors.[2]

Participation in Contemporary South Africa

Contemporary possibilities for citizen participation in South African politics are deeply shaped by the country's apartheid history. There were no legal rights or avenues for Black participation in political self-governance until 1994. The government was highly centralized, deeply authoritarian and secretive, and ensured that fundamental public services were not accessible to Black people. The struggle against apartheid took place outside the spaces of governance, and sought to mobilize community participation in order to transform South Africa's repressive government. Until 1976, a largely passive dream for liberation existed amidst unspeakable forms of oppression and exploitation. Dormant as its actualization remained, this allowed at least imagined spaces of participation.

The murder of Steve Biko in September 1977 signalled the need for not only community organization and mobilization at grassroots level but also community control. In subsequent years, spaces of community organization and mobilization multiplied throughout South Africa, culminating in the birth of the United Democratic Front (UDF) in 1983. The UDF claimed operational spaces against the apartheid state throughout South Africa, sustaining community forms of liberatory struggles at street and neighbourhood levels, often in the name of the banned liberation movements such as the African National Congress. From 1984 to 1989 the struggle against the apartheid state intensified, extending from local to international arenas, resulting in a range of divestment campaigns and cultural boycotts. This period created spaces of ungovernability throughout South Africa. The period from 1990 to 1994 saw the unbanning of the liberation movements and the beginning of the consensual politics of negotiation, leading up to and beyond the end of white minority rule.

The period since 1994 has been one of 'transitional governance', involving the negotiation of demands for democratization and deep social change. In this context, community participation has literally become synonymous with legitimate governance. This began with the negotiated settlement of a range of promissory spaces of participation, such as the Reconstruction and Development Programme of 1994 and the Constitution of South Africa of 1996: the former the outcome of community participation and the latter ensconcing the right to participate in local government planning programmes.

From 1996 to 2000, the need for visible, experientially significant forms of social change gave rise to various types of 'development' partnerships mediated by socio-historical relations of power and trust, resulting in largely truncated spaces of participation. Since 2000, there has been a manifest shift from euphoria to disappointment, from generative hope to existential despair at the slow pace of change. Yet this despair, too, has given rise to new transformative spaces such as the Treatment Action Campaign, Jubilee 2000 and a myriad other local initiatives that seek to democratize politically liberated spaces. At present, then, community participation finds a strong place in rhetorics of governance, but with mixed results on the ground, as entrenched power relations shape the possibility of this participation being meaningful.

These broad dynamics play out in local government politics. Until the early 1990s, local government had no constitutional safeguard, as it was perceived as a structural extension of the state and a function of provincial government. In the wake of the abolition of apartheid in 1990, local government assumed an important role vis-à-vis institutional transformation. Thus, with a view to ensuring bottom-up, people-centred, integrated development planning at grassroots level, the South African constitution states that '[t]he objective of local government is to encourage the involvement of communities and community organizations in the matters of local government' (RSA 1996: subsection 152e). This is a radical posture, but one that encounters profound structural limitations in the midst of bureaucratic institutions and uneven relations of power.

There is reason for concern that in South Africa ordinary people serve mainly as endorsers of pre-designed planning programmes and objects of administrative manipulation in which bureaucratic elites impose their own truncated version of 'community participation' on particular communities. Consent for governance is not earned through rigorous policy debates of the merits and demerits of specific social programmes; rather, political acquiescence is manufactured through skilful manipulation by a host of think-tanks, self-styled experts, opinion polls and media pundits. Indeed, often community participation is managed by a host of consulting agencies on behalf of pre-designed, party-directed planning programmes and is quite clearly not fostered to empower local communities.

What possibilities exist, then, for meaningful spaces of participation? Some of the limitations of these spaces, and also some of their possibilities, are evident in Health Facility Boards (HFBs), which are meant to contribute towards the institutional transformation of hospitals, yet are shaped and constrained by the complex legacies of institutionalized racism and exclusion. In what follows, I consider the operation of two HFBs, one at Heimwee Hospital, a peri-urban institution, the other at the rural Vorentoe Hospital, revealing both challenges facing spaces of public participation and ways of attempting to negotiate these challenges.[3]

Health Facilities Boards

The Health Facilities Boards Act of 2001 established HFBs as vehicles of institutional transformation – a way of ensuring greater community participation in the provision of healthcare services at grassroots level (Act 7 of 2001, sections 9 and 10). HFBs have broad mandates: they are responsible for approving the mission, vision and values of their hospital facility; advising in its management; strategic planning; monitoring performance; attending to patient grievances; fund-raising; appointments; and inspection (RSA 2001). The South African Medical Bill of 2003 reinforces these community-driven controls of healthcare. The Health Facilities Boards Act (section 6, subsection 4) makes it explicit that community representatives must constitute at least 50 per cent of an HFB. Theoretically, at least, this means that communities are now able to influence the formulation, implementation, monitoring and revision of hospital business plans, hospital staffing and the quality of hospital services.

HFBs represent vehicles for popular participation in institutional change not only because of their mandate and composition, but because of their link to Transformation Units (TUs). TUs were established by the National Department of Health in the late 1990s, at different levels of governance. Membership of TUs and HFBs often overlaps, although this was not an official requirement. Replaced in 2003 by Quality Care Committees, the TUs had significant institutional effects. The Deputy Director of Human Resources [Transformation] in the Western Cape suggests that TUs succeeded in making hospital management aware of *Batho Pele* ('People First') principles, established some cooperative relations with some hospitals such as Vorentoe and, in some small measure, brought people together across ethnic divides, at least to talk about institutional change at hospitals.

Yet a close look at HFBs shows the extent to which these partici-patory spaces of transformation remain hostage to their context, including the history of the institution and associated power relations, resource/capacity constraints, understandings of citizenship, norms and expectations of health services, and the material conditions of the surrounding population. HFBs operate in a context of profound divisions and glaring material inequalities, not merely between Black and white in general, but also between white and Black healthcare workers.

Demographic disconnections

The demographics of Heimwee hospital show the extent to which apartheid legacies shape contemporary conditions. The ethnic profile of patients is 5 per cent 'Whites', one per cent 'Indian', 29 per cent 'Black' Africans and 65 per cent 'Coloureds'. Top management, by contrast, consists of 66.6 per cent 'Whites' and 33.3 per cent 'Coloureds'. Middle management is a small step closer to representing the broader population: 13 per cent 'Whites', 3.4 per cent Black Africans and 82 per cent 'Coloureds'.[4] This disconnection between hospital management and the demographics of the surrounding community is echoed in Vorentoe, where the former Municipal CEO trenchantly comments:

> Their finances might well be in order, as they have been in order dur-ing the days of apartheid, but where is their transformation plan? How many Black doctors do they have? How many Black staff members do they intend appointing in the next few years in compliance with the government's requirement for 'demographic representivity' in public insti-tutions? This is a new South Africa! It cannot be business as usual when under the guise of 'competency and experience' apartheid continues by other means![5]

In keeping with this comment, we can note that neither the Heimwee nor Vorentoe Hospitals have a single Black medical doctor.

HFBs were brought into being as participatory vehicles for institutional transformation, yet the under-representation of Blacks in hospital management is mirrored in the HFBs themselves. The Heimwee local population is 19.6 per cent 'White', 30 per cent 'Coloured' and 50.3 per cent 'Black', yet the HFB, with ten members, is 40 per cent 'White', 50 per cent 'Coloured' and 10 per cent 'Black'.[6] Members are between 50 and 60 years of age; and there are almost twice the number of men as women. In Vorentoe there are fourteen board members – four women and ten men, between 45 and 55 years of age. They are all white except a priest representing the faith-based community in the village of Klawer (approximately 25 kilometres outside Vorentoe). Yet only 20.6 per cent of the area population is 'White', whilst 70.5 per cent is 'Coloured' and 8.9 per cent are Black Africans. HFB memberships are also skewed in favour of hospital management: in both Heimwee and Vorentoe the same nurses and doctors who constitute the majority in the HFBs are also part of the hospital management structures.

Recruitment to the HFBs is done via advertisements in the *Government Gazette*, calling for nominations from community organizations. Any nomination has to be accompanied by a verified copy of the constitution of the nominating organization. These procedures favour the historically well-connected white communities and exclude organizations without constitutions, such as Black youth organizations in Vorentoe and Heimwee. An absence of rules obliging the nomination of women, together with a historically entrenched patriarchy only recently beginning to be addressed, also ensures a relatively low proportion of women.

The implications of skewed membership for the conduct of HFBs comes out clearly in the comments of a senior Black male nurse at Heimwee Hospital, who rues the missed transformative possibility of HFBs: 'While the post-1994 health-related acts are very progressive, problems arise with regard to ensuring the rights of communities to participate in the healthcare service delivery programmes.' A key explanation, he suggests, is the relative economic privilege of those serving on the boards, which detaches them from an understanding of problems of service delivery:

> When you look at the members of the HFB at Heimwee Hospital, most of the members, with the exception of one or two, do not use hospital services because they all have medical aid that provides them access to private medical services. This, in effect, means that their knowledge regarding services rendered, why they are rendered and to what extent they are rendered, is very sketchy. Therefore, their understanding of patient flow within the hospital is also suspect. I am not sure that they have a clear understanding of their role and function in respect of service delivery.

The nurse offers a picture of an HFB that is closely tied to hospital management, opaque to other hospital constituencies, and unconnected to grassroots perspectives and needs:

The personnel have never had any introduction to the HFB members and minutes of meetings have never been circulated. There has never been a suggestion or enquiry from the HFB to improve some aspect of service delivery. For example … no one has ever asked what would be needed to improve patient waiting times.… It could be that hospital management gives the HFB satisfactory answers in their monthly meetings. It could also mean that the question never was asked because of lack of insight on the part of the HFB. Health is always a very contentious issue and therefore there are always a myriad questions, even from the most illiterate of people, and the HFB is supposed to represent the people, be their mouthpiece so their voices could be heard at a platform that could give some validation to their plight. Unfortunately this does not seem to be the case.… Many people are not even aware of the HFB's existence.[7]

A case in point is the presence of a white-owned security company at Vorentoe Hospital, appointed by the white management staff of the hospital, controlling the visiting hours of predominantly Black patients. According to the only Black councillor on the HFB, this company frequently prevents Black families from visiting their sick relatives in hospital, causing them to phone him in the middle of the night to address their frustrations. In the councillor's own words, 'Why do they have to do this to poor people? Where is their respect for the basic rights of patients and their family members? Why should families have to call me to sort out this totally unnecessary form of power, of control, and abuse?'[8]

During the interviews it was made quite clear that Black people do want to participate on HFBs as they are mostly poor and dependent on these hospitals for healthcare, whereas most whites can afford private care. Influencing HFBs, their agenda, their decisions, their programmes and their daily activities is therefore necessary to advance the interests of the essentially poor Black communities they serve.

Sustaining the Status Quo?

It is not only the composition of HFBs that works against their being agents of institutional transformation. Their culture and design also serve to perpetuate the dominance of whites, and sustain existing hierarchies of power and privilege. A first of such features of HFBs concerns rules for formal agenda-setting and control of topics: the board secretary constructs the agenda, although nominally every board member can introduce issues. The chairperson of the board is equally influential in determining the extent to which issues are discussed or whether they are immediately referred to a subcommittee for further investigation.

A second feature involves the dynamics of authority and deference. It seems that often issues are not discussed with the requisite rigour for fear of offending people of significant social standing on the board. Moreover, HFB members typically participate as recipients of information: they are told what has been decided or what has already happened. It was announced without discussion, for example, that ward C in Vorentoe Hospital had been privatized to cater for the needs of patients who could pay for medical services.

Third, the procedures and protocols of HFBs are inflexible and ritualized. Ms Archer, a senior citizen and former nurse, spoke eloquently of the constraining protocols of these meetings at a board meeting of April 2002:

> This is how we speak,
> This is how we look,
> This is the image we want to project,
> This is taboo to us,
> This we do not tolerate.[9]

The culture of HFBs conditions not only the topics that arise (what is sayable and unsayable), but how topics are treated. Introducing a topic with a sense of seriousness or with nonchalance influences its course. For example, the issue of the Vorentoe October musical festival was introduced casually to the board, belying the fact that it is a contested calendar event, largely unlegitimated by the Black community.

Assessing the Contribution of HFBs

The composition, structure and design of HFBs together work to limit their accomplishments. Their ostensible aim was to make hospital services more responsive to the needs of surrounding communities by giving members of those communities an active, participatory role in policymaking. Yet there has been far too little movement on the part of hospitals to respond to the needs of the most impoverished and marginalized groups. Health needs of Black residents in both Heimwee and Vorentoe, who confront unemployment and poverty levels ranging from 50 to 70 per cent in some communities,[10] are wide-ranging and include malnutrition and related diseases. The attention of the boards, however, is on matters quite distant from the most pressing community priorities. The Heimwee HFB, for example, appointed two psychologists in a hospital where none of the patients has behavioural problems. In the words of one senior Black nurse, 'one psychologist would still have been a nice-to-have, two is certainly extravagant!'[11]

The overall orientation of HFBs is towards narrowly defined management goals, and particularly goals of fiscal discipline. Indeed, Vorentoe prides itself on being one of the few hospitals in the country that regularly records financial compliance with the statutory require-ments of sound governance. Yet its model of effective management is flawed in the sense that not only do the hospital's decision-making powers remain unconnected to the communities they serve, but its effectiveness is also measured with barely any reference to the Black community who constitute the majority of its patients. A Black nurse at Vorentoe comments: 'To a certain extent the HFB serves a purpose, but they really do not make a contribution to society as a whole. They do not go out to the public and ask them what they want. They only implement things they think the community needs.' In both the Heimwee and Vorentoe hospitals there appears to be a 'charitable' attitude among white HFB members that serves to reduce the concept of public participation to an efficiency model of financial management.

Whose Voice? Issues of Inclusion and Representation

One of the most pressing challenges that emerges in this context is to make sense of the dramatic under-representation of Blacks on HFBs. Previous studies, as well as the research on which this chapter is based, point to a tension between the apparent efficiency of healthcare services and residual racist attitudes, lack of communication and indeed lack of opportunities to participate in HFBs. Further dimensions emerge when we distinguish between representation of Blacks from the community at large, and from the community of healthcare workers.

From the community at large

Though the Athlone community, a predominantly middle-class suburb of the City of Cape Town,[12] in general favours public participation in the delivery of healthcare services, not a single respondent could cite an example where they were consulted by healthcare workers, or a committee meeting that engaged them on issues of service provision. Rather, members of the Athlone community are strikingly unaware of HFBs as vehicles for possible participation. Indeed, a study we began on patient attitudes towards HFBs was redesigned to focus on nurses once we discovered that no members of our initial sample of patients at Heimwee Hospital even knew that HFBs existed. We surmised that if patients themselves do not know about the existence of the HFB, it is likely that the surrounding Heimwee communities, especially the historically disadvantaged ones, are also largely ignorant of it; and that in Vorentoe and elsewhere in the Western Cape the situation is likely to be similar. Lack of effective communication of the existence of HFBs in these areas clearly contributes to the lack of participation in them by Black communities.

Our survey in Athlone showed that members of the community get their information about health services through complex communication networks. Almost a third (32 per cent) of the residents indicated that they get healthcare information through their families; 30 per cent through health professionals; 26 per cent through the community, and 12 per cent through friends. Newspapers and radio seem much less effective in communicating information about health services to the community, and yet it is these avenues that were employed in publicizing HFBs.

The creation of HFBs was preceded by awareness-raising programmes through advertisements in the daily newspapers, local community newspapers, and by information sessions on public radio stations. According to the Deputy Director, Legal Adviser in the Health Department of the Provincial Administration of the Western Cape, the response from Black communities was 'pathetically low' especially in areas such as Vorentoe. In his view, urban areas such as Cape Town had a much better response rate, as reflected by the greater 'ethnic balances' on the HFBs in Metropolitan Cape Town.

The limitations of newspapers as vehicles for raising awareness of HFBs in the broader community are reiterated by an Anglican priest who has lived in the area for more than thirty years:

Black people are very poor in Vorentoe and cannot afford these [news] papers. Also, the legacy of the apartheid mindset in Vorentoe is still very strong and therefore whites generally do not communicate with Black people on an equal footing. Indeed, there is a need to involve civil society organizations and the churches in particular to draw the people's attention to their constitutional right to participate in the provision of healthcare services in their communities. People will indeed participate if they are granted the opportunity to do so.[13]

The combination of inappropriate mechanisms of publicity and intercommunal division and lack of trust in excluding Blacks from participation on HFBs is substantiated by comments from the Deputy Director of Human Resources and Transformation for the West Coast Winelands Region, Malmesbury:

Black people are generally poor, and cannot afford the newspapers. Consequently, they do not know of the invitation to serve on the HFB. There is no other form of communication with people at grassroots level. This means white people are able to dominate the nomination/election of the HFB. And because Black and white people do not interact beyond a master–servant relationship [domestic servants/maids], the election of the HFB is not made known to the poorer sections of especially the Black communities. We must not forget that apartheid divisions still exist and the only contact that whites have with Black people is still largely through their domestic servants/maids, surely not a good measure of the leadership potential of politically literate, educated Black people. More importantly, perhaps, both in Vorentoe and Heimwee, Black people simply do not trust whites!… Thus talking about cooperation is still merely talk.[14]

The role of internalized racism in reinforcing Black exclusion from HFBs is brought out by comments from a young Black businesswoman in Vorentoe, who described Black non-participation in socio-historical and psychological terms:

Black people do not participate because they feel inferior to white people. Participation requires special knowledge and Black people do not have the necessary knowledge to engage white people on matters such as health. These negative self-concepts are reinforced by the fact that Blacks and whites do not mix. In short, Blacks and whites do not trust each other. Still, if Black people do get the opportunity to participate on the HFB, they most probably will do so.[15]

The exclusion of Blacks from HFBs can also take place through more direct and intentional forms of racism, as this narrative from a Matzikama Municipal Counsellor on the Vorentoe HFB reveals:

It is an error to assume that apartheid is over. This is not true....When nominations were invited for the present HFB, I was nominated as chairperson of the HFB. The white people came to know about my nomination and did not like it. Indeed, they consider the hospital their property. They consequently lobbied the powerful Dutch Reformed Churches – of which there are two in Vorentoe. And, given their resources and influence, the white community managed to re-elect van der Spuy as the chairperson, for the fifteenth year running!

Interestingly, our survey in Athlone shows a high level of satisfaction with health services: 92 per cent of the respondents considered healthcare services to be adequate, and only 8 per cent disagreed. However, satisfaction with health services does not mean satisfaction with the range of services. During follow-up interviews with some participants a need for a holistic approach to healthcare was expressed, as well as for specialist services. For example, it was suggested that poor tuberculosis patients need meals as well as direct observation treatment (DOT); an eye clinic was also identified as a need.

Survey respondents clearly supported community participation in healthcare: 46 per cent of the respondents indicated that the community should have the final say in decisions affecting healthcare service delivery, whilst exactly the same proportion said that healthcare professionals should have the final say. Some 18 per cent said that decision-making should be a partnership between healthcare workers and the community, and only 6 per cent said that they did not know. When it came to what 'participation' meant there was more unanimity: 80 per cent of respondents said that community participation means involvement in decision-making about the types of healthcare services.

That there are opposing views on community participation in healthcare suggests that the Athlone community is not a monolith, even though it is largely a 'Coloured' middle-class constituency. Participants vary, not merely in terms of their gender, ethnic background, language use, religious affiliation and knowledge base, for example, but they also have differential access to information and ability to make sense of it. These differentiations shape different understandings of and perspectives on community participation. Indeed, some middle-class residents may feel that since they pay taxes they are entitled to good healthcare without the additional effort of participation in the governance of health services. Social differentiations such as these also shape the likelihood of participation being effective in ensuring good healthcare, especially among Black communities. One senior Heimwee nurse identified lack of access to capital resources on the part of some communities as a major reason for the failure of one community–private partnership in healthcare:

> In a predominantly 'Coloured' lower-middle-class community in Eerste River, some 25 kilometres outside Cape Town, there were attempts to introduce private health care, based on a community–private partnership. Very soon, however, cashflow problems emerged and this community had to abandon the partnership ... and refer their patients to Tygerberg Hospital.... Unless you are well-connected to largely white capital, as is the charity organization Heimwee Hospital Action Group, which raises money for the Heimwee Hospital, whatever partnerships are launched are bound to fail. For historical reasons, there is ... a very strong relationship between private capital, sound health care and sustainable public–private partnerships. It is access to these forms of capital that Black communities must seek to secure to ensure sustainable and meaningful public–private partnerships.... Unfortunately, at this point, white capital still largely controls both the form and substance of these partnerships. This is also the case in Vorentoe, where Ward C has been privatized for the use of both Black and white private patients.[16]

From health practitioners

HFBs include representation from the community at large, and also from members of the hospital community. The above discussion reveals how ineffective publicity, formal and informal exclusion, and internalized racism all play roles in keeping Black members of the community at large from participating on HFBs. What, though, of Blacks on staff at hospitals?

In Heimwee, twenty nurses (nineteen Black and one white) were each asked about the extent of their knowledge of HFBs, their willingness to participate in them and their general opinion of them. Knowledge of the boards was widespread: with the exception of one nurse, all knew of the existence of the HFB. There was, however, a relatively low level of unconditional willingness to participate on the HFB: 25 per cent said they would participate; 20 per cent said they would participate conditionally; 35 per cent said they would not participate, and 20 per cent said they did not know.

Reasons for willingness to participate included the ability to influence the HFBs' agenda and activity programme. Reasons for unwillingness included time-consuming jobs in a situation of staff shortages, as well as worries about the effectiveness of HFBs in influencing hospital priorities or working conditions. One interviewed nurse identified the Union as a potentially more effective site for negotiating service provision policy as well as working hours and career support.

Prospects for Change?

The above analysis offers a pessimistic portrayal of HFBs: notwithstanding their broad mandates for institutional transformation of hospitals, the boards have tended to focus on a combination of trivial issues and management concerns, while paying little attention to the pressing healthcare needs of the broader population, and especially of Blacks. Our analysis has suggested that the failure of HFBs to act as transformative institutions is connected to the narrowness of their membership, with Blacks dramatically under-represented and hospital management over-represented.

Yet the story is not entirely negative: since their creation, HFBs have managed to enact positive changes that provide grounds for hope. The entrenchment of fundamental rights in the South African Constitution, and broader social and political movements towards institutional change, have attuned the HFBs to pressures for transformation, resulting in the creation of a Transformation Unit at some hospitals such as Vorentoe. There the hospital representative has already attended several workshops, as a result of which the management has established contacts with other hospitals experiencing similar transformation challenges. Similar contact networks have been formed with local, provincial and national governments, for example in Malmesbury, Heimwee and Cape Town. The approach to healthcare has changed from being curative in nature to one that is primary and holistic, addressing the impacts of socio-economic issues such as unemployment and poverty on the well-being of the community. Vorentoe, for example, now supports a rural clinic programme.

The minutes of HFB meetings are also becoming considerably more detailed and are providing a more comprehensive account of board activities. This may reflect a movement towards greater democratic commitment. Moreover, the presence of *any* Black community members on HFBs is a lesson for white participants: by sharing institutional space with their historically separate 'White' counterparts, these (predominantly middle-class) Blacks demonstrate to racial bigots that it is possible for Black and white to cooperate at local level, even if the HFBs do little to address the most pressing Black community concerns.

The under-representation of Blacks at HFB meetings is also officially recognized as a problematic reiteration of historic patterns of exclusion: the Department of Health is currently concerned to construct and present public participation programmes at the hospitals under its jurisdiction.

Towards More Inclusive Representation

The key question, then, is how the membership of HFBs can be rendered more representative of the broader community, so that the participatory, transformative intent of these democratic spaces can be more fully realized. There is a widespread view, articulated in many of the interview narratives, that there would be a strong willingness on the part of Blacks to take part in HFBs under the right conditions. As a young Black businessman in Vorentoe stated: 'If there is an opportunity for Black people to participate on these boards they will definitely do so.'[17] This conviction finds support in the literature: Patterson (2000), for example, argues that non-participation in community representative spaces does not necessarily mean apathy towards the democratic process. On the contrary, entering space as a subordinate, unfamiliar with the forms and meanings of deliberative discourse and hidden transcripts, undermines participation as a rational, open and empowering democratic practice.

Our analysis reveals a number of changes that might encourage participation by marginalized members of communities and hospital staff in HFBs. We have seen the limitations of conventional forms of publicity in informing poor and marginalized Black communities of the existence of HFBs as invited spaces: poor communities cannot afford expensive daily newspapers and have limited access to radios and television. Informing this population of HFBs as avenues of transformative participation thus requires other, more effective and accessible means of communication, which might include rallies, flyers, door-to-door visits and so forth. This lesson accords with the broader claim that in poor communities informal communication strategies (such as street theatre) can serve to conscientize and inform the marginalized about community issues and their rights vis-à-vis public institutions (Bratton and Alderfer 1999).

Our analysis shows how both subtle and overt forms of racism, as well as internalized racism, shape the ability and propensity of Blacks to serve on HFBs. This dynamic is likely to be aggravated by associations of healthcare with charity and paternalistic provision, whereas in fact healthcare is entrenched in the South African constitution as a legal right (section 27; RSA 1996). Treating both healthcare and participation in HFBs as rights, to be defended and used as such, might constitute an important vehicle to encouraging and securing greater Black participation.

The dominance of privileged elites in the current operation of HFBs is reinforced by aspects of the culture and design of these spaces, including the authority over agendas possessed by secretaries and chairs, dynamics of authority and deference, inflexible and ritualized procedures and protocols, and the tone that surrounds the treatment of topics. In order for poor, historically marginalized communities to participate in HFBs, the social relations of power undergirding these invited spaces must be opened to critique, and procedures rendered sufficiently flexible and open-ended to accommodate a broader range of participants and topics.

Steps should be taken to ensure that HFBs as invited spaces are not dominated by the articulate middle-class and conscious members of the community, but that working-class constituencies are directly involved in the formation of community participatory spaces. For this to be realized, changes in the rules of representation are required. The current practice of nomination of registered organizations should be replaced by the election of representatives from among all users, with the reservation of seats for women and Blacks. Greater publicity is needed to ensure that a broader section of the community are aware of the HFBs and their role, and are able to put themselves forward as candidates. Proactive efforts are needed to change the racial balance, seeking out Black community organizations such as taxi associations, ratepayers' associations, community police forums and youth groups in Heimwee. In Vorentoe, where there are virtually no civil society organizations in Black residential areas, political parties and the Farm Workers' Advice Office could function as a catalyst to organize and mobilize poor people to claim their constitutional right to be represented on HFBs.

The above steps to transforming the membership and procedures of HFBs can each be fostered in so far as community organizations serve as intermediaries between the boards and members of broader communities. Recall the voice of the Deputy Director of Human Resources and Transformation for the West Coast Winelands Region, who pointed out the gulf between Blacks and whites that perpetuates exclusion on HFBs; he goes on to say that

> Attempts must be made to bring the two groups together. And, in my view, this can best be done through youth networks. In this regard, the churches in both rural and urban areas are starting to play a role. Indeed, building social relations based on trust and human solidarity, even if it must be done primarily through the churches, is perhaps the only genuine way to move away from white racism and Black oppression. In the fullness of time these 'new' relationships will affect how institutions in South Africa are run, including the composition and management of HFBs.[18]

Conclusion

This chapter has identified three possible reasons for the racially skewed nature of HFBs: the historical dominance of whites in institutions of governance; the procedures for election which favour the literate and influential; and the culture of deference to professional authority which undermines substantive dialogue.

It has also pointed to reasons for hope: more representative, less hierarchically structured HFBs could be dynamic networks of dialogue and engagement, triggering feelings of identification, trust and self-reliance in opposition to historical paternalism in healthcare and the infantalization of Black people in general. There are nascent signs of trust emerging. These take three forms: identification with the need for participation; the development of solidarity and collective engagement on issues; and increased self-reliance and achievement, which can induce people to take public participation seriously – if provided the opportunity to participate.

Thus pursued, participatory spaces would, indeed, constitute living community networks of engagement, reflection and transformation. More than 350 years of a charitable stance towards Black participation in institutions of governance preceded the formation of HFBs at the dawn of the twenty-first century. Thus, only the future will tell whether or not Blacks will indeed become co-shapers and governors of their lives via HFBs, not merely in policy design but in practice.

Notes

I wish to thank David Kahane for his valuable contribution to this chapter – he translated my turgid prose into readable, coherent and concise text. However, all remaining errors are mine.

1. The South African Constitution, Act 108 of 1996, describes the historically disenfranchised sections of the population, the Africans, 'Coloureds' and 'Indians', as 'Black'. For the sake of historical and textual clarity, this chapter also refers to the apartheid racial categories of 'Blacks' (African), 'Coloureds' and 'Indians', while recognizing their sociological and scientific weakness.
2. This chapter is based on fieldwork carried out in the Western Cape in 2003–05, using a mix of survey and interview methods. It also makes use of the results of a 2003 opinion survey on community participation in the provision of healthcare in Athlone, historically a 'Coloured' middle-class suburb of the City of Cape Town (Mabuya 2003).
3. Both of these hospitals have been given fictitious names.
4. Source: Hammers, Garfield, information provided on request, 2004
5. Interview, 9 July 2004.
6. Source: Hammers, Garfield, information provided on request, 2004.
7. Interview, 24 May 2005.
8. The Security Company usually relents after the Councillor's intervention – i.e. it allows Blacks to visit their sick family members.
9. Source: Archival records: Health Facilities Board Minutes, 11 April 2002.
10. Respectively Stellenbosch and Vorentoe Integrated Development Plans, 2004/05, supported by interviews with councillors from these municipalities.
11. Interview, 23 August 2005.
12. The City of Cape Town does not have an HFB, but a Medical Officer of Health, who is responsible for healthcare services in terms of the City's Integrated Development Plan. Community participation takes place in terms of the Municipal Systems Act, Act No. 32 of 2000, which regulates Integrated Development Planning.
13. Interview, 20 May 2005.
14. Ibid.
15. Ibid.
16. Interview, 23 August 2005.
17. Interview, 20 May 2005.
18. Ibid.

References

Bratton, M., and P. Alderfer (1999) 'The effects of civic education on political culture: evidence from Zambia', *World Development* 27(5): 807–24.

Mabuya, G.D. (2003) 'Community participation in the delivery of primary health care services in the City of Cape Town: an evaluative study of the Athlone Health District', unpublished thesis, University of the Western Cape.

Patterson, P.M. (2000) 'Nonvirtue is not apathy – warrants for discourse and citizen dissent', *American Review of Public Administration* 30(3): 225–51.

RSA (Republic of South Africa) (1996) *Constitution of the Republic of South Africa, Act 108 of 1996*, Pretoria: Government Printers.

RSA (Republic of South Africa) (2000) *Local Government: Muncipal Systems Act, Act 32 of 2000*, Pretoria: Government Printers.

RSA (Republic of South Africa) (2001) *The Western Cape Health Facility Boards Act 7 of 2001*, Pretoria: Government Printers.

Heimwee Hospital Board Minutes, Archives.

6

Civil Organizations and Political Representation in Brazil's Participatory Institutions

Graziela Castello, Adrián Gurza Lavalle and Peter P. Houtzager

There is considerable evidence that civil organizations such as advocacy NGOs, membership organizations and community associations have become *de facto* and *de jure* representatives of particular segments of the population and interests in the design, implementation and monitoring of public policy. Governments are, for a variety of reasons, inviting this set of collective actors into institutionalized spaces for policymaking, in either a consultative or a deliberative role. Conversely, many civil organizations are themselves pressuring governments to create such spaces, in order to gain access to policymaking centres. The institutions that have been created over the past twenty years to link these actors and policymakers, such as the systems of deliberative development councils in Guatemala and of policy councils in Brazil, are often part of larger democratic decentralization reforms that, at least formally, seek to redistribute power within the state and between state and society (Heller 2001; Grindle 1999).

Students of the new participatory institutions and the role civil organizations play in them have not identified the issue of political representation as an important one, because this issue is masked by the emphasis put on 'citizen participation', which is seen as the foundation of contemporary democratization. Institutions such as the councils in Brazil are often referred to as spaces for 'citizen participation', even though more often than not they bring collective actors (rather than individual citizens) into contact with public officials (Gurza Lavalle et al. 2005). We are not witnessing simply an increase in opportunity for citizen participation, but a broader process of *reconfiguration of political representation* in which civil organizations play a central role.

The contribution of this reconfiguration to greater political inclusion and democratization hinges in part on how the dilemmas of civil organizations' *representativeness* are resolved. We believe, on the one hand, that as networks of advocacy NGOs, membership organizations and community associations acquire a new role in political representation, the current processes of the reconfiguration of representation around the executive may converge to produce more inclusive democracy. Similar to the emergence of mass political parties, which contributed to the expansion of institutions of political representation and of democracy itself in the early decades of the twentieth century, the contemporary shifts in forms of political representation involve changes in the workings of the traditional institutions of representative government and an expansion of the locus and the functions of political representation.

On the other hand, the consequences of this reconfiguration for political inclusion and democratization depend in some measure on the answers to two linked questions. Who do civil organizations represent when they act as representatives in the polity, and in what terms is this representation constructed? The large majority of organizations that engage in political representation do not have electoral mechanisms through which they can establish their representativeness – that is, build a mandate and ensure accountability – and most are not membership-based. Furthermore, there are no well-established or widely accepted models of how civil organizations could establish their representativeness beyond these two classic mechanisms. Civil organizations therefore face a significant challenge when it comes to establishing their representativeness.

This chapter explores some of the efforts to meet this challenge using the findings of a survey of 229 civil organizations – that is, neighbourhood or community associations, membership organizations, NGOs, and coordinators of networks of these organizations – in the city of São Paulo (population 10 million, within municipal boundaries). The survey was undertaken in 2002 and used sampling criteria that favoured organizations that were actively working with (or on the behalf of) the urban lower middle class, the working class and the poor.[1] Because this universe of organizations works with or for social groups that are said to be marginalized in classic representative institutions and from centres of political power, their role as representatives is especially relevant to the debates on the direction of contemporary democracy and whether greater political inclusion is in the offing.

São Paulo is a 'forerunner case' that may reflect what lies on democracy's horizon. The city is the largest and politically most diverse in Brazil, a country that has since its democratic transition in 1985 become a democratic laboratory of enormous dimensions. It has a tradition of councils linked to left-wing actors, has experimented with participatory budgeting and other participatory institutions, and has a long-standing presence of societal actors linked to popular sectors, such as the housing and health movements. Civil organizations in São Paulo and elsewhere in Brazil have, furthermore, achieved notable influence in various areas of public policy since the end of the military dictatorship in 1985, and particularly since the 1988 Constitution. As the research agenda on the democratization of democracy suggests, with its empirical focus on Brazil and other middle- and low-income countries, perhaps for the first time democracy and the cutting edge of democratizing reforms are being imagined and constructed in the southern hemisphere.

Civil Organizations, Representation and Democracy

The processes of state reform that have unfolded in recent years, and in particular the wave of institutional innovations that have created new opportunities for citizen participation in policy processes, have intensified the political protagonism of civil organizations. In the case of São Paulo, almost two-thirds of our sample of organizations that work with or for the urban poor participate in at least one of the new participatory institutional arrangements, namely the participatory budget or the policy councils (Houtzager et al. 2004). Furthermore, the actors have a broad representative commitment in São Paulo – almost three-quarters explicitly assert that they represent the social groups that take part in or benefit from their activities. And, when we take into account the different forms of political representation that lie within reach of these actors, we find that claims of engaging in political representation are associated with actual political practices during which representation is likely to occur. The inverse relationship is as consistent: civil organizations that carry out few or no practices of representation tend *not* to define themselves as representatives of their publics.

This ability of particular types of civil organizations to enter and potentially represent interests of poorer sectors in different policy arenas and in the polity more generally, where these interests are often absent, is also an important reason to pay careful attention to the nexus of societal and political spheres, and their institutional sedimentation. Whether or not a civil organization claims that it is representative of its public is, in São Paulo, closely linked to its relationship with traditional political structures. More precisely, whether or not an actor supports political candidates is by far the best predictor of assumed representation, followed at some distance by two characteristics – registration as a public interest organization (*utilidade publica*) or mobilization and demand-making on public authorities.

There is no *a priori* guarantee that the potential political representation provided by civil organizations will in fact be representative, simply because this form of representation is constructed within a 'societal,' rather than political, sphere. If they function as effective new channels of mediation between the population and electoral processes or, as occurs in Brazil, between the population and public administration in the design and implementation of policies, civil organizations can only contribute to the democratization of democracy if they themselves are representative, or if they are able to maintain the core tension in the relationship between representatives and the represented. Clientelism and patrimonialism of various kinds, for example, also tend to occur at this level of 'societal' organizational activity.

Paradoxically, the crucial dilemma of the representativeness of civil organizations' representation – who do they represent exactly, and through what mechanisms is the relationship between representatives and those represented established? – has not been taken up in the literatures on the reconfiguration of representation or on democratizing democracy. Neither has explored this novel form of representation empirically in any kind of systematic manner, nor in terms of its implications for democracy or democratic theory. The former works with the legitimate model of political representation that exists – that is, representative mandate through elections – which was historically inspired by a set of actors, and for carrying out particular roles, that do not fit in any way with the profile of civil organizations or the political roles they play. The latter literatures do not address the issue of representation, in any form.

Studies of the democratization of democracy have focused their attention on institutional innovations that embrace various forms of participation in institutional structures for the design and implementation of public policies.[2] Yet this broad field of study – that composed by work on deepening democracy social accountability, empowered participation, deliberative democracy and civil society – does not recognize the issue of political representation by civil organization, because it is (in these studies) masked by the emphasis put on 'citizen participation' and 'civil society', which are seen as the foundations of the contemporary democratization. In this literature there obviously are different emphases, focuses and analytical categories. Nonetheless, most share two traits that have the effect of blocking the ability to conceive of a role that civil organizations might play in political representation. First, to a greater or lesser extent they rely on stylized conceptions of civil organizations, often grouped under the heading of civil society and assumed to have a particular unifying logic. This conceptual, and normative, step eliminates relevant internal differences between societal actors as well as the interactions present at the interface of political institutions and civil organizations. Civil society is said to rationalize public action and democratize political decisions because 'it' is guided by dialogue and has capacities and convictions that are previously defined because they have emanated from genuine and 'pre-political' roots in the life-world. Thus there is an assumed continuity or natural connection between a group of societal actors and society, or some segments of it – that is, between civil society and society – undermining the investigations into the processes of representation that link the two together. It is worth remembering Pitkin's (1967: 60–91) observation that representation by definition presumes difference and not identity between the representative and those who are represented.

Second, research agendas and policy interventions concerned with the democratizing of democracy are strongly attached to the idea of participation, be that the direct presence of those eventually affected or benefited by public decisions or face-to-face deliberation. The debate about political representation is incompatible with radical criticisms of representative democracy that denounce the inevitable distorting, dividing effects between those represented and representatives and that in different ways advocate direct democracy. In fact, as long as direct democracy operates by means of self-presentation, the problematic of representation is eliminated entirely (for instance, see Tenzer 1992; Keane 1984). The direct participation of those sectors of society considered under- or badly represented in classic representative institutions is understood as a critical means to improve the quality of democratic institutions, by making these more inclusive. If at times the very idea of participation appears burdened by the expectations of its ultimately positive effects on the quality of democracy, however, the idea also appears cognitively impoverished when we consider that in places like Brazil innovative participatory institutions – independently of whether or not they have stimulated direct citizen involvement – have produced the intense 'participation' of civil organizations.

Studies that explore the reconfiguration of political representation, in turn, offer interpretations of a transformation in progress at the level of the party system, where the relationship between elected representative and represented citizen is believed to be in flux (Manin 1997; Novaro 2000; Miguel 2003a, 2003b; Roberts 2002; Hagiopian 1998). In these studies, representation fundamentally resides in the electoral process, and for this reason there is no need even to explore whether civil organizations are acquiring any role in political representation in contemporary democracies. Asserting that civil organizations lack representativeness, either because they have no identifiable mechanism to establish a mandate or authorize their representation – elections – or because they do not have any accountability mechanisms, voids rather than illuminates the problematic that is explored in this chapter. The possible role of civil organizations in a reconfiguration of representation is defined *a priori* as irrelevant (see Przeworski 2002; Chandhoke 2003).

There are good reasons for some scepticism about the representativeness of civil organizations. In addition to the absence of clear and obligatory accountability mechanisms between the actors and the social sectors they represent (Przeworski 2002), the line between the public and private roles of these organizations is ambiguously defined. As a result, various authors point to the functional role these organizations play in the logic of privatization and of redistribution of responsibilities between society, the state and the market (Houtzager et al. 2002; Cunil 1997; Dagnino 2002). There are other relevant reservations as well, including the possible proliferation of claims based on substantive representation, such as race and gender, which are alien to the formal and universal logic of modern political representation, or the weakening of civil organizations' capacity to act as agents of social protest and to dispute the political agenda as their involvement in state programmes or participatory institutions increases, or even the public's lack of recognition and expectations of civil organizations (Chandhoke 2003, 2004).

We believe, however, that it is wise to defer any conclusion based on such reservations, because most take a traditional configuration of political representation or representative mandate as their point of departure. Civil organizations do not, and cannot, hold a representative mandate on these terms – that is, as public officials elected through universal franchise. Judging them according to this standard may not be a productive exercise. In fact, the boundaries, achievements and constraints of existing notions of representation within the universe of civil organizations are the subject of great political dispute today. Setting aside the reservations mentioned above allows us to continue to reflect on the analytical challenge that exists. The actors themselves are not waiting for theorists to discover or come to terms with their new political role. Among civil organizations today one finds a diversity of partially constructed notions of representation that are used to defend publicly their representativeness. The content of some of these notions is compatible with the expansion of democracy, while that of others clearly is not.

Assumed Representation by Civil Organizations

In the absence of historical or theoretical models for examining political representation by civil organizations, we argue for an analytic strategy that is inductive but guided by the constitutive duality of the concept of representation, on the one hand, and the importance of representatives' genuine (subjective) commitment to the interests of the represented (Burke 1949), on the other. The strategy consists of shifting the question of representativeness from the actual to the symbolic level, centring attention on the representative's commitment to representation, on their identification with those represented, and, in sociological terms, on their own perception of their representativeness. It entails taking seriously civil organizations' self-definition as representative: actors' public acceptance or rejection of the idea of being representatives, together with the justifications or congruency arguments used by them to defend publicly the genuineness of their commitment to represent.

The constitutive duality of political representation is the autonomy of the representative and the mandate given by the represented (Pitkin 1967). The existence of representation does not guarantee representativeness – its correspondence to the will of those being represented – and the strength of representativeness cannot be accomplished by removing the autonomy of the representative. As Sartori (1962) and Pitkin (1967) have meticulously demonstrated, maintaining analytically only one of the two poles in this duality is the quickest way to empty out political representation of its meaning – either it loses its substantive meaning of acting in the interests or on behalf of those represented, or it loses its political nature as institutional crystallization for governing society.

Publicly assumed representation is not equivalent to effective representation, but commitment to the interests of the represented is a vital component of representation. Ultimately, Burke (1949) argues, the best measure to guarantee authentic representation – that is, its representativeness – is the existence of a genuine representative commitment. Given the contingent nature of this subjective factor, formal institutional mechanisms are both necessary and desirable to ensure this representative commitment is not displaced or lost. Although the subjective dimension of representation has become systematically devalued among theories of democracy, institutional rules and designs are powerless when representatives are not stimulated or moved by a 'feeling of representation'. More precisely, if representation cannot be reduced to merely assumed representation, representativeness cannot do away with the commitment of representing, and this is found in abundance in civil organizations.

Six Notions of Representation

The idea of 'assumed representation' allows us to avoid the question of whether actual representation is taking place, and thus of an actor's representativeness. It introduces distinctions that help explore the problematic of civil organizations' representativeness in a different form – as justification attached to assumed representation. Justifications are an inherent part of assumed representation. The range of arguments an actor can invoke to defend a claim to represent a public makes explicit the basis of the authenticity of that self-definition, from the perspective of that actor, of course. The typology of congruency arguments condenses this broad range and categorizes their key elements. What is considered here are the motives and reasons actually furnished by civil organizations to address the thorny question of their representativeness, once they have assumed the position as representatives of their public. Therefore the typology is a result of the research. It disregards normative conceptual elements and does not say anything about the way in which civil organizations *should* construe their roles of political representation, or about the appropriate mechanisms of accountability or responsiveness that would connect these organizations to those they ultimately represent.

Six congruency arguments prevail among civil organizations (Table 6.1). They are classical-electoral, proximity, services, mediation, membership and identity. Each argument is made up of the same components, although these are related to each other in different ways. Broadly speaking, representation combines three components: *those represented*, always people whose will is bound together in a way that is to a greater or lesser degree direct and concrete (vote, demand, petition) or in a way necessarily indirect and abstract (nation, tradition, common good); *the representative*, mediator and guardian of interests of those represented, whose role lies in diverse levels of institutionalization, authorization, and duty to those represented; and *the locus*, which is simultaneously the jurisdiction where representation is exercised and the interlocutors to whom it is addressed. In this case, where the figures of traditional political representation prove to be inadequate, those represented tend to coincide with the publics of the organizations, usually outlined in quite broad terms such as 'the excluded', 'the poor', 'the community' and 'citizens'. The representative corresponds to the civil organization that is authorized as such by self-definition, and the locus, only implicitly specified in the majority of cases, as a rule centres on the public authority and less frequently on other social institutions and before other societal interlocutors.

Although the three components appear in all of the congruency arguments, in each argument the components relate to each other in a particular manner, the distinguishing mark of which lies in the emphasis placed by the actor on the part and content of those relationships which are used by them as proof of the authenticity of their assumed representation.

The findings reveal that the congruency arguments civil organizations make to support their representativeness appear to be

Table 6.1 Typology of congruency arguments

Congruency arguments	Frequency No. (%)	Emphasis of relationship	Dimensions of the argument	Examples
Classical electoral	8 (4.2)	*Vertical*: From represented to representative	Electoral process	'Because we are elected to respond politically for this population…'
Membership	13 (6.8)	*Internal*: From the representative to the represented	Membership	'Because we are part of the movement as affiliated members…'
Identity	9 (4.7)	*Internal*: From the represented to the representative	Identity/ substantive	'We are an integral part; we talk because we are.'
Mediation	60 (31.1)	*Vertical*: From the representative to the locus	(a) Advocacy (b) Mediation	(a) 'Because we fight for children's rights…' (b) 'Because we have been their voice before the public authorities…'
Proximity	52 (27.1)	*Horizontal*: From the representative to the represented	(a) Emancipation (b) Openness (c) Commitment	(a) 'Because we provide the conditions for this group to develop a political conscience…' (b) 'Because we work in partnership with these people…' (c) 'Because the aims of the organization are centred on this group, supporting their development…'
Services	45 (23.4)	*Vertical*: From the representative to the represented	Service non-profit	'Because we try to provide some structure to the families, distribution of milk, basic supplies'
Others	5 (2.6)			
Total	192 (100)			

crystallizing around a small number of notions of representation. Of the six arguments made by civil organizations, those that have received the most attention in scholarly works – the identity, electoral and membership arguments – are surprisingly rare. They account for only 16 per cent of the actors who assume representation of their publics. In contrast, mediation, proximity and services are by far the most common arguments (ranging from 31 to 23 per cent of actors).

Who uses these congruency arguments and how do they relate to the potential exercise of representation? The fact that actors overwhelmingly use a single argument suggests that they are consciously and purposefully constructing justifications of their assumed representation. Only 1 per cent make use of three arguments to justify their representativeness, 13 per cent use two arguments, and 86 per cent use only one. Of the six arguments, those most used are mediation (31 per cent) and proximity (27 per cent), followed by the service argument. In contrast, membership, identity and classical-electoral mechanisms are invoked only infrequently.

There is an elective affinity between particular congruency arguments and specific types of organization, reflecting the logic of the arguments themselves (Table 6.2). Service non-profit organizations do not cite the classical-electoral, membership or identity arguments even once, while they use the service argument with notable frequency. Local associations use the proximity argument the most, and they do not use the membership argument. Together with the coordinating bodies, local associations are the only actors to use the classical-electoral argument. The coordinating bodies in turn account for almost all the membership cases cited and centre the reasons for their representativeness on the mediation argument. Advocacy NGOs also make the mediation argument more frequently, followed closely by the proximity argument, although, differently from the coordinating bodies, they totally dismiss the classical-electoral argument.

Is there a relationship between practices of political representation – (i) new forms of representation within the executive; (ii) direct mediation of demands vis-à-vis specific public agencies; (iii) political advocacy by means of aggregation of interests through traditional electoral channels; and (iv) political advocacy – and the different congruency arguments? Table 6.3 shows that the classical-electoral and membership arguments, which conform to representation structures accepted in mass democracies, are used by organizations that in fact score more highly in their number of the above four activities

Table 6.2   Arguments for assumed representation by civil organizations (%)

Congruency arguments	Advocacy NGOs	Local associations	Service non-profits	Coordinating bodies	Others
Classical electoral	0.0	8.3	0.0	8.5	0.0
Membership	6.7	0.0	0.0	23.4	0.0
Identity	6.7	6.3	0.0	4.3	0.0
Mediation	33.3	27.1	25.9	36.2	42.9
Proximity	30.0	29.2	14.8	19.1	21.4
Services	16.7	27.1	55.6	6.4	35.7
Others	6.7	2.1	3.7	2.1	0.0
Total	100.0	100.0	100.0	100.0	100.0

ultimately linked to political representation. The identity argument in turn performs similarly, albeit scoring slightly lower. The large majority of organizations that cite these arguments carry out at least three of the activities considered in the analysis. On the other hand, the mediation and proximity arguments are cited by only a small group of organizations which do not carry out at least one of the activities linked to political representation. The congruency argument based on service delivery has the weakest relationship to activities of representation – it is used by actors that in their majority (70 per cent) only carry out up to two activities.

These findings from São Paulo suggest a surprising affinity between notions and actions of representation and they interrogate in authoritative and multiple ways some of the assumptions central to the research agendas on reconfiguration of representation and on the democratization of democracy. For example, 73 per cent of organizations assumed representation, and for these organizations the relationship with political institutions is of central importance to their claiming the status of representatives. By far the best predictor of their propensity to assume their representation of the publics for which or with whom they work is whether the organization has supported political candidates in elections. Furthermore, those who assume

Table 6.3 Representational activities according to congruency arguments (%)

Arguments of representation	Activities of representation					
	0	1	2	3	4	Total
Classical electoral	0.0	0.0	12.5	62.5	25.0	100.0
Membership	0.0	7.7	30.8	61.5	0.0	100.0
Identity	0.0	0.0	44.4	44.4	11.1	100.0
Mediation	5.0	15.0	25.0	41.7	13.3	100.0
Proximity	9.6	7.7	25.0	44.2	13.5	100.0
Services	13.3	26.7	20.0	33.3	6.7	100.0
Others	40.0	20.0	40.0	0.0	0.0	100.0

representation are far more likely to engage in actual representational activities than those who state they are not representatives. Contrary to the assumptions of the two research agendas, this suggests not only that a majority of civil organizations working with or for lower income groups self-consciously engage in political representation, but also that the dynamics of this political representation are closely related to those of traditional political channels of representation. They are *not* parallel to or separate from traditional channels.

Among the congruency arguments reconcilable with democratic principles, the *mediation* argument appears the most promising. The argument is made by roughly a third of the actors – principally NGOs, community associations and coordinators. It suggests that the representation exercised by civil organizations is not an alternative to that of traditional institutions of political representation, but rather an additional form of mediation that connects segments of the population otherwise poorly or under-represented in the state and in electoral politics. Actors who make the mediation argument overwhelmingly engage in political activities in which actual representation is likely to occur.

Recent innovative experiments in institutional participation and state reform in Brazil are reflected within this mediation argument for assumed representation. These political-institutional changes have altered the dynamics of representation among civil organizations over the past two decades, and in particular they have led this representation to acquire explicit political dimensions. Civil organizations who make the mediation argument affirm their commitment to a mediating role that connects poorly or under-represented segments of the population, on the one hand, to the state and, on the other, to electoral politics. What is being discussed therefore is an argument that situates civil organizations as a new form of mediation between representatives and those represented.

Conclusion

Innovative institutional spaces that bring civil organizations into the process of designing and supervising public policy are expanding the boundaries of political representation beyond their original locus and functions, towards the executive. In São Paulo ordinary citizens are not, by and large, the principal protagonists in these new participatory spaces; but, rather, civil organizations legally invested as representatives of the social sectors envisaged by these policies have assumed this protagonism. Furthermore, it is the civil organizations that actively cultivate political support and build alliances with traditional political actors in order to carry out their objectives that take on the assumed representation of their public.

Confirming that civil organizations are playing a substantial role in the reconfiguration of representation in São Paulo does not say anything about the positive or negative consequences for political inclusion and the quality of democracy. These consequences depend, among other things, on the nature of the representativeness of civil organizations, and the extent to which notions of political representation among these actors meet democratic requirements.

The evidence examined here indicates that one should avoid constructing a single stylized model of representation by civil organizations, as diverse models of representativeness are used in the public justifications of the authenticity of their assumed representation. Undoubtedly, a substantial number of organizations conceive the legitimacy of their representation in terms that have perverse consequences if they are projected into the political arena. Nevertheless, congruency arguments reconcilable with democratic requirements do exist and these are made by a majority of actors. Among these, the notion of representation we call *mediation* is explicitly political and compatible with the contemporary processes of the reconfiguration of representation.

Notes

This chapter draws heavily on Gurza Lavalle et al. 2005. More systematic empirical support for the claims we make in this chapter can be found in this and in Houtzager et al. 2003, available for download at www.ids. ac.uk/gdr/cfs/research/Collective%20Actors-pubs.html.

1. The sample was constructed using a snowball technique, particularly useful for accessing 'hidden' populations (Atkinson and Flint 2003). For further details, see Houtzager et al. 2003.

2. For literature on deepening democracy, see Fung 2004; Fung and Wright 2003; Santos Boaventura 2002. For social accountability approaches, see Peruzotti and Smulovitz 2002. For a focus on empowered participation, see Fung and Wright 2003. For a perspective on deliberative democracy, see Habermas 1993, 1996a, 1996b; Bohman and Rehg 2002; Elster 1998. On civil society, see Keane 1988, but especially Cohen and Arato 1992; Costa 2002; Avritzer 1994, 1997, 2003; and Panfichi 2003.

References

Atkinson, R., and J. Flint (2003) 'Accessing hidden and hard-to-reach populations: Snowball research strategies', *Social Research Update* 33, www.soc.surrey. ac.uk/sru/ SRU33.html.

Avritzer, L. (1994) 'Modelos de sociedade civil: uma análise específica do Caso Brasileiro', in L. Avritzer, ed., *Sociedade civil e democratização*, Belo Horizonte: Del Rey.

Avritzer, L. (1997) 'Um desenho institucional para o novo associativismo', *Lua Nova* 39, CEDEC.

Avritzer, L. (2003) *Democracy and the Public Space in Latin America*, Princeton: Princeton University Press.

Bohman, J., and W. Rehg (2002) *Deliberative democracy*, Massachusetts: MIT Press.

Burke, E. (1949) [1774] 'Speech to the Electors', in R.J.S. Hoffman, *Burke's Politics*, New York: Alfred A. Knopf.

Chandhoke, N. (2003) 'Governance and the pluralisation of the state: implications for democratic pratices in Asia', University of Delhi, mimeo.

Chandhoke, N. (2004) 'Revisiting the crisis of representation thesis: the Indian context', University of Delhi, mimeo.

Cohen, J. and A. Arato (1992) *Civil Society and Political Theory*, Cambridge MA: MIT Press.

Costa, S. (2002) *As cores de Ercília: Esfera Pública, democracia, configurações póstnacionais*, Belo Horizonte: UFMG.

Cunil, G.N. (1997) *Pensando lo publico a traves de la sociedad: nuevas formas de gestión pública e representación social*, Caracas: Nueva Sociedad/CLAD.

Dagnino, E. (2002) 'Sociedade civil, espaços públicos e a construção democrática no Brasil: Limites e possibilidades', in E. Dagnino, *Sociedade Civil e Espaços Públicos no Brasil*, São Paulo: Paz e Terra.

Elster, J., ed., (1998) *Deliberative Democracy*, Cambridge: Cambridge University Press.

Fung, A. (2004) *Empowered Participation: Reinventing Urban Democracy*, Princeton: Princeton University Press.

Fung, A., and E.O. Wright (2003) 'Thinking about empowered participatory governance', in A. Fung and E.O. Wright, *Deepening Democracy: Institutional Innovation in Empowered Participatory Governance*, London: Verso.

Goodman, L. (1961) 'Snowball sampling', *Annals of Mathematical Statistics* 32(1).

Grindle, M.S. (1999) *Audacious Reforms: Institutional Reform and Democracy in Latin America*, Baltimore: Johns Hopkins University Press.

Gurza Lavalle, A., P.P. Houtzager and G. Castello (2005) 'In whose name? Representation and civil organisations in Brazil', IDS Working Paper No. 249, Institute of Development Studies, University of Sussex, Falmer.

Habermas, J. (1993) 'La soberanía popular como procedimiento: Un concepto normativo de lo público', in M. Herrera, ed., *Jürgen Habermas – Moralidad, Ética y Política: Propuestas y Críticas*, Mexico: Alianza Editorial.

Habermas, J. (1996) 'Three Normative Models of Democracy', in S. Benhabib, ed., *Democracy and Difference: Contesting the Boundaries of the Political*, Princeton: Princeton University Press.

Habermas, J. (1998) *Between Facts and Norms: Contributions to a Discourse Theory of Democracy*, Cambridge MA: MIT Press.

Hagiopian, F. (1998) 'Democracy and political representation in Latin America in the 1990s: pause, reorganization, or decline?', in F. Agüero and J. Stark, eds, *Fault Lines of Democracy in Post-Transition Latin America*, Miami: North–South Center Press.

Heller, P. (2001) 'Moving the state: the politics of democratic decentralization in Kerala, South Africa, and Porto Alegre', *Politics & Society* 29(1).

Houtzager, P., J. Harris, R. Collie and A. Gurza Lavalle (2002) 'Rights, representation and the poor: comparisons across Latin America and India', LSE Working Paper Series No. 2–3, London School of Economics.

Houtzager, P., A. Gurza Lavalle and A. Acharya (2003) 'Who participates? Civil society and the new democratic politics in São Paulo, Brazil', IDS Working Paper No. 210, Institute of Development Studies, University of Sussex, Falmer.

Houtzager, P., A. Gurza Lavalle and A. Acharya (2004) 'Atores da sociedade civil e atores políticos – participação nas novas políticas democráticas em São Paulo', in L. Avritzer, ed., *Participação política em São Paulo*, São Paulo: UNESP.

Keane, J. (1984) *Public Life and Late Capitalism: Toward a Socialist Theory of Democracy*, Cambridge: Cambridge University Press.

Keane, J. (1988) *Democracy and Civil Society*, London: Verso.

Manin, B. (1997) *The Principles of Representative Government*, Cambridge: Cambridge University Press.

Miguel, L.F. (2003a) 'Representação política em 3–D: elementos para uma teoria ampliada da representação política', *Revista Brasileira de Ciências Sociais* 51(18), February.

Miguel, L.F. (2003b) 'Impasses da accountability: dilemas e alternativas da representação política', paper presented to XXVII Congresso Anual da AN-POCS, Caxambu, October.

Novaro, M. (2000) *Representación y Liderazgo en las Democracias Contemporáneas*, Rosario: Homo Sapiens Ediciones.

Panfichi, A. (2003) *Sociedad civil, esfera pública y democratización en América Latina: Andes y Cono Sur*, Fondo de Cultura Económica, Universidad Veracruzana.

Peruzzotti, E., and C. Smulovitz (2002) 'Accountability social: la otra cara del control', in E. Peruzzotti and C. Smulovitz, eds, *Controlando la política – Ciudadanos y medios den las nuevas democracias latinoamericanas*, Buenos Aires: Temas.

Pitkin, F.H. (1967) *The Concept of Representation*, Berkeley: University of California Press.

Przeworski, A. (2002) 'Accountability social en América Latina y más allá', in E. Peruzzotti and C. Smulovitz, eds, *Controlando la política – Ciudadanos y medios den las nuevas democracias latinoamericanas*, Buenos Aires: Temas.

Roberts, K.M. (2002) 'Party–society linkages and democratic representation in Latin America', *Canadian Journal of Latin American and Caribbean Studies* 27(53).

Santos, B. de Sousa (2002) *Democracia e Participação: O Caso do Orçamento Participativo de Porto Alegre*, Porto: Edições Afrontamento.

Sartori, G. (1962) 'A teoria da representação no Estado Representativo moderno', *Revista Brasileira de Estudos Políticos*, ed. Bernardo Álvares, Minas Gerais.

Tenzer, N. (1992) *La Sociedad Despolitizada. Ensayo sobre los fundamentos de la política*, Barcelona: Ediciones Paidós.

7

Inclusion and Representation in Democratic Deliberations: Lessons from Canada's Romanow Commission

Bettina von Lieres and David Kahane

In both Northern and Southern contexts it is now widely affirmed that public deliberation leads to more effective and legitimate policy-making, increases public trust and social capital, cultivates citizen character and engagement, and reduces controversy when policies are implemented. However, whereas in many Southern contexts new democratic deliberative spaces are often localized and rarely involve large-scale, society-wide deliberations, in Northern contexts there has been a recent proliferation of extensive deliberative consultations with citizens on issues of national importance.[1] These consultative exercises raise distinctive questions about citizenship and inclusion, especially when it comes to including marginalized groups in deliberative processes. This chapter explores these issues of deliberative inclusion through an examination of the role of Aboriginal people in the deliberative components of the Romanow Commission, established in April 2001 by the Canadian government to deliberate with citizens on the future of healthcare in Canada.

The Romanow Commission's mandate was to review Canada's healthcare system, engage Canadians in a national dialogue on its future, and make recommendations to enhance the system's quality and sustainability. The range of the Commission's consultations was vast: it commissioned forty expert reports and convened nine expert panels over its one-and-a-half-year mandate; it partnered with broadcasters, universities, business and advocacy groups, and the health policy community in a 'four-phase national dialogue'; and it sponsored explicitly deliberative consultation methods, designed to 'probe deeply not only Canadians' current views, but also how those views evolve as citizens work through difficult trade-offs in dialogue with each other and try to reconcile those views with deeper values' (CPRN 2002: 2). The Commission was amply resourced in these tasks: with a staff of forty-seven, the Commission ultimately cost between Can$15 and 20 million.

There is a strong tendency in deliberative democratic theory and practice to treat deliberation as involving generic, individual citizens in dialogue about the common good. In this model, political deliberation demands that citizens take up a reflective stance toward their own interests and attachments, so that collective conclusions are based on the force of better reason emerging from unconstrained dialogue (Fishkin 1991; Habermas 1990). Critics of this paradigm have argued, however, that the dynamics of political deliberation are heavily conditioned by relations of power: marginalized groups are less likely to participate in deliberation and their perspectives are less likely to influence outcomes, even though these groups may be especially vulnerable when it comes to the policy contexts about which citizens are deliberating (Fraser 1993; Tully 1995; Williams 1998). From the point of view of these critics – and we number ourselves among them – the challenge is to design political delib- erations in ways that make space for marginalized perspectives and empower these to influence collective decisions.

The challenge of empowering the perspectives of marginalized groups in political deliberations is acute in Canada, especially when it comes to Aboriginal people. The complex legacies of colonization have left First Nations, Metis and Inuit people in Canada at the bottom when it comes to a wide range of indicators of well-being, including economic status, education, housing quality, and health outcomes. These legacies also have cultivated a deep sense of al- ienation, disenfranchisement and mistrust on the part of Aboriginal people towards the Canadian state. Complicating matters yet further is the fact that many Aboriginal peoples claim self-government rights, often based in centuries-old treaties; so there are conflicting views of what political units are involved in dialogues on the territory called 'Canada', and whether Aboriginal peoples are properly subject to the rule of the Canadian state.

The Romanow Commission engaged in complex and sometimes contradictory ways with questions of Aboriginal inclusion and Abo- riginal health. On the one hand, the final report of the Commission devoted a chapter to questions of Aboriginal health, based upon careful consultation with Aboriginal people. On the other hand, the explicitly deliberative elements of the Commission's work were with statistically representative groups of 'unaffiliated citizens' and, though they included Aboriginal people, did not focus on questions of Aboriginal health, or overtly build in devices to allow Aboriginal participants to overcome dynamics of marginalization.

In what follows, we first sketch the political context within which the Romanow Commission worked, laying out the controversies that define current debates over Canadian healthcare, and the distinctive situation of Aboriginal peoples when it comes to questions of health. We next describe the activities of the Romanow Commission, showing how citizen deliberation fits into the work of the Commission as a whole, and how the Commission structured a separate track for consultation with Aboriginal people. We then look more closely at the design of Citizen Dialogues, and at the day-long Aboriginal Forum that was the closest the Commission came to making space for deliberative engagement with Aboriginal people.

We suggest that the successes and shortcomings of the Romanow Commission in including Aboriginal people in deliberations are tied to three key features of deliberative design:

1. The extent to which the process is *reflexive*, in the sense of giving participants a deliberative say in defining the terms of their participation, the issues they will address, and the form deliberation will take.
2. The extent to which public involvement is *recursive*, so that citizen deliberation takes place from the beginning, applying to the range of decisions made.
3. The existence of *separate spaces* in which members of marginalized groups can reflect on dynamics of power and exclusion, and negotiate questions of common agendas, strategies and identities. These separate spaces can take many forms, from parallel deliberative processes to opportunities for caucusing within heterogeneous deliberations.

Our discussion of the Romanow process reaffirms the importance of these design choices, and shows their significance in enabling the negotiation by marginalized groups of the complex politics of recognition and representation. The chapter concludes with lessons

from the Romanow process for the design of deliberative spaces in
other contexts.

The Context for the Romanow Commission

Canada's healthcare system is a publicly funded, single-tier system.
The federal government funds about 50 per cent of healthcare
expenditures, with the balance provided by the provinces. The federal
contribution is contingent on provinces following the principles of
the Canada Health Act (CHA), which stipulates that care should be
universal, portable, comprehensive, accessible and publicly funded.
There is an ongoing struggle between provincial governments and the
federal government over questions of jurisdiction and funding, and
over the flexibility that the CHA allows to provinces for experimentation with forms of healthcare funding and delivery (e.g. user fees,
privately available diagnostic services, paying for-profit companies to
provide government-insured services). There also are Canada-wide
challenges of sustainability, growing waiting lists, shortages of health
professionals, access to care in rural and remote regions, fragmentation,
pressure for more privatization or expansion of the public system,
and the challenges of Aboriginal health.

The historical relationship between Aboriginal people and the
Canadian state has had three broad consequences that cast shadows
on any discussion of health policy. First, a history of colonization
has contributed to endemic social and health problems in Aboriginal
communities. Second, treaties and the process of colonization together
established special federal responsibilities for Aboriginal health, though
the nature of these 'fiduciary' responsibilities is contested. Third, the
troubled history of relationships between diverse Aboriginal peoples
and the Canadian state makes democratic policymaking on Aboriginal
issues extremely complex: 'Aboriginal' is a loose umbrella term for
a culturally, linguistically, economically, socially and politically diverse
assemblage of communities and nations, including First Nations, Inuit
and Metis peoples.

The poor health status of Aboriginal people in Canada, and the
complex constitutional status and political construction of Aboriginal
health issues, formed an inevitable part of the backdrop to the
Romanow Commission's work on the health of Canadians. Aboriginal
issues also played an ambivalent part in the citizen deliberations set
up by the Commission.

Deliberation and Aboriginal Voices in the Romanow Commission

Royal Commissions form part of Canada's British parliamentary heritage: they are struck by governments to investigate issues of public concern (or, more cynically, to allow governments to defer dealing with fraught political issues). In the 1990s, public support for the Canadian health system declined in the face of problems such as long waiting lists for surgical procedures, shortages of trained medical personnel, and lack of access to health services in rural and remote areas. Polls conducted in 1991, 1995 and 1999 showed the percentage of Canadians rating the health service as 'excellent' or 'very good' declining from 61 per cent to 52 per cent to 24 per cent (Shulman and Raza 2003: 38). Infusions of federal funding in the late 1990s temporarily defused public anxiety, but it was widely recognized that this would provide only short respite. And so the Canadian government struck a commission to canvass Canada's citizens' views on healthcare and 'to ensure over the long term the sustainability of a universally accessible, publicly funded health system, that offers quality services to Canadians' (Privy Council of Canada 2001: 569). The Commission was to be led by Roy Romanow, the former premier of Saskatchewan.

The mandate of the Commission was open, requiring that there be a fact-finding stage of work followed by an interim report, and then dialogue with the Canadian public and interested stakeholders based on that report. It is important to note that nowhere in the official mandate of the Commission is there mention of Aboriginal health; indeed, in the early months of the Commission's work there was considerable uncertainty about whether Aboriginal health even fell within the mandate (Forest, interview, 2005).

In the end, the Commission engaged in a range of consultative mechanisms, which Romanow describes as follows:

> We began by analyzing existing reports on medicare and by inviting submissions from interested Canadians and organizations. To clarify our understanding of key issues, we organized expert roundtable sessions and conducted site visits, both in Canada and abroad. Where we identified knowledge gaps or needed a fresh perspective, we commissioned independent experts to conduct original research. Finally, I met directly with Canada's foremost health policy experts to hear their views, challenge them and have them challenge me. We also worked hard to engage Canadians

in our consultations, because medicare ultimately belongs to them. We partnered with broadcasters, universities, business and advocacy groups, and the health policy community to raise awareness of the challenges confronting medicare... I also had the privilege of leading one of the most comprehensive, inclusive and successful consultative exercises our country has ever witnessed. (CFHCC 2002: xv)

The 'inclusive and successful' consultation with Canadian citizens took a number of forms, including televised fora, open public hearings, and a consultation workbook. It is the National Citizens' Dialogue, however, that most stands out: here the Commission stepped beyond conventional forms of citizen input to construct an intensively deliberative form of citizen consultation, one that sought to move participants beyond their preformed understandings and interests, to positions informed by careful exchanges of perspectives and reasons.

The National Citizens' Dialogue

The Order in Council that established the Romanow Commission specified that the work of the inquiry should include 'dialogue with the Canadian public', and the Commission took this part of the brief seriously. It sought ways to take citizen involvement beyond consultation – hearing the views of citizens and stakeholders – to *deliberation:* engaging citizens in a dialogue that challenged their existing understandings, confronting them with the sorts of trade-offs called for in health policy, and urging them to define paths to healthcare reform that fit with their deepest values. The Commission partnered with the Canadian Policy Research Network (CPRN), a think-tank with extensive experience in researching and designing invited spaces for citizen dialogue.[2] The CPRN in turn partnered with Viewpoint Learning, a private consulting firm specializing in structuring dialogues in both business and public policy contexts using a 'ChoiceWork' dialogue methodology.[3] The process that emerged from this partnership was the Citizens' Dialogue on the Future of Health Care in Canada.

The Citizens' Dialogue was designed in explicit contrast to two models of citizen involvement used by past Royal Commissions. A first contrast was with public hearings, which make space for the voices of self-selecting citizens, but 'do not create the ambience where average citizens can present their views and participate actively in the public debate' (CPRN 2002: 15). A second contrast was with the National Forum on Health between 1994 and 1997: this task force 'explicitly set out to learn Canadians' core values in relation to healthcare by having focus groups discuss a series of scenarios that presented discrete issues and personal situations. However, the Forum did not find a method that enabled citizens to make the trade-offs needed to come to terms with difficult reform choices.' The Citizens' Dialogue, and the ChoiceWorks methodology it used, were designed to avoid these pitfalls: 'to probe deeply… how views evolve as citizens work through difficult tradeoffs in dialogue with each other and try to reconcile those views with their deeper values' (CPRN 2002: 2).

The Citizens' Dialogue convened twelve one-day sessions across the country, each involving about forty citizens. Participants were randomly selected, although healthcare professionals and managers were screened out, as were those under 18, and those who could not take part in a dialogue in English or French. The cost of the dialogues is estimated at Can.\$1.3 million.

The Commission developed a workbook[4] for participants. The workbook focused on three characteristic challenges confronted by the Canadian healthcare system: growing costs, public dissatisfaction with the quality of care, and varying levels of coverage across the country. It then laid out four scenarios for responding to these challenges, meant to serve as a starting point for discussion:

- Putting more public investment in doctors, nurses and equipment, either through tax increases or by reallocating funds from other government programmes.
- Introducing shared costs and responsibilities (e.g. user fees or co-payments) to discourage overuse of the system and increase government revenue.
- Increasing private choices for patients via a restructuring of the healthcare system that includes private-sector providers.
- Reorganizing service delivery (e.g. teams of doctors, nurses and other professionals working together) to improve efficiency and cost-effectiveness.

The morning sessions of each dialogue began with time to read the workbook and complete a questionnaire to measure participants' initial judgements of the four scenarios. The results showed that no particular change was overwhelmingly supported; favourable judgements of each scenario (scores of 5–7 on a seven-point scale) ranged from 34 per cent (for increasing private choice) to 56 per cent (for reorganizing service delivery) (CPRN 2002: 27–8). In the next step, each participant spoke briefly about an issue of concern. Issues raised at this stage included universality and accessibility; affordability and sustainability; inefficiency and abuse; prevention and health education; expanding services covered; and privatizing services to increase individual choice.

Next, participants worked in self-facilitated groups to define the healthcare that they desired, then reconvened in plenary to build a composite goal. The ideal healthcare system defined in the morning 'was remarkably consistent in the twelve dialogues held from coast to coast': access is based on need; coverage is universal; accountabilities are clear for all the players; individual needs are met in a more patient-centred system; wellness and prevention are emphasized; care is integrated, multi-disciplinary and convenient; and the system is efficient and affordable (CPRN 2002: 27–8).

The afternoon sessions pushed participants to consider the choices and trade-offs that they would be willing to make in pursuit of these values and ideals, working first in their groups, then in plenary to identify common ground:

> Facilitators emphasised the importance of developing a list of steps that are mutually consistent and affordable; to be as specific as possible on the steps that should be taken and how they would be paid for. They underlined: 'If we do not make the choices and trade-offs they will be made for us, and they may not be the choices we want…' (CPRN 2002: 35)

The reforms that emerged in the afternoon sessions centred on reorganizing service delivery; increasing public funding (rejecting a parallel private system, ambivalence about user co-payments); and building stronger accountability and transparency into the system (on the part of providers, drug companies, administrators and governments).

The final step was for participants to complete the same questionnaire they had filled in at the start of the day. Overall, the number of undecided responses diminished, support for the status quo dropped, and support for all four scenarios increased (the scenarios were not necessarily disjunctive). Support for 'reorganize service delivery' rose from 56 per cent to 79 per cent; support for 'more public investment' rose from 48 per cent to 61 per cent; support for 'share costs and responsibilities' rose from 45 per cent to 50 per cent, and support for 'increase private choice' rose from 34 per cent to 39 per cent. These changes in participants' prescriptions for healthcare reform seem to substantiate the contrast that the space-makers drew between deliberative engagement and the sorts of perspectives elicited through more conventional forms of public consultation.

The Citizens' Dialogues proved important in the deliberations of the Romanow Commission, belying elite views that citizens are incapable of nuanced understandings of issues in healthcare reform and unwilling to make tough trade-offs. Maxwell et al. (2003: 1033) write that the dialogues contradicted elite preconceptions that citizens would not sign up with a primary care network, would reject having their personal data in an electronic health record, were unconcerned with health education and prevention, and lacked useful views on governance: 'One important lesson is that the abilities (and desire) of the general public to engage in this way should not be underestimated.'

The final report of the Commission was influenced in three key ways by the Citizens' Dialogue. First, it clarified Canadians' core values around healthcare, in a way that defined and framed the Commission's recommendations. Second, demands for transparency and accountability that emerged from the Dialogue were unexpected – the Commission had not perceived these as important values on the part of citizens – and came to inform the final report (Forest, interview, 2005). Third, the Dialogue instantiated an active role for citizens in healthcare policymaking and governance, a role that was emphasized by the Commission's final report: 'The principles of public participation and mutual responsibility were entrenched in a proposed health "covenant" between governments, providers, and the Canadian public. And the report recommended regular reruns of the dialogues' (Maxwell et al. 2003: 1033).

Members of the Romanow Commission speak with justifiable pride about the Citizens' Dialogue, which engaged large numbers of Canadians in disciplined reflection on complex questions of healthcare provision, and yielded considered judgements that informed policy recommendations. Yet when it comes to including the perspectives of marginalized groups – and particularly Aboriginal people – there is room to question its success. While some Aboriginal people were included in the dialogues, neither their design nor their outcomes include even a whisper about Aboriginal health issues. We suggest that this absence results from a failure of the Citizens' Dialogue to engage overtly with the complex politics of representation involved in any public deliberation: with questions of who needs to be at the table and in what numbers; who is typically marginalized in political dialogues; and how dynamics of exclusion and marginalization can be thematized and managed within the deliberation. It is our view that a serious engagement with these politics of representation would have required changes in the extent to which the Citizens' Dialogue process was *reflexive* (giving participants a deliberative say in the terms of their participation), *recursive* (so that participants have a say from the beginning to the end of the process), and involved *separate spaces* for caucusing and deliberation by marginalized groups.

A first set of design choices that bear on including the marginalized involves the *reflexivity* of the process. We would argue that questions of deliberative inclusion and representation are always complex and politicized, in so far as a goal of deliberation is to include the voices of social groups that are typically disadvantaged in political dialogues. Issues of inclusion and representation deserve the close attention of space-makers before deliberation takes place, but there are both practical and normative reasons why they cannot be settled in advance. Practically speaking, even a diverse group of space-makers will be unable to anticipate how issues of inclusion and voice will play out in a deliberation, or the questions that will arise; space needs to exist within the deliberative space for these issues to be raised and addressed. From a normative point of view, the very justification of democratic deliberation is based on connections between political legitimacy and unconstrained dialogue (Habermas 1990; Bohman 1996; Chambers 1996); so there is reason to worry when the terms of dialogue and the questions to be addressed are established by elites, outside of the deliberative exercise itself.

The Citizens' Dialogues were designed from the top down: the topics and conduct of the deliberation were carefully structured, and highly structured at that. This predetermined structure focused participants' attention on what they shared as generic, individual citizens. Indeed, it is a linchpin of the ChoiceWorks process that dialogues are most successful when participants are 'unaffiliated citizens', rather than stakeholders who self-consciously represent some particular identity or interest group in society.[5] The language of the workbooks, and indeed of the Romanow Commission more broadly, encouraged a focus on the common values of Canadians, so that the particularity of individual citizens could be folded together into a set of shared goals. This orientation toward 'unaffiliated citizens' also played out, we would suggest, in the selection procedure for the Citizen Dialogues, where what mattered most was getting a statistical cross-section of the population; this contrasts with selection procedures that focus on groups most affected by decisions, or groups typically marginalized in discussions of a given policy area.

Had there been a greater degree of reflexivity in the Citizens' Dialogues, participants would have been able to deliberate together about the terms of their conversation – about the proper sequence and duration of discussion, the scenarios to be discussed, the relative importance of the shared and the divergent. This reflexivity would have made the Citizens' Dialogues much less predictable, and more complex to manage; it might also, however, have made them more meaningfully democratic.

These issues of design – of how much is decided beforehand, and how much within deliberation itself – also connect with how *recursive* the process is. Where reflexiveness refers to participants' ability to consider the terms of their conversation, recursiveness describes the ways in which deliberation is treated as ongoing. From the standpoint of each participant, the Citizens' Dialogues were non-recursive: each dialogue was a single, eight-hour, bounded process. Elites decided on both the structure of the Dialogue and how to assimilate outcomes of the Dialogue into the Commission's reports.

We can imagine much more recursive versions of citizen delibera-tion. First, the design of the Citizens' Dialogue might itself have involved deliberation by citizens. And second, there are many ways in which deliberating citizens could have played an ongoing role: they could, for example, have been given a voice in how their day's work was taken up by the Commission, or on the adequacy of the Commission's final report.

The Citizens' Dialogue was heard and interpreted by Romanow and the Commission staff and seems to have had an important influence on the Commission and the final report. But its role was purely consultative: the outcome of the dialogue had no formal authority in the construction of recommendations, and participants in the Dialogue had no agency in the interpretation of the ses-sions. This non-recursiveness would seem to speak to a particular construal of the role of citizen representatives, relative to experts and elites, in producing knowledge and recommendations around health policy. Notwithstanding the rigorous and extensive quality of citizen deliberation, it had a non-authoritative place within the Commission.

A third key dimension of deliberative design is the existence of *separate spaces* for marginalized groups. As already noted, the ChoiceWorks methodology, taken at face value, treats participants as individuals. As the workbook explains, 'All dialogue participants speak for themselves, not as representatives of special interests' (CPRN 2002: 94). Given this methodology, issues of group-based marginalization and inclusion can be dealt with, at most, as issues of protocol, equal speaking time, and imprecations to take all views seriously – for example, 'Listen with empathy to the views of others: acknowledge you have heard the other *especially* when you disagree' (CPRN 2002: 94). This individualistic orientation in dialogue design may not take seriously enough the complex ways in which marginalization may be perpetuated in deliberative spaces, for example in the privileging of certain kinds of reasons, leaving mainstream criteria of authority and credibility in place, or favouring certain tones and structures of argument (Williams 1998; Young 1996).

The participation of Aboriginal people in the Citizens' Dialogue substantiates some of these concerns (given demographic variations across Canada, Aboriginal people were present in all sessions, and in the largest numbers in western sessions). Organizers were disappointed, overall, in the degree to which the dialogue was able to engage Aboriginal participants, who often didn't show up to sessions once recruited, and who typically were very quiet in the dialogue sessions. Interestingly, there were two significant (if ad hoc) attempts, as the dialogue process proceeded, to intervene in these dynamics. First, organizers worked to cluster Aboriginal participants in small group discussions to build confidence and voice. Second, in advance of the Winnipeg session organizers sought to bring more Aboriginal people to the dialogue than dictated by the representative sampling methodology by extending extra invitations through the Winnipeg Native Friendship Center. Neither of these ad hoc innovations had much effect, however, and few strong Aboriginal voices emerged in the Citizens' Dialogue (Maxwell, interview, 2005). This experience points to the difficulty of engaging and empowering members of marginalized groups within invited deliberative spaces, and to the limitations of piecemeal innovations in surmounting these difficulties. Giving Aboriginal people a more influential voice would have required changes to the basic structure of the dialogue, at which point the tension with the individualistic premisses of the ChoiceWorks method would have been acute.[6]

The two ad hoc attempts to build Aboriginal voice in the Citizens' Dialogues sought to lessen the isolation of Aboriginal people during deliberation by letting them work together, and by increasing their relative numbers. Separate deliberative spaces are a more concerted way to build voice for marginalized groups, through mechanisms such as group caucusing, or separate deliberative streams. Mechanisms such as these enable members of marginalized groups to develop strategies for naming and countering dynamics of exclusion; build confidence and capacities; reflect upon and consolidate common goals and identities; and make space for differences within the group (Mansbridge 1993). Separate spaces for Aboriginal participants in the Citizens' Dialogue would have been one route to mitigating the marginalization of Aboriginal perspectives, while also taking seriously the distinctiveness of issues of Aboriginal health in a context where constitutional and jurisdictional issues are very much in question.

Creating separate spaces for Aboriginal deliberation would have real potential benefits, and costs. A first benefit would be to offer a space within which Aboriginal values and claims could be sorted through concertedly and deliberatively, without the ongoing need to translate and justify Aboriginal perspectives to make them intelligible to non-Aboriginal people. In such contexts, culturally specific modes of communication and self-representation can find expression and roots. Second, separate spaces provide room for the internal complexity of Aboriginal perspectives to be dealt with democratically and deliberatively; in more heterogeneous spaces, by contrast, Aboriginal people can feel pressure to present a common front (downplaying differences, say, between on-reserve and off-reserve Aboriginal people, or Metis, First Nation and Inuit perspectives) in order to make their voices intelligible to others, and to exercise some minimal influence on deliberations. Third, separate spaces may allow greater reflexiveness about how issues are framed. This is especially important in connection with cross-jurisdictional issues like healthcare, given the extent to which Canadian state sovereignty over Aboriginal people is itself contested. Separate deliberative spaces leave open the question of whether Aboriginal people are properly

considered Canadian subjects whose views should be folded into a
nationally shared understanding.

There would have been costs to creating separate deliberative
spaces for Aboriginal people in the Romanow process. A first, obvious
cost is that the Citizens' Dialogue, and the work of the Commission as
a whole, would have had to be conducted differently, and quite possibly in more time-consuming and resource-intensive ways. Second,
creating separate spaces itself enacts presumptions about individual
and collective identities – both in treating Aboriginal people as a
bounded (if internally complex) group, and by supporting narratives
of separateness or incommensurability between Aboriginal and non-
Aboriginal beliefs and interests (Kahane 2004). Third, if there is no
additional space in which the values and perspectives of Aboriginal
and non-Aboriginal people can be brought into deliberative contact,
neither side can fully consider the trade-offs and sacrifices they
are demanding from the other, nor discover how the perspectives
of each side might be changed in dialogue with the other. Given
the dense and inescapable interconnections between Aboriginal and
non-Aboriginal communities, only this sort of common dialogue
could take account of the interpenetration of policy decisions on
Aboriginal health, and on the health of Canadians.

If these are the issues that arise at the abstract level in considering
separate Aboriginal and non-Aboriginal dialogues within the work of
the Romanow Commission, a host of other questions emerge when
we notice that the Commission *did* in fact run parallel dialogues: in
addition to the Citizens' Dialogue there was a day-long Aboriginal
Forum that provided input into Chapter 10 of the final report, 'A
New Approach to Aboriginal Health'.

The Aboriginal Forum

On 26 June 2002, the Romanow Commission partnered with the
National Aboriginal Health Organization (NAHO) to host the
Aboriginal Forum in Aylmer, Quebec. The Forum represented the
centrepiece of the Commission's engagement with Aboriginal groups.
The overall aim of the Forum was framed by Dr Judith Butler,
chairperson of NAHO Board of Directors, as sharing 'successes and
to provide an opportunity for participants to share their views on
the future of health care' (NAHO 2002: 3).

The Aboriginal Forum represented an important turning point in the Commission's deliberations with Aboriginal peoples. Prior to the Forum, special attempts had been made to ensure Aboriginal participation in a number of different consultative spaces which highlighted important shortcomings in the Commission's strategy for Aboriginal consultation. According to the director of the health desk of Canada's national Inuit organization, Inuit Tapiriit Kanatami, the workbook, for example, was largely ineffective among Inuit people, as 'Inuit culture is a verbal culture and for many Inuit the written format cannot be translated into dialogue, although some regions are completely connected to high-speed Internet' (Randell, interview, 2005). But it was during the public hearings that the real challenges of Aboriginal participation became evident.

The regional public hearings consisted of twenty-one days of 'open' meetings in which individual Canadians and healthcare stakeholder and advocacy groups presented their views on the future of the Canadian healthcare system. Many regional and national Aboriginal organizations participated in these consultations. Despite their participation, however, it quickly became clear that issues of Aboriginal health featured minimally. According to Michel Amar, the communications director of the Romanow Commission, the Saskatchewan health minister was the only regional health minister to mention Aboriginal health in his contribution. The brevity of the hearings provided little space to explore the deeply political context of Aboriginal health, and its context-specific challenges. The hearings were not well attended by Aboriginal organizations and participants, as many found it difficult to organize and mobilize their members in remote and rural areas. Key groups such as the Labrador Inuit were not represented at all (Amar, interview, 2004–05).

The hearings showed that the 'the one-size-fits-all approach' to consultation was a weakness in the overall consultation strategy with Aboriginal groups. As Randell pointed out, there were other forms of consultation that would have been more effective for Inuit groups: more local visits and tours by Romanow in the Arctic regions to raise the profile of the Commission, more use of 'verbal' media like the radio and opportunities for Inuit to phone in, and more community-based fora (Randell, interview, 2004). In particular, the consultation failed to address group-specific forms of communication and underestimated logistical constraints. It soon became clear that there were also important challenges of political representation.

During the first half of the Commission, Aboriginal participation had been structured around individual organizations and unaffiliated citizens. What was needed was a space in which Aboriginal groups could meet separately, not only in order to discuss the specific challenges of Aboriginal health but also to construct legitimate and effective representative processes.

The Commission then asked NAHO to co-host a more effective consultation process with Aboriginal groups. A joint decision-making process was set up to identify the best consultative model for securing appropriate engagement. The Commission adopted a 'hands-off' approach to the design of the Forum. One of the very few guidelines it gave NAHO was to 'include all key Aboriginal groups equally' (Amar, interview, 2004–05). About a hundred people participated in the Forum. Participants consisted of practitioners (health technicians, policy analysts), ordinary members of organizations and leaders. They were figured as affiliated and unaffiliated citizens, some representing the views of their organizations, and others speaking in a non-representative capacity as individual users of the Aboriginal health system.

The Forum opened with prayers led by elders on behalf of First Nations, Inuit, Metis and Urban Aboriginal Peoples, and then held group-specific workshops in which participants met to discuss the challenges faced by their specific indigenous community. This was viewed by some delegates as a positive element of the design process as it allowed participants to articulate challenges specific to their own group. The second half of the Forum featured a televised town-hall style interaction where individuals could present their concerns in person, or via telephone link-ups, directly to Commissioner Romanow. Each group's moderator synthesized their morning's discussion into a fifteen-minute presentation, which was handed over to Romanow in the afternoon.

The Aboriginal Forum had a number of strengths as a mechanism of democratic consultation. It offered a context within which Aboriginal values and claims could be sorted through concertedly, without the ongoing need to make them intelligible to non-Aboriginal people. Culturally specific modes of communication and self-representation may have been able to find greater expression, and it seems clear that a range of shared commitments among Aboriginal participants could be taken for granted. It also provided room for the internal complexity of Aboriginal perspectives to be dealt with democratically: the Forum involved a clear differentiation by subgroups, which many delegates viewed as important. In assessing the impact of the Commission's consultation process on distinct Aboriginal peoples such as the Inuit, Randell pointed out that the Commission gave the four Inuit regions a 'common project' and that 'it forced Inuit groups to focus on their common agenda'. She praised Romanow for listening to Inuit-specific demands. 'Romanow actually listened. He was the first commissioner to actually mention Inuit' (Randell, interview, 2004).

Many participants assessed the Aboriginal Forum's partnership with the Romanow Commission positively:

> There was a good process, no vague understandings, clear parameters, and sufficient opportunity for a dialogue between Romanow and Aboriginal leaders... Romanow was one of the few commissions who engaged in a partnership with Aboriginal groups. [The] Commission's reporting-back format has set the pattern for subsequent meetings between cabinet and Aboriginal groups. (Jock, interview, 2004)

The fact that there was a 'partnership' in the planning and design stage of the Forum was one of the reasons why the consultation process was seen as successful by participants.

The Aboriginal Forum also had a number of weaknesses from the standpoint of inclusive democratic deliberation. First, it is not clear how 'deliberative' the Forum was: it had a relatively conventional format, with highly structured and formal discussions, especially in the afternoon sessions. This leaves room for questions about whether there was in fact room for culturally distinctive or appropriate modes of communication to flourish. Second, the fact that the Forum was a *separate space* entailed certain costs, since it limited deliberation about relationships between Aboriginal and non-Aboriginal people. Just as the Citizens' Forum didn't take up issues of Aboriginal health, there was no systematic discussion in the Forum of issues *beyond* Aboriginal health. Third, the Aboriginal Forum – a one-day event designed in advance – was not especially *reflexive*: it is not clear that the discussions were rooted in in-depth explorations of the complex politics surrounding Aboriginal health; nor was there any extended discussion of the terms of the dialogue of the Forum, who was and was not there, and so on. The Forum did not obviously allow for the articulation of political values, treaty claims, and deeper political challenges to the framing of the process. Fourth, the Forum was not *recursive*: while Romanow and his staff may have gleaned important insights from hearing the proceedings, participants in the Forum had no further input into the Commission's deliberations, much less an opportunity to react collectively and deliberatively to the Commission's final report.

A further aspect of recursiveness seems especially salient to issues of Aboriginal representation, and that is the ability of participants to be in dialogue with their communities over the course of a deliberative process. This hardly seems possible in the space of a one-day event; yet the legitimacy of the Forum as a representation of Aboriginal perspectives would have been enhanced by a structure that allowed a back-and-forth between discussions among direct participants, and conversations between these participants and their peoples and communities.

After Romanow: Institutionalizing Citizen Participation

The Romanow Commission's final report recommended a new approach to Aboriginal healthcare – one that tackled the root causes of health problems for Aboriginal peoples, cut across administrative and jurisdictional boundaries, and focused squarely on improving the health of Aboriginal peoples. Specific actions were recommended: to consolidate fragmented funding for Aboriginal health; to create new models to coordinate and deliver healthcare services and ensure that Aboriginal healthcare needs were addressed; to adapt health programmes and services to the cultural, social, economic and political circumstances unique to different Aboriginal groups; and to give Aboriginal people a direct voice in how healthcare services are designed and delivered (CPRN 2002). While it is too early to evaluate the full impact of these recommendations, they have made an identifiable difference in the treatment of Aboriginal issues within the Canadian health system. It is less clear, however, that this real progress was a result of the deliberative democratic elements of the Commission's work, as represented by the Citizens' Dialogues and the Aboriginal Forum.

Taken together, the Citizens' Dialogues and the Aboriginal Forum represented an important attempt to include a differentiated citizenry in a large-scale public participation process. However, both processes were also fairly isolated parts of a large, complex process where the ultimate interpretive authority resided with an elite (Romanow and his staff). It is crucial to recognize the extent to which the deliberative spaces of the Citizens' Dialogue and the Aboriginal Forum were localized, surrounded by decisions and processes that were much less broadly based. The mandate of the Commission was established in the elite space of the Canadian government's Privy Council; this mandate was interpreted by Romanow and his staff, who had authority to decide how citizens would be consulted; the deliberations of citizens in the Dialogue were subject to interpretation by Romanow, and were in no way binding; and the final report of the Commission was Romanow's to construct. The success of the Citizens' Dialogue and the Aboriginal Forum as deliberative spaces needs to be evaluated, then, not only in terms of its internal structure and what this enabled to happen but also in terms of its connection to a broader range of spaces that constituted the Commission's activities as a whole.

So the strengths and weaknesses of these deliberative spaces – which we have parsed in terms of norms of reflexivity, recursiveness and separate spaces – may only partially hit their target, because the Romanow Commission was not *meant* to be deliberative all the way down. And so we really are forming judgements on a complex terrain, not only because the dynamics of deliberation in heterogeneous public spheres are elusive, but because our politics are not entirely democratic – nor do space-makers want them to be; there are roles preserved for expertise, representative legislatures, entrenched interests, judicial review, and so on.

In so far as what we want is democratic deliberation, the issue of including the marginalized should be key. The Romanow case sheds light on a number of underlying issues raised by the incorporation of marginalized groups into mainstream deliberative processes. Key among these is the challenge of creating space for 'affiliated' marginalized citizens and the complex processes in and through which their representative identities are established in the course of deliberation.

Notes

Research leading up to this chapter began as a solo effort by von Lieres. The final chapter is a collaboration, representing equal contributions from Kahane and von Lieres. We would like to thank Merrick Zwarenstein for bringing to Bettina von Lieres's attention the innovative consultative methods of the Romanow Commission. We would also like to thank all the members of the 'Spaces and Places' working group of the Development Research Centre on Citizenship, Participation and Accountability at the Institute of Development Studies, University of Sussex, for their comments on earlier drafts of the chapter. In Canada, Michel Amar was extremely generous with his time in responding to our many questions. The original research was made possible by a grant from the Rockefeller Foundation.

1. These large-scale exercises use a range of consultative methods: prominent among these are the 'Twenty-First Century Town Meetings' organized by AmericaSpeaks and 'Deliberative Opinion Polls' pioneered by James Fishkin. For a useful overview of methods, see Gastil et al. 2005.
2. http://cprn.ca.
3. www.viewpointlearning.com.
4. The workbook is reproduced as an appendix to CPRN 2002.
5. Conversation with Dan Yankelovich.
6. For a discussion of issues of sampling and inclusiveness in connection with James Fishkin's 'deliberative opinion polls', see Kahane 2002.

References

Bohman, J. (1996) *Public Deliberation: Pluralism, Complexity, and Democracy*, Cambridge MA: MIT Press.

CPRN (Canadian Policy Research Network) (2002) *Report on the Citizens' Dialogue on the Future of Health Care in Canada*, Ottawa, 26 June, www.hc-sc.gc.ca/english/pdf/romanow/pdfs/Dialogue_E.pdf.

Chambers, S. (1996) *Reasonable Democracy: Jürgen Habermas and the Politics of Discourse*, Ithaca: Cornell University Press.

CFHCC (Commission on the Future of Health Care in Canada) (2002) *Building on Values: The Future of Health Care in Canada*, Final Report, Ottawa.

Fishkin, J.S. (1991) *Democracy and Deliberation*, New Haven: Yale University Press.

Fraser, N. (1993) 'Rethinking the public sphere: a contribution to the critique of actually existing democracy', in Bruce Robbins, ed., *The Phantom Public Sphere*, Minneapolis: University of Minnesota Press.

Gastil, J., and P. Levine, eds (2005) *The Deliberative Democracy Handbook: Strategies for Effective Civic Engagement in the 21st Century*, San Francisco: Jossey-Bass.

Habermas, J. (1990) 'Discourse ethics: notes on a program of philosophical justification', in S. Nicholsen, ed., *Moral Consciousness and Communicative Action*, Cambridge MA: MIT Press.

Kahane, D. (2002) 'Délibération démocratique et ontologie sociale', *La démocratie délibérative*, special number of *Philosophiques* 29(2).

Kahane, D. (2004) 'What is culture? Generalizing about aboriginal and newcomer perspectives', in D. Kahane and C. Bell, eds, *Intercultural Dispute Resolution in Aboriginal Contexts*, Vancouver: UBC Press.

Maxwell, J., S. Rosell and P. Forest (2003) 'Giving citizens a voice in healthcare policy in Canada', *British Medical Journal* 326: 1031–3.

Mansbridge, J. (1993) 'Using power/fighting power', *Constellations* 1(1): 53–73.

NAHO (National Aboriginal Health Organization) (2002) 'Dialogue on Aboriginal health: "Sharing our Challenges and Successes"', Draft Proceedings, 26 June.

National Forum on Health (1997) *Canada Health Action: Building on the Legacy*, Values Working Group Synthesis Report, Ottawa: Health Canada.

Privy Council of Canada (2001) P.C. 2001–569, Minute of a Meeting of the Committee of the Privy Council on 3 April 2001: Mandate of the Commission on the Future of Health Care in Canada.

Shulman, R., and S.N. Raza (2003) 'Canadian health care at a cross-roads: a review of the Romanow report', *McMaster University Medical Journal* 1(1), September.

Tully, J. (1995) *Strange Multiplicity: Constitutionalism in an Age of Diversity*, Cambridge: Cambridge University Press.

Williams, M. (1998) *Voice, Trust, and Memory: Marginalized Groups and the Failings of Liberal Representation*, Princeton: Princeton University Press.

Young, I.M. (1996) 'Asymmetrical reciprocity: on moral respect, wonder, and enlarged thought', *Constellations: An International Journal of Critical and Democratic Theory* 3(1).

Interviews

Amar, Michel. Communications Director, Romanow Commission 2002–03 (November 2004; June 2005).

Forest, Pierre-Gerlier. Research Director, Romanow Commission (May 2005).

Jock, Richard. Executive Director, National Aboriginal Health Organization in 2002 (March 2004).

Maxwell, Judith. President, Canadian Policy Research Network (May 2005).

Randell, Onalee. Director of Health, Inuit Tapiriit Kanatami (November 2004).

Yankelovich, Daniel. Chairman, Viewpoint Learning (June 2005).

The Politics of Institutionalized Participation

The Politics of Institutionalised Paternalism

8

Democratizing the Governance of Health Services: The Case of Cabo de Santo Agostinho, Brazil

Andrea Cornwall

The growing body of work on innovations in participatory governance draws attention to a series of conditions that contribute to making citizen participation meaningful: an overarching political project in which there is explicit ideological commitment to popular participation; legal and constitutional rights to participate; committed bureaucrats; strong and well-organized civil society organizations; and effective institutional designs that include procedures for broad-based civil society representation (Coelho, this volume; Fung and Wright 2003). This chapter is set in a context where all these factors were in place. It focuses on the Municipal Health Council of Cabo de Santo Agostinho, a municipality of around 150,000 people in the north-eastern Brazilian state of Pernambuco, and on the motivations, personal histories and experiences of those who were part of Cabo's Municipal Health Council in 2003–05.

Drawing on interviews with founding members and those elected to the council for a two-year term in 2003, the council's archives of minutes, and participant observation in council meetings over the course of 2003–05, I ask: what brings people to participating in the health council?[1] What visions and versions of participation animate them? What contributions do they see themselves and other participants in the health council making to democratization and the improvement of health services in the municipality? And what challenges do they identify to achieving the potential of the council in democratizing the governance of health services in Cabo?

This chapter seeks to address two questions that lie at the heart of debates about the democratizing potential of participatory sphere institutions. The first is whether such spaces can expand and deepen democracy by serving as crucibles for the creation of new political subjects and subjectivities and bring about shifts in identification from clients and beneficiaries of favours to citizens with rights (Tatagiba 2002; Cornwall 2004). And the second is whether these spaces can serve to promote new forms of communication, collaboration and understanding between citizens and the state, which can begin to transform residual political culture and redress inequalities of power (Abers 2001; Heller 2001; Fung and Wright 2003; Gaventa 2004). I begin by setting the context for the analysis that follows, with the story of the institutionalization of Cabo's Municipal Health Council. I go on to examine the narratives of representatives of health service users, health workers and the municipal government. I explore what they have to say about their own participation in the council and what they see as its principal challenges. I conclude by reflecting on what the perspectives of those who participate in it tell us about the challenge of democratizing democracy through participatory sphere institutions.

Spaces for Change?

The ambitious democratic innovation of institutionalizing citizen oversight and engagement in framing health policies in a system of health councils and conferences at each tier of government was a conquest of Brazil's radical health reform movement of the 1970s and 1980s, the *movimento sanitarista*. A key demand of this movement was for *controle social* (literally 'social control'), for a role for citizens and their organizations in holding government to account and in shaping the governance of health services through active engagement in deliberation over policies, plans, programmes and priorities. The ideals embodied in the principle of *controle social* were given shape in the 1988 Citizens' Constitution and formalized in the Basic Health Law of 1990, which made the existence of deliberative health councils and their approval of accounts, budgets and health plans a condition for the transfer of federal funds to state and municipal governments (de Carvalho 1998). The health councils are designated as deliberative, rather than consultative. It is worth pointing out that the term 'deliberative' – *deliberativo* – carries a different meaning in this context to that used in writings on deliberative democracy in the USA and Europe (Bohman and Rehg 1997; Habermas 1996; Fung and Wright 2003): while Habermasian deliberation implies a search for communicative consensus, the Brazilian notion emphasizes binding decisions which may be reached without consensus.[2]

The health councils are mandated to monitor health budgets, approve health plans and track their implementation, and hold the government to account to follow through on resolutions passed at the health conferences that take place at municipal, state and national levels every two to four years. There are now some 5,500 health councils across Brazil's twenty-six states and 5,656 municipalities (Coelho 2004), and the councils and conferences have opened up space for several hundred thousand Brazilian citizens to participate in deliberation over health policy. Representation is stipulated by law to follow a principle of parity between governmental and civil society representatives: 50 per cent of seats are set aside for user representatives, 25 per cent for health workers, and the remaining 25 per cent for political appointees to posts in health service management in local government and representatives of private health providers who have contracts to deliver services to the municipal health system. Beyond this requirement, municipalities are advised to enable the representation of particular interest groups, such as disabled people or people living with HIV/AIDS, and those who work with particularly vulnerable groups. Each municipal health council has, however, discretion over how the rules of representation are formulated and over their own internal regulations.

The growing literature on Brazil's health councils paints a mixed picture of the success of these institutions in democratizing the governance of health services (see Coelho, this volume). Set in a context where traces of authoritarian and clientelistic political culture, high levels of bureaucratization, and variable degrees of civic organization complicate the democratizing aspiration of *controle social*, few participatory councils appear to have achieved sufficient independence from established political interests and sufficient citizen competence in relation to the technical, managerial and financial aspects of the health system to serve as genuinely deliberative spaces. Three principal dilemmas surface from these analyses. The first is that of autonomy, and the extent to which the councils are able effectively to hold to account a state with which its members have multiple and complex linkages (Hayes 2004). The second is that of representation, and the extent to which the councils genuinely reflect the diversity of social actors and interests (Tatagiba 2002; Galvanezzi 2003; Coelho 2004). And the third is that of embedded inequalities of knowledge and power between citizen representatives and health workers and managers (Rodrigues dos Santos 2000; Dal Poz and Pinheiro 1998; Avila Viana 1998). The democratic legitimacy, as well as the democratizing potential of the councils, depends on addressing these issues. How do these dilemmas for democracy play out in the case of Cabo? And what lessons might be learnt from the perspectives and experiences of its councillors?

Creating Cabo's Municipal Health Council

Cabo is, in many respects, a microcosm of the Brazilian north-east, with a largely urban population, high levels of poverty, violence and unemployment, and a mix of the infectious diseases and malnutrition associated with deprivation and the chronic-degenerative complaints characteristic of modern urban societies. Over the period 1997–2004, striking improvements in health outcomes were achieved in Cabo, which can be directly attributed to successful reforms in the health system. Investment by senior bureaucrats and active engagement by health workers and well-organized civil society organizations have contributed to making Cabo's Municipal Health Council one of the most successful in the region. In what follows, I set the scene for analysing the perspectives of those who participated in the council over the period 2003–05 with a brief account of the council's history.[3]

Cabo's Conselho Municipal de Saúde (Municipal Health Council) was inaugurated in 1994, as regulations requiring the establishment of councils as a prerequisite for receiving federal health monies came into force. It was born at a time of transition from a progressive municipal government to a right-wing Partido da Frente Liberal (PFL) administration with scant interest in popular participation. Over the period 1994–97, the council functioned in name but was widely perceived as being packed with government appointees and used to rubber-stamp the decisions they wanted to see made. Intense pressure from a coalition that brought together progressive elements from the Catholic Church, the feminist movement, unions and neighbourhood associations representing the *movimento popular* (popular movement), sought to force the PFL government to hold a health conference and fulfil its statutory obligations to open democratic space for the deliberation of health policy.

It was not until 1998, however, that the council began to gain institutional vitality, with the election in late 1997 of the 'post-communist' Partido Popular Socialista (PPS), a party with close connections with social movements and a commitment to popular participation, into municipal government. To revitalize Cabo's ailing health system, the new PPS mayor, Elias Gomes, brought in an energetic health reformer, Cláudio Duarte. A radical democrat, one of the founding members of the Partido dos Trabalhadores (PT, Workers' Party) in the region, Duarte brought to Cabo a passionate commitment to enhancing public involvement in health policy so as to create more accountable and responsive local government. Like many medics of his generation, Duarte was a veteran of the radical public health movement, the *movimento sanitarista*. The process of democratizing Cabo's health system that Duarte began was to continue over the years that followed.

At the 3rd Municipal Health Conference, in 1998, a new cohort of health councillors was elected. Among the ten health user representatives was Silvia Cordeiro, the leader of the established Cabo-based feminist NGO, Centro das Mulheres do Cabo. A doctor with a history in the *movimento sanitarista*, Silvia was to become, in 2000, following the 4th Municipal Health Conference, the health council's first civil society president. The process of constructing a viable democratic space was one that absorbed health council members in intense debate over the months that followed Silvia's election as president. From norms of representation that would permit optimum inclusiveness of the diversity of Cabo's social actors and constituencies, to mechanisms for decision-making, to establishing subcommittees to undertake tasks like inspecting clinics and examining budgets, the task of institution-building was a considerable one. In a context where it is more common for these institutions to be dominated by political interests within local government, rather than actively taken up as political spaces by citizen groups, there were few precedents to draw on.

The 5th Municipal Health Conference in 2003 saw all that had been planned come to fruition. A series of pre-conferences across the municipality expanded participation in deliberation over health policy, gathering locality-specific demands and priorities. From each, delegates were elected to the municipal health conference. Debates raged, propositions and suggestions for reforms were placed on the table, 183 resolutions were passed, and delegates voted new health service user and health worker representatives onto the municipal health council. The twenty health service users elected as title-holders and substitutes represented a diversity of Cabo's poorer citizens; most were lower middle class or working class. Among the ten title-holders, men and women were in equal proportions, with ages ranging from the early twenties to the late sixties. Three councillors had only primary-level education, and only one had studied beyond secondary school. Four of them were unemployed, and a number of others worked part-time or for the organizations represented in the council, which made their attendance at afternoon meetings possible. Those with connections to leftist political parties, principally the PT, were in the majority. Most had no previous experience of engagement with the health sector, and little technical knowledge of the health system, budgeting or planning.

At its inaugural meeting, the council swiftly moved to elect a president. Defeating the Municipal Health Secretary, the president elect, a PT member and representative of the Movement of Christian Workers, Adson da Silva, was, again, a health service user representative. And he epitomized the democratizing potential of these spaces: black, from a lower-class background and with primary-level formal education. Under Silvia Cordeiro's leadership, the council had achieved some measure of functionality and, through collaboration and consensus-seeking with the municipal health secretariat, had begun to engage in shaping health policy. Adson's mission focused on another dimension of *controle social*, that of *fiscalização*, auditing and ensuring probity in government spending. As leaders, they could not have been more dissimilar; in many respects, as I return to reflect, they manifested the very polarities inherent in the ideal of *controle social*.

The everyday business of the health council ranges from listening to presentations by organizations that deliver services, to being informed about the plans of the municipal health secretariat, to discussing specific incidents that have been reported by members of the public concerning the provision of health services. Meetings last around three hours, and are held monthly. There is little deliberation, in the Habermasian sense, on matters of health policy; health plans are prepared by the government, without any attempt to engage the participation of health councillors in their formulation, and presented to the council for their approval, along with periodic presentations of the accounts. Minutes of meetings and participant observation reveal heated debates about procedure, and combative exchanges between the more vocal of the health service user and health worker representatives and the Secretary of Health. Over the course of 2003–05, much of the substance of these exchanges concerned the presentation of the municipal accounts.

Participation in Cabo's Health Council

What did 'participation' mean to the health councillors who became part of the council in 2003? Why had they got involved? What did being part of the council do for them – as people, as professionals, as political actors? And, from the diversity of backgrounds, passions and positionalities that brought them into the council, what did they make of the council's potential as a participatory governance institution? In what follows, I consider the perspectives of the three distinctive segments that constitute the council on their and others' engagement in the health council: health service users, health workers and health managers.

Health service users

A mix of missions, personal as much as political, brought user representatives to the council. Some were seasoned social actors, with backgrounds in social movements, a strong affiliation to leftist parties and experience in community mobilization. It is these kinds of actors who might be expected to extend their attempts to influence local politics and policy into participatory sphere institutions; and they were conspicuously more vocal in the council's debates. Others were completely new to this arena, having got involved because of personal experiences with the health system that enraged and engaged them, in search of career opportunities and new experiences, a wish to ensure continued financial support for their organizations from the municipal government, and a desire to do good for their communities. Others still entered the council as representatives of organizations that had previously had a representative, stepping into the shoes of a more experienced leader.

Most of the organizations represented on the council had links of some kind with the municipal government.[4] Many of the neighbourhood associations in Cabo were established in the early to mid-1980s, during a progressive administration in the final years of the military dictatorship and received *subvençoes* (subsidies) from the municipal government for their activities; several of the non-governmental organizations, most of which were established in the late 1990s, had *convenios* (contracts for services) with the government. These connections motivated engagement; they also posed a challenge for the autonomy of these organizations, and the council itself, from the municipal government. As one community activist charged: 'Those who don't agree are today those without *subvençoes*.'

Health service user representatives' accounts of the purpose of the council varied from those who saw its primary role as that of holding the state to account and enforcing the right to health, to those who saw a broader role for the council in defining public policies, developing projects and engaging communities in improving health services (Cordeiro, Cornwall and Delgado 2004). These different purposes evoke some of the paradoxes of civil society engagement in participatory sphere institutions, and the tension between the close, collaborative relationship with the authorities that may be needed to facilitate popular participation in shaping health policies and in developing joint projects, and the distance required to elicit accountability. Divergent understandings of the purpose of the council also shape perceptions of what the everyday business of the council should be. For those concerned with accountability, time spent grilling officials over spending is time well spent; for those anxious to see more discussion about strategic health priorities, there was a certain measure of frustration over the turn the council had come to take in recent times.

What did participating in the council mean to its health service user representatives on a personal level? From activists with years of experience to those completely new to this kind of engagement, their own participation was often described in terms of *crescimento* (growing), gaining experiences that they might otherwise never have had: opportunities to travel beyond the borders of the municipality and the state; to mix with new people, hear how things were being done in other parts of the country, to broaden their horizons; to go on courses, to learn things that they hadn't thought they'd ever understand; to gain knowledge, skills and understanding that they could make use of personally and put to the service of their communities. Yet sceptical views were voiced by some on the participation of some of their fellow health service users. Among the most vocal and the most silent were those perceived by fellow representatives to see the council as a springboard for other opportunities – jobs in the municipal government, seats as elected councillors, and greater prominence, financing and prestige for their own organizations.

Resonating with Castello, Gurza Lavalle and Houtzager's findings in this volume and elsewhere (Houtzager, Gurza Lavalle and Acharya 2003), many user representatives saw themselves as intermediaries. Their narratives captured a variety of intermediary roles. For one neighbourhood association representative, a librarian who had come to be involved in the politics of health through indignation at the treatment her daughter had received when she fell sick, user representatives were advocates for those who might know that they have rights but lacked the courage, confidence or knowledge to articulate their demands. She spoke of the fears people have – of not speaking properly and being ignored, of arriving in old and shabby clothes and having the doors barred to them – and of the need for people like herself who can go to the streets to convince them that 'you can lift your head, because you have the same rights as me'.

For a number of other neighbourhood association representatives, being on the council enabled them to be intermediaries for information about new programmes or projects that could benefit their communities and conduits who could bring their communities' experiences and demands for improvements in service delivery to the attention of the authorities. In this intermediary role, health councillors parallel the responsibilities of elected councillors; and they have the potential actively to undermine clientelistic politicians' claims to have personally secured health improvements in the locality and their uses of health as a favour. A representative of the radical Catholic Church, with long years of involvement in neighbourhood activism, described how much closer people like him were to communities and the part they could play in changing political culture at the local level by letting people know 'that health is a right, not a favour'. With echoes of Cohen and Sabel's (1997) vision of 'directly-deliberative polyarchy', he also talked of the Council as a space for people like him to bring their knowledge of what was being said on the street and experiences of poor health services directly into the ambit of those responsible for provision.

Among those with backgrounds in social movement activism, the council was talked of as a space for democracy – a 'school for citizenship', as one put it – that should embody and promote new and different practices from the authoritarianism and clientelism that characterized politics in other spaces. They used the language of *cidadania* (citizenship) to talk about the obligation of the state to deliver on social rights; their vision of the council was as a space for stimulating new expressions of *cidadania* that could extend to society at large – a narrative that has been promoted by Brazilian social movements in the post-dictatorship era (Dagnino 2005). *Cidadania* also framed, for them, a sense of indignation at the lack of respect for their rights by the government. 'We are all citizens', one health service user representative said, 'but the municipal government doesn't respect this. Look at the queues in our clinics, the lack of medicines, the lack of doctors. We deserve more than this.'

The majority of health service user representatives were affiliated to leftist political parties, predominantly the PT.[5] Frictions within the council were often attributed to what people called the 'partyization' of debates.[6] For party activists, the council was in many respects an extension of other available political spaces. They brought into the council not only political positions – such as the principled opposition to the contracting-out of services (*terceirização*) that united health service users, health workers and managers (Cordeiro, Cornwall and Delgado 2004) – but also political postures and conduct learnt in party meetings. One party activist who had been involved with the council since the outset, alternating between being a representative and speaking from the floor as a member of the public, spoke of the delight he took in wrestling directly with the government and denouncing unfairness and undemocratic practice, using tactics and a style of politics learnt in the party. For him, the council was a more productive political space than those of formal politics: 'I would never want to be a *vereador* [elected local government councillor]', he told me. 'Here is where I belong.' Energetic in promoting local health councils, he sketched out a capillary vision of democratic institutions seeded in multiple sites that broadened the scope and reach of politics by creating new and more qualified leaders at the local level, that would create 'didactic' waves that begin at this level and ripple out from there to the municipal, state and federal levels, creating a new, more just, political system.

Continuities with the formal political arena emerged in other visions of the council's role. They arose in critiques of those health managers who saw the council simply as an extension of the executive. And these continuities were central to the perspective of the health council president, who described the council as 'an *instancia* [instance] of government ... that exists to contribute to government'. His style of engagement, learnt from hours of watching elected councillors battling in the municipal assembly, was that of insistent questioning, hounding the government representatives for answers on questions of accountability. With repeated recourse to the law, and a taste for formal politics that had led to an unsuccessful attempt at election as a *vereador*, his view of the council was less as somewhere where new norms and policies are deliberated than as an institution mandated to ensure accountable implementation. A sheaf of letters in the council's files, demanding information and follow-up on promised actions, attest to the seriousness with which he took this duty.

Contrasting visions of the council's purpose and a complex mix of motivations, expectations and understandings of what it meant to be a 'health service user representative' emerge from this account. As Morita (2002) argues, while the category *usuário* (health service user) may be seen as an undifferentiated 'them' by health managers, considerable diversity exists within this category; networks, allegiances and identifications span the different segments of the council, creating the potential for conflict as for collaboration. Three preoccupations emerged from health service users' analyses of the shortcomings of the council: the overt politicization of the council; the council's lack of effective independence, a factor both of inadequate resourcing and of the dependencies of many of its members on financial support and employment from the municipal government; and the gap between what health managers say about participation and what they actually do. As an NGO leader, with years of grassroots experience, reflected: 'in the space of the council, the government listens and the councillors grow as citizens. But to do this the councillors need to be listened to and respected by the municipal government.' It was this, he felt, that was the biggest brake on the council's role in facilitating *controle social*.

Health workers

A quarter of the seats in the Council are allocated to health work-ers, who are also selected at the Municipal Health Conference. As a primary care doctor, with years of experience in Cabo and a political history within the PT, pointed out, health workers are a very heterogeneous group. They are difficult to mobilize as a group, in part because of the hierarchical nature of the health system and the nature of their contracts. Many are employed on temporary contracts; fearing dismissal for speaking out, they feel keenly the need to be, as one health worker put it, 'diplomatic'.

Health workers occupy positions which many of them recognize as ambiguous. They may be perceived by health bureaucrats and citizens alike as part of the government, to which they are expected to demonstrate loyalty. Yet, as frontline health workers – doctors in community clinics, auxiliary nurses and community health workers – they see at first hand some of the deficiencies in the health system, and have other loyalties, to patients and to the communities where they work. And they are, as an auxiliary nurse pointed out, also citizens and able to exercise their own independent judgement: 'As I explained once here in the Council, what everyone thinks in their own minds is theirs, it's not the government who teaches us to think.'

One of the PPS administration's most impressive achievements is a sharp reduction in the infant mortality rate, from 42 per 1,000 to 18 per 1,000 over the course of their two terms of municipal administration. This has been due, in no small part, to the introduction of a national primary healthcare programme, the Programa Saúde e Familia (Family Health Programme, now Saúde em Casa, 'Health at Home'). This programme led to the recruitment of hundreds of community health workers (*agentes de saúde*), who are from the communities they serve, and work to monitor the health of the households in their area, introducing preventive health measures and referring patients to clinics if sicknesses develop. As Tendler (1997) describes for the nearby state of Ceará, these community health workers bring to their work a commitment to their communities' health, relationships of trust with communities that create internal pressures for accountability and a real sense of pride in their achievements. In Cabo, this sense of pride and the commitment it engenders is palpable.

One young community health worker, recruited as part of the Programa Família e Saúde, spoke with animation of how much being involved in the council meant to her. She saw her participation as a way of valuing the role of community health workers. For her, the council was fundamental to effective *controle social*, something to which she was politically committed as a PT activist. It was also a space into which she could bring her passion for politics. She told me:

> I've been participating like this since I was twelve. I never liked playing with dolls, I wanted to be involved in these kinds of discussions. My daughter, who is 5, is just the same. She leaflets with me, she knows what a strike is, she prefers talking with adults to playing with dolls.

For another young community health worker, her involvement began at a pre-conference in her locality: it gave her not only a taste of participation, but the confidence to go forward to the municipal level. What she valued most about the health council is that it provided, as she put it, the opportunity for bringing together 'different worlds'; and for giving health workers, as well as citizens, an idea of what makes health managers tick. It was also the experience of participating at the local level, in one of the more successful local health councils, that brought another health worker representative, an auxiliary nurse, to the health council. She spoke of the exhilaration of having been part of successful mobilization, together with the community, to make demands on the municipal government for waste removal, and of the opportunity she saw for being an intermediary between the community she served and the powers that be. She took great pride in being someone that people in her community felt they could count on. For her,

> We come to learn, to discuss, to grow as people – not just as a professional, but as a person – and in the case of user representatives, they will pass this onto their community, when someone comes criticizing certain services, they'll know how to explain that service.

Striking in their dedication, never missing a meeting and participating actively in subcommittees, lower-level health workers were often reserved in council meetings. Health service hierarchies quickly reasserted themselves in this space, a factor less of the technical nature of issues under discussion than of the inequalities in positional power of representatives from this sector and the insecurity of contractual work. For several of the health workers, like a number of the health service users, one of the main challenges the council faced was the attitudes and behaviour of the health managers. In the analysis of the primary-care doctor cited earlier, the root of the problem is that health managers find it hard to see themselves as partners with the council: 'They come there with the stance of the boss, the stance of the manager, and not the stance of the councillor.' What is needed, she argued, is for them to begin sharing problems and working together with councillors to find solutions: 'they treat the council as if they really didn't know anything.' They are missing a trick, she noted. The council could be a help rather than a hindrance, serving in yet another intermediary role: to defend health managers to communities and to the municipal authorities.

Health workers occupy multiple subject-positions, with identifications as citizens, and as members of communities, churches and political parties, as workers and as professionals. This makes for complexity in terms of their positionality and allegiances. I witnessed several occasions when small groups of health workers and health service users, linked by party affiliation or a shared commitment to an issue of policy or procedure, strategized together outside meetings. Yet, as professionals, they were also sometimes frustrated by health service users' complaints and demands, knowing full well just how limited the resources they and their colleagues had at their disposal actually were. Health workers, like health service users, talked of how they had grown through gaining opportunities to acquire new knowledge, broaden their horizons and extend their networks through engagement in the councils. Their role as intermediaries, and the effects that being in the council have on them as professionals and as people, deserve greater attention than they have been given to date.

Managers

Unlike other members of the council, those representing the government occupy seats by virtue of their positions.[7] Health service managers are political appointees. They enter office with values shaped by their party political affiliation as well as their medical training. And they are keenly aware of the political fallout that failures to deliver on health improvements might produce. Representing the municipal government on the health council are those with *cargos de comando* ('positions of command') in the health service: the director of the largest municipal hospital, the director of primary care, the director of public health and the municipal health secretary. They are, in effect, the highest officials the municipality has to offer: and the disparities in knowledge and power between them and most, if not all, other councillors are acute.

How do these officials view popular participation in the councils? How do they see their own role in promoting civic engagement and facilitating *controle social*? A number of the senior health managers I interviewed had been student activists in the *movimento sanitarista*. The passion this had given them for popular participation reverberated in their accounts of the council as a political as well as a management space. Their narratives were often more overtly politicized than those of health worker or user representatives, conveying in often eloquent terms their ideological commitment to *controle social*. They saw the presence of senior bureaucrats in the council as essential for its viability, and engagement with social movements as vital for its legitimacy. As the Municipal Health Secretary put it,

> The orientation of this government is that it's necessary to listen to the population, to listen to social movements, and that they are the fount of orientation as to how health policies should be implanted and implemented.... If you don't have the government there to discuss, you don't have decision-making power, influence, deliberation [i.e. decision-making] together with the government.

As noted earlier, the incoming PPS administration of 1997 brought a dynamic health reformer, Cláudio Duarte, to Cabo to revitalize the health system. Reflecting on what was needed to make the councils viable institutions for *controle social*, Duarte identified a number of factors. These included the importance of explicit recognition by the municipal government of the importance of the council, backed with material resources, including the provision of infrastructure; a style of management 'in which information should always be available to councillors even if it is largely technical and they may not fully understand it'; and regular meetings attended by senior local government staff who signalled their desire to act on the council's decisions. He deemed essential clear procedures regulating representation and the conduct of meetings. For user representatives to be effective in this space, he argued, they need to be trained so as to avoid simplistic solutions and excessive medicalization.

For Duarte, the council was a space in which *convivencia constructiva* – 'constructive coexistence' – could be achieved through transparency and commitment on the part of government representatives, which would convince citizens of their seriousness. He was also only too aware of the disabling effects of residual political culture, and of tensions between managers and citizens over the scope the council

might have for deciding on issues that managers might see as more properly under their jurisdiction. He emphasized the importance of experiential learning, of exchanges of knowledge and experience between councillors, and of municipal health conferences as an 'educative moment'. And he spoke of the need to set the councils in time, as nascent institutions in which new forms of leadership and new democratic practices were emerging through processes that were beginning to change residual cultures of bureaucratization, clientelism and authoritarianism in local government.

Duarte's successors were described to me by health service users as weaker leaders, who were less effectual in following through on the promise of popular participation. One of them, Rivanildo Santana, was, however, described to me as 'inspiring'. I sought him out at the busy Recife maternity hospital that he now directs. Echoing Duarte's sentiments on the importance of popular participation, he emphasized the importance of the council being seen not as part of the government, but as an institution in its own right: a *partner*. To achieve this independence, he argued, the council needs certain institutional conditions that guarantee continuity: secretarial assistance, archives, a computer to register organizations, its own meeting space. It also needs to serve as a space to generate new leaders, who, over time, come to secure the council's independence. For this, the Municipal Health Conference is essential: 'I love the conferences because it is there that new leaders arise ... new faces'. He recognized the extent to which state reluctance to give up control over decision-making limited the scope of the council:

> The council is defined as a consultative institution and as a deliberative institution. In my experience, the Council has been not been very deliberative... sometimes it stops being deliberative because decisions have already been made and the institution with power wants to execute them.

For the senior health managers who took up positions in the 2003–05 council, or were called upon to explain themselves at council meetings, *controle social* offered a bridge to the community. One spoke of how the councils are an opportunity for government to learn from the 'collective intelligence of society' by bringing together different visions of how services might be managed and implemented. 'It's an opportunity', she said, 'for people to grow, to deepen democracy, to create a debate – in this city, where we have such diversity'. Motivation for citizens to participate came, in the view of another, from the relationship people have with health, as something that 'stirs passions and polemic because it touches people's very skin, sensibility and pain', which helps organize and motivate popular participation, and which in turn creates 'a consciousness that they are citizens'. Difficult as it was to be on the receiving end of demands and complaints, all recognized how vital this was to fulfilling the promise of *controle social* and improving health services.

Issues of representation loomed large in health service managers' narratives. Two concerns predominated: the extent to which the councils create a generation of leaders who begin to behave like elected representatives and seek to maintain their foothold, weakening the broader democratizing effects of constant renovation and capacity-building of user representatives; and the fragility of links between those who speak for communities and those they purportedly serve, which translates into a failure to disseminate information about programmes and policies, and to facilitate discussion at community level about priorities and concerns for health. One senior manager reflected:

> It preoccupies me that some people become militants and they are always the representative of the organization and of the community, they come to assume a role, a profile, a personality that seems that they dominate the situation and don't respond to their bases. Then there's the problem of not renewing representation in the council. This is also something that training should address.

The answer for the managers consistently lay in training. Yet this is far from a magic bullet. Training is all very well, one health manager argued, but the council is constantly changing: new people arrive, replacing those whose non-attendance at meetings causes their expulsion, or new association leaders, 'and you're at square one again'. Constrained by available time, as well as finance, densely packed training courses tend to focus on the main priorities: understanding budgets and accounts and gaining an elementary grasp of the health system.

Managers' accounts reveal a tension between their politicized vision of public health and the realities of what health service users have to bring to realize it. One senior manager noted how disorganized and ill-informed user representatives tended to be, and how their lack of knowledge and parochial preoccupations detracted from the real business at hand: running an effective health service. But there is equally a recognition that the kinds of changes that are needed go much deeper than providing health service users with information about how the health system works. As one senior manager observed,

> Changing behaviour isn't something simple, easy and linear. It implies processes, that go backwards and forwards ... you can't change someone's behaviour just through information, only by raising questions that can change consciousness ... and it's not only through conscious processes, educative processes, but in many cases also through processes that can be painful, that affect people's very sensibility.

The challenge of orientating and informing health service users is enormous, she argued: not just on their role in *controle social*, but on how to carry it out effectively. It is too easy to get stuck on the basics, without any discussion of strategic issues that can advance the health system: she gave as an example the extent to which the presentation of the municipal accounts had dominated meetings over the last year.

Amidst a recognition that the council had achieved some measure of maturity, there was also some ambivalence among managers about how far it could go. Pressurized by the need to move plans and budgets through the system as quickly as possible, they were only too aware of the tension between efficiency and inclusive deliberation (Warren 2000). And, as several of them observed, if managers were to respond only to health service users' demands, then their agenda for improving health through extending preventive services might well be scuppered. A very real tension arises over where the boundaries of appropriate expertise come to be placed. Yet for citizens, being told that there were complexities that they would not be able to grasp and technical decisions that needed to be made reaffirms suspicions that managers have no desire to cede control. I witnessed one such exchange in a health council meeting. A senior manager commented that the matter at hand was a technical issue that he would not elaborate on as the councillors would not understand it. One councillor piped up: 'try us, you may be surprised... and if we don't understand, we will find someone to teach us so that we will be able to understand.'

The health managers' ideological commitment to *controle social* sits awkwardly alongside the defensiveness I witnessed in meetings in the face of irate health service users, and the complaints of users and workers about managers resorting to technocratic obfuscation, failing to provide adequate information and withholding the resources needed to guarantee the functionality of the council. Even though health managers all emphasized the importance of timely access to information and material support, proposals were often rushed through with little scope for debate, to meet federal deadlines, although, on several occasions, the council demanded extraordinary meetings to discuss them in more depth. And despite the allocation of a budget for the council, the fact that the purse strings were held by the Secretary of Health, who could grant or refuse requests for travel or materials and required elaborate bureaucracy to access, limited the council's independence.

Democratizing the governance of health service calls for more than providing the training, resources and support that make popular participation viable, and inviting civil society organizations to participate. As several health managers reflected, the state has a role to play in developing what one described as 'political consciousness, critical consciousness and consciousness of being a citizen' among those whom it serves: provoking, in so doing, the cultural changes needed to engage them in *controle social*. Yet, as health service users and workers pointed out, making *controle social* effective also calls for state actors to relinquish some of their power and control, open the black-boxed 'technical' domain to citizen engagement, and recognize that 'constructive coexistence' requires not only ideological commitment but also real changes in their own attitudes and conduct. For all managers' talk about training, they themselves fail to attend training courses; some training might be in order, health service users and workers pointed out, to teach them to listen and respect health service users more. The political will was certainly there: it was, perhaps, as a number of health service users and health workers commented, that for all the will in the world bureaucrats used to making decisions and running the show have not yet acquired the skills with which to participate as partners.

Conclusion

At a participatory workshop in April 2004, Silvia Cordeiro posed the question to the health service users and health workers we'd gathered together: had the council succeeded in realizing the promise of *controle social*? Their answer was, resoundingly, that yes, significant strides forward had been made; but that the struggle for *controle social* continues. *Controle social* is inherently political and inevitably politicized. The dimensions and dynamics of participation to which I draw attention here have implications for both the construction of political subjectivities and the creation of new relationships between citizens and the state, with which this chapter began.

For the citizens who entered the arena of municipal policy and politics for the first time with their election as user or health worker representatives, it is evident that their experiences have shaped new political subjectivities as they have come to learn to participate. Their narratives suggest the new awareness of their rights, new-found confidence and new knowledge that they have gained in the process. For more experienced activists, the council has offered opportunities for extending networks and connections within and beyond the municipality, as well as an arena in which to negotiate demands directly with the government – whether for better services or for accountability. As a 'school for citizenship', the health council has taught them many lessons, affirming that citizenship is something actively demanded rather than bestowed (Kabeer 2005). Frustrations abounded in their narratives, but there was a tangible sense that being part of the council was, for many of its health service users and health worker members, a rewarding experience that enriched them personally and professionally (see Baocchi 2001; Labra and St Aubyn 2002).

The promise of participatory governance lies well beyond the small numbers of people who come to participate in institutions such as health councils. Health service user perspectives on what citizen participation could contribute to democracy signalled some of this promise. The capillary effects of the expansion of democratic spaces, as described by one of the health service users, is consistent with the democratising vision that animated the creation of new democratic spaces such as the health councils. Through the creation of multiple interfaces with the state, the expansion of the participatory sphere holds the potential of repopulating politics with new energy, new faces, and new practices. That in some parts of the municipality user engagement is reconfiguring representation at the community level, undermining politicians who use health as a favour, and creating new forms of intermediation that work to enhance awareness of rights, suggests that slowly some transformation in political culture is happening, although old ways still retain their hold.

For health service users and health workers alike, it was the reluctance of managers to realize their part of the *controle social* bargain and concede some of their managerial powers to the council that was the brake on further progress. Managers' concerns about gatekeeping and the low rotation of representatives (see Cohn 2003) raised other questions: about democratic legitimacy and the extent to which political practices of clientelism and authoritarianism were being reproduced within and by civil society. Civil society emerges in their view less as the motor of democratization than as a site in which residual political culture is very much alive; for them, it was a task for the progressive state to democratize its *un*civil tendencies (Chandoke 2003), educate citizens about their rights and teach them how to participate. The question then arises: who is democratizing whom? As long as managers see the councils as spaces to which they are doing the 'inviting', the council's democratizing effects might fail to rub off on *them*, leaving other dimensions of entrenched political culture – not least the exercise of technical and bureaucratic power – intact.

The differences that emerge in the narratives of health service users, workers and managers evoke a paradox, captured in the tension between, as Duarte put it, 'constructive coexistence' and the task of *fiscalização*, that of monitoring the government and holding it to account. Constructive coexistence requires a degree of collaboration, trust, respect for the knowledge and opinions of others, and willingness to shift positions to accommodate consensus. Perceptions of being patronised and denied information and respect by government representatives, the reproduction of elements of existing political culture – with its echoes of older citizen–state relations of authoritarianism or clientelism – in interactions within the council and the overt politicization of the council makes this coexistence an uneasy and often fractious experience for all.

Where the paradox emerges is that while 'constructive coexistence' depends on building trust and creating the basis for partnership, the task of holding the state to account may come to depend on an altogether different dynamic. For a start, it calls for sufficient distance for the council's members to be free to probe into financial irregularities and draw attention to the government's shortcomings in implementing policies, decisions or programmes. This requires a measure of autonomy that is difficult to envisage given the complex dependencies that exist between the government and many of those who represent health service users. And being involved in auditing activities that expose deficiencies in health service management is not going to be easy for health workers, with their contracts as well as their colleagues to think about. For some user representatives, however, it is precisely their role in pressing the government to be accountable that defines what the council exists to do. For those with histories of activism, the more confrontational stance that might be needed to get answers to their questions is one with which they are entirely familiar. From the narratives drawn on in this chapter, it is easy enough to see how the council can end up getting locked into cycles of unproductive wrangling; but it is also salutory to recognize what it means, in a setting such as this, for user representatives to be able to directly challenge, argue and engage with the powerful health bureaucrats who manage the services on which their and their communities' health depends.

There is a tendency in writing on participatory governance to focus primarily on the citizen 'side of the equation' (Gaventa 2004), and pay less attention to the role that state actors have to play in ensuring the viability and legitimacy of participatory institutions. Experience in Cabo suggests that there is much that the state might do to make real its constitutional obligation to *controle social*. Real resources need to be committed to ensuring the functionality of the councils, whether for infrastructure and administrative support, funding for councillors to travel to attend conferences and network with other councillors in other parts of the country, or training to equip citizens with the capabilities to participate and to facilitate the emergence of new grassroots leaders (Daniel 2000; Gohn 2002). Inadequate information and limited technical knowledge – whether of budgets and accounts, or the health system – poses as much a barrier to effective citizen oversight as it does to constructive collaboration. Training is, as some of the managers insisted, key; and the opportunities for capacity development offered to sequential waves of health councillors may in itself have broader democratizing effects as they move on to other arenas. Yet, as users and health workers pointed out, *they* are not the only ones in need of educating. Making *controle social* effective calls for activating citizens, but realizing its promise depends on the capacity of state actors to engage, listen and respond – and this is something that, for all their political commitment, Cabo's health managers might yet do much to improve upon.

Notes

This chapter owes many insights to a DFID-funded participatory research project conducted with Silvia Cordeiro and Nelson Giordano Delgado in 2003–04 (Cordeiro, Cornwall and Delgado, 2004), which I continued in three further periods of fieldwork over 2004–05.

I am profoundly grateful to Silvia Cordeiro for all that I learnt from her about Cabo and the Municipal Health Council and for all the support she and the Centro das Mulheres do Cabo gave me, and to Nelson Giordano Delgado, with whom I conducted several of the interviews I draw on here. I owe Surama Lins a huge debt for all her help, as I do members of the health council. Many thanks too to Lucy Hayes for her research assistance and to Alex Shankland, Mark Robinson, John Gaventa and David Kahane for their comments.

1. I draw directly here on interviews with six health managers, including two previous secretaries of health, five health worker representatives, fifteen people who serve or have served as user representatives, the private-sector representative and the executive secretary of the council. My analysis also builds on impressions gained through participant observation at council meetings and interviews with a further twenty people, including civil society leaders, NGO workers and a local politician.
2. I am grateful to Alex Shankland for this point.
3. See Cordeiro, Cornwall and Delgado 2004 for a more detailed account of the process of institutionalizing participation in the health council.
4. This echoes Gurza Lavalle, Acharya and Houtzager's (2005) findings for civil society organizations in São Paulo.
5. This is also observed by Gurza Lavalle et al. 2005.
6. This became acute around the time of the 2004 elections and resulted in the expulsion of the two Communist (PCdoB) Party members on the council, instantly reducing the representation of young black men.
7. The private sector has not been a particularly active participant in the council. The one private-sector representative on the council was an administrator from a local private hospital. He was generally silent in meetings, and spoke of how being on the council allowed him where necessary to defend the interests of his hospital.

References

Abers, R. (2001) *Inventing Local Democracy: Grassroots Politics in Brazil*, Boulder CO: Westview Press.

Ávila Viana, A.L. (1998) 'Desenho, modo de operação e representação de interesses do sistema municipal de saude e os conselhos de saúde', *Ciência e Saúde Coletiva*, 3(1): 20–22.

Avritzer, L. (2002) *Democracy and the Public Space in Latin America*, Princeton: Princeton University Press.

Baocchi, G. (2001) 'Participation, activism, and politics: the Porto Alegre experiment and deliberative democratic theory', *Politics and Society* 29(1): 43–72.

Bohman, J., and W. Rehg (1997) *Deliberative Democracy: Essays on Reason and Politics*, Cambridge MA: MIT Press.

Carvalho, A.I. de (1998) 'Os conselhos de saúde, participação social e reforma do estado', *Ciência e Saúde Coletiva* 3(1): 23–5.

Chandoke, N. (2003) *The Conceits of Civil Society*, Delhi: Oxford University Press.

Coelho, V.S. (2004) 'Brazil's health councils: the challenge of building participatory political institutions', *IDS Bulletin* 35(2): 33–9.

Coelho, V.S., and J. Veríssimo (2004) 'Considerações sobre o processo de escolha dos representantes da sociedade civil nos conselhos de saúde em São Paulo', in L. Avritzer, *A Participação em São Paulo*, São Paulo: Unesp.

Cohen, J., and C. Sabel (1997), 'Directly-deliberative polyarchy', *European Law Journal* 3(4), December: 313–40

Cohn, A. (2003) 'State and society and the new configurations of the right to health/ Estado e Sociedade e as reconfigurações do direito á saúde', *Ciencia e Saúde Coletiva* 8(1): 9–18

Cornwall, A. (2004) 'Introduction: new democratic spaces? The politics and dynamics of institutionalised participation', *IDS Bulletin* 35(2): 1–10.

Cornwall, A. (2000) *Beneficiary, Consumer, Citizen: Perspectives on Participation for Poverty Reduction*, Stockholm: Sida, www.sida.se.

Dal Poz, M.R., and R. Pinheiro (1998) 'A participação dos Usuários nos Conselhos Muncipais de Saúde e seus Determinantes', *Ciência e Saúde Coletiva* 3(1): 28–30.

Dagnino, E. (2005) 'We all have rights, but… Contesting concepts of citizenship in Brazil', in N. Kabeer, ed., *Inclusive Citizenship: Meanings and Expressions*, London: Zed Books.

Daniel, C. (2000) 'Interview: conselhos, esfera pública e co-gestão', in M.C. Carvalho and A.C.C. Teixeira, eds, *Conselhos Gestores de Políticas Públicas*, São Paulo: Polis.

Dryzek, J.S. (1996) 'Political inclusion and the dynamics of democratization', *American Political Science Review* 90(3): 475–87.

Fox, J. (1996) 'How does civil society thicken? The political construction of social capital in Mexico', *World Development* 24: 1089–103.

Fung, A., and E.O. Wright, eds (2003) *Deepening Democracy: Institutional Innovation in Empowered Participatory Governance*, London: Verso.

Galvanezzi, C. (2003) 'A representação popular nos conselhos de saúde: um estudo sobre os conselhos distritais da zona leste e o conselho municipal de São Paulo', research report, São Paulo: CEBRAP, FABESP.

Gaventa, J. (2004) 'Towards participatory governance: assessing the transformative possibilities', in S. Hickey and G. Mohan, eds, *From Tyranny to Transformation*, London: Zed Books.

Gohn, M.G.M. (2002) 'Papel dos Conselhos Gestores na Gestão Pública', in *Informativo CEPAM*, Conselhos Municipais das Áreas Sociais, São Paulo: Fundação Prefeito Faria Lima.

Gurza Lavalle, A., A. Acharya and P. Houtzager (2005) 'Beyond comparative anecdotalism: lessons on civil society and participation from São Paulo, Brazil', *World Development* 33(6): 951–64.

Habermas, J. (1996) 'Three normative models of democracy', in Seyla Benhabib, ed., *Democracy and Difference: Contesting the Boundaries of the Political*, Princeton: Princeton University Press.

Hayes, L. (2004) 'Participation and associational activity in Brazil: the case of the São Paulo Health Councils', M.A. dissertation, Institute of Development Studies, University of Sussex, Falmer.

Houtzager, P., A. Gurza Lavalle and A. Acharya (2003) 'Who participates? Civil society and the new democratic politics in São Paulo, Brazil', IDS Working Paper No. 210, Institute of Development Studies, University of Sussex, Falmer.

Kabeer, N., ed. (2005) *Inclusive Citizenship: Meanings and Expressions*, London: Zed Books.

Labra, M.E., and F.J. St. Aubyn (2002) 'Associativismo, participação e cultura cívica, o potencial dos conselhos de saúde', *Ciencia e Saúde Coletiva* 7(3): 537–47.

Mansbridge, J. (1999) 'On the idea that participation makes better citizens', in S. Elkin and K. Soltan, eds, *Citizen Competence and Democratic Institutions*, University Park: Pennsylvania State University Press.

Mercadente, O. (2002) 'Conselhos Municipais de Saúde', in *Informativo CEPAM*, Conselhos Municipais das Áreas Sociais, São Paulo: Fundação Prefeito Faria Lima, 41–44.

Morita, I. (2002) 'Conselho e Conselheiros Municipais de Saúde: Que trama é esta?', Ph.D. thesis, Anthropology, PUC–São Paulo.

Santos, N.R. (2000) 'Implantação e funcionamento dos Conselhos de Saúde no Brasil', in M.C. Carvalho and A.C.C. Teixeira, eds, *Conselhos Gestores de Políticas Públicas*, São Paulo: Polis, 15–21.

Tatagiba, L. (2002) 'Os conselhos gestores e a democratização das políticas públicas no Brasil', in E. Dagnino, ed., *Sociedade Civil e Espaços publicos no Brasil*, São Paulo: Paz e Terra.

Tendler, J. (1997) *Good Governance in the Tropics*, Baltimore MD: Johns Hopkins University Press.

Valla, V.V. (1998) 'Comentários a "Conselhos Municipais de Saúde: a possibilidade dos usuários participarem e os determinantes da participação"', *Ciência e Saúde Coletiva* 3(1): 31–2.

Vargas Cortes, S.M. (1998) 'Conselhos Municipais de Saúde: a possibilidade dos usuários participarem e os determinantes da participação', *Ciência e Saúde Coletiva* 3(1): 5–17.

Warren, M. (2000) *Democracy and Association*, Princeton: Princeton University Press.

9

Subverting the Spaces of Invitation? Local Politics and Participatory Budgeting in Post-crisis Buenos Aires

Dennis Rodgers

The worst crisis in Argentina's recent history came to a head during the night of 19–20 December 2001, when the country was racked by a series of mass protests that came to be known collectively as the *Argentinazo*. Following President Fernando de la Rúa's desperate and unsuccessful attempts to prevent capital flight and defend the value of the Argentinian peso, thousands descended into the streets demanding his resignation and an immediate end to austerity measures. This rapidly escalated into rioting and violent clashes with the police that left twenty-eight dead and plunged the country into unprecedented turmoil. De la Rúa resigned, and there were three interim presidents in ten days before Eduardo Duhalde was appointed head of state by the Argentinian Senate, with a limited mandate to serve out the remainder of de la Rúa's term until December 2003.[1] The peso was deregulated and lost three-quarters of its value, the country defaulted on its foreign debt of US$132 billion – the largest sovereign default in history – and businesses ground to a standstill, precipitating soaring unemployment and a massive increase in the proportion of the population living under the poverty line, from 38 per cent in October 2001 to 54 per cent in June 2002 (Fiszbein et al. 2003; Manzetti 2002).

Although the economic dimensions of the crisis are clearly important, it is critical not to underestimate its simultaneously political character. There is no doubt that the demonstrations were protests against ongoing processes of pauperization and exclusion, but they clearly also reflected a more general disillusion with Argentinian politics and politicians, as was paradigmatically reflected in the ubiquitous slogan of the demonstrators, *Que se vayan todos* ('Out with the lot of them'). The *Argentinazo* can be said to have highlighted 'the limits to Argentina's democratic culture' and 'the absence of political channels capable of providing for the more systematically and proactively deliberative articulation of interests' (Tedesco 2002: 469). It was a moment 'when people bypassed politics as usual' (López Levy 2004: 10), and led to Argentina becoming a 'political laboratory' (Dinerstein 2003: 187), as an unprecedented groundswell of bottom-up mobilization led to a range of 'alternative' forms of political participation aiming to transform the nature of Argentinian political culture and society.

These included *asambleas populares* (spontaneous neighbourhood assemblies), *clubes de trueque* (barter clubs), *empresas recuperadas* (worker-occupied enterprises) and *piqueteros* (organized groups of unemployed). In the years since December 2001, however, the first three forms have either disappeared or steadily declined, while most instances of the latter have become institutionalized as a new form of political clientelism. This suggests that none constituted a sustainable mode of alternative political participation. At one level this is easily explained: politics, at its most basic, is about resource distribution decisions, and none of the above practices controlled anything significant in the way of resources or access to resources. They furthermore all positioned themselves in opposition to an Argentinian state that they decried as 'weak' or 'irrelevant', but that in fact, following the crisis, rapidly embarked on a wide-ranging programme of social assistance in order to mitigate its effects and to shore up its dominant position within the institutional fabric of Argentinian society.[2]

The issue of the relationship with the state is an especially important one. As Kohli and Shue (1994) have pointed out, state–society linkages are a critical political interface, perhaps the most significant in the modern era. Although such relations are highly variable – neither states nor societies are monolithic entities, and the boundaries between them are often blurred – they inevitably constitute a particular sociological space of cohabitation between a generally manifold 'society' and a 'state' that is a privileged social institution in terms of political scope and flows of power. The alternative forms of political participation described above that emerged in post-crisis Argentina arguably occurred in what Brock et al. (2001: 23) have termed 'autonomous spaces': that is to say, spaces that have opened not in interface with the state but rather against or in indifference to it. This has critical ramifications for the political possibilities of such spaces. Although they might conceivably be imagined as 'insurgent' forms of political participation that could eventually 'conquer' or 'replace' the state (Holston 1999), both history and the continuing strength of the post-crisis Argentinian state caution against such an interpretation, and as such it can be contended that they effectively constitute 'dead end' forms of transformative politics.

Implicitly for this very reason, Cornwall (2004: 2) argues that there is a crucial distinction between the political possibilities accorded by 'autonomous' spaces of participation, on the one hand, and what she labels 'invited' spaces, on the other. These are political spaces opened up by the state to non-state actors, which, because they intrinsically involve *both* society and the state, potentially offer greater scope for reconfiguring power relations and extending democratic practices (see also Fung and Wright 2003; Gaventa 2004; Harriss et al. 2005). A rapidly growing literature has emerged on the issue, including in particular on the famous Porto Alegre 'participatory budgeting' (PB) initiative in Brazil, which by all accounts has been remarkably empowering and democratizing (Abers 1996, 1998; Baiocchi 2001; Genro and De Souza 1997). This literature is, however, arguably characterized by a range of normative assumptions, including in particular the notion that the simple existence of invited spaces will automatically lead to better decision-making, better outcomes, and the creation of better citizens. Cornwall (2004: 9) points out that this is by no means always the case, and suggests that to truly understand the dynamics of invited spaces it is necessary 'to situate them in institutional landscapes as one amongst a host of other domains of association into and out of which actors move, carrying with them relationships, knowledge, connections, resources, identities and identifications'.

Arguably the most important issue in this regard are the political configurations within which invited spaces are embedded. Indeed, these are frequently considered to be *the* key factor determining the success or failure of participatory initiatives, in so far as oppositional politics and the excessive politicization of participatory processes are widely thought to lead to deficient and non-meaningful participation (Cooke and Kothari 2001). This chapter takes a closer look at political factors surrounding the introduction and implementation of PB in the Autonomous City of Buenos Aires in 2002–03, during which it was remarkably effective despite a manifest process of politicization.[3] Based on ethnographic research and interviews carried out over a six-month period (April–September 2003) with a range of individuals and groups involved in the process, it explores the micro-level politics of PB in the central Buenos Aires neighbourhood area of Abasto in order to understand this apparent paradox. It shows how PB overlay existing social practices and relations; how different actors perceived and acted upon the process according to distinct and often contradictory agendas; and how the empowering nature of the PB process itself all combined to make it work in an autonomous and effective manner. This raises a number of interesting issues about the politics of participation in invited spaces, including the necessity to take into account local-level socio-political dynamics, as well as the practically transformative nature of participatory processes.

The Macropolitics of PB in Buenos Aires

The official 2003 PB information brochure explicitly suggests that its introduction in 2002 was a direct response by the Government of the City of Buenos Aires (GCBA) to the *Argentinazo*:

> We live in an epoch in which the institutions of democracy lack repre-
> sentation and legitimacy in unprecedented ways. The citizenry demands
> new answers, new channels of accountability and participation, new ways
> of doing politics. Bridging the gap that today separates the state from
> society is the key to maintaining a fully democratic life. In this context,
> the Government of the Autonomous City of Buenos Aires has opened
> a space for the direct participation of local neighbourhood inhabitants in
> public affairs. The Participatory Budget Plan has the objective of chan-
> nelling the demands of society and granting citizens a central role in the
> democratic life of the city. Citizen participation is the best means possible
> to attain a more democratic control over the government's administration
> of the city. (GCBA, 2003a: 4, my translation)

Considering the underlying logic and aim of 'empowered deliberative democracy' initiatives such as PB (Fung and Wright 2003), this
arguably constituted a logical response to the crisis. At the same time,
PB was by no means an obvious initiative to implement in Buenos
Aires. The idea was first suggested by the independent Central de
Trabajadores Argentinos (CTA, Argentinian Workers' Central) trade
union, which campaigned successfully to have 'the participatory

character of the budget' established in Article 52 of the 1996 Constitution of the Autonomous City of Buenos Aires (GCBA 2003b: 19). The city legislature, however, subsequently failed to establish consultative procedures regarding the assignation of resource priorities due to a combination of lack of interest and suspicion towards PB on the part of the city's major politicians and political parties. Only a few limited pilot projects in specific Buenos Aires localities took place before 2001.

To a large extent, the full-scale introduction of PB in Buenos Aires can be characterized as a case of 'unintentional democratization', in so far as it was a contingent consequence of changes in the city's political balance of power following the *Argentinazo* (Rodgers 2005). The crisis tore apart the ruling Frente Grande (Broad Front) party and forced the mayor of the city, Aníbal Ibarra, to seek new configurations of support both within and outside of his party. Among those he turned to was Ariel Schifrin, the leader of an important but previously marginalized faction within the Frente Grande party, the Grupo Espacio Abierto (Open Space Group). Schifrin agreed to support Ibarra, but made overseeing the introduction of PB in the city a condition for his support, and consequently became head of the city administration's Secretaría de Descentralización y Participación Ciudadana (Secretariat for Decentralization and Citizen Participation) in February 2002. He was clearly less interested in PB as a form of empowering democratization than as a mechanism to build up the Frente Grande – and, more specifically, Grupo Espacio Abierto – political networks, and moved rapidly to insert loyalists throughout the city's sixteen decentralized administration and participation centres (the Centros de Gestión y Participación, CGPs), with the brief to establish a strong party presence by means of the PB process that was now being instituted through the CGPs. As one of these loyalists based in the CGP no. 2 Norte (North) told me during an interview on 11 August 2003,

> The Open Space Group now has a better territorial development than before, precisely because Ariel is the Secretary of Decentralization and he's worked the CGPs well, and of course the PB is a good tool to extend the presence of the party and impose ourselves at the local level, especially vis-à-vis the Radicals [the traditionally dominant political party in Buenos Aires].

At the same time, despite this manifest politicization of PB, by all accounts it was a process that worked very well during the first two years of its application. As Navarro (2005: 108–9) has succinctly summarized, the process began with a one-month *Plan de Prioridades Barriales* (Neighbourhood Priorities Plan) pilot project in June 2002, involving 4,500 individuals in 16 neighbourhoods who participated in 250 meetings and identified 338 budgetary priorities, which were then incorporated into a special annex of the city's 2002 budget. By May 2004, 165 of these priorities had been executed (49 per cent), 101 were in the process of being executed (30 per cent), and 22 were being disputed (7 per cent). A full-scale *Plan de Presupuesto Participativo 2003* (2003 PB Plan) followed this pilot project between July and September 2002, where 9,450 individuals in 43 neighbourhoods participated in 450 meetings and voted 189 priorities. By May 2004, 65 of these priorities had been executed (34 per cent), 45 were in the process of being executed (24 per cent), and 10 were being disputed (5 per cent). The *Plan de Presupuesto Participativo 2004* (2004 PB Plan) was carried out between March and September 2003 in 51 neighbourhoods: 14,000 individuals participated in the identification and voting of 1,000 priorities, 600 of which were incorporated into the city's 2004 budget (those rejected were considered unfeasible or inappropriate).

To a certain extent, these impressive achievements were due to intelligent institutional design. PB in Buenos Aires involved the devolution of authority for the determination of municipal action from the city government to local neighbourhood inhabitants, who debated and established their local needs over a period of several months, first in neighbourhood assemblies, and then in six local thematic commissions, respectively on socio-economic development, public works and environment, education, health, culture and security. Once proposals were decided on by each commission, a final neighbourhood assembly was held where participants voted on which thematic clusters they felt contained the most urgent proposals, ranking the top four. The proposals were then sent to relevant city government departments, and discussed in a city-wide plenary bringing together neighbourhood inhabitants and city government bureaucrats. Proposals found to be technically feasible were then ranked in relation to each other according to a formula that took into account population differences, the number of voters in neighbourhood assemblies, and the relative wealth and poverty of neighbourhoods, in order to put all neighbourhoods on an equal footing. An 'action matrix' for the whole city was then drawn up of all the ranked proposals and integrated into the municipal budget, providing the order in which city public resources were to be expended until depleted. In many ways, PB in Buenos Aires was therefore arguably more an exercise in participatory planning than PB per se, but this meant that it avoided many of the problems linked to a lack of public funds that have plagued other PB processes (and that would moreover have been particularly critical in post-crisis Argentina).

While it is important to take into account the institutional design of the Buenos Aires PB initiative, it was not a counterweight to the process's politicization. Indeed, the design was continuously being tinkered with by the PB Provisional Council – a council of elected neighbourhood delegates and NGO representatives, which theoretically supervised the whole process but in practice deferred to the Secretariat for Decentralization and Citizen Participation – and its provisions were often ignored or imperfectly executed by both local and central GCBA PB Technical Coordination teams. To this extent, the reasons underlying the unlikely success of PB in Buenos Aires are likely to be found elsewhere. One reason is undoubtedly the fact that a significant proportion of the members of the central PB Technical Coordination team, as well as some of the local teams, shared something of a technocratic public service outlook and sought to promote PB for the process's sake rather than with any party political agenda. As such, they constituted something of an anti-political 'Trojan Horse' within the politicized PB process (indeed, many of the cases of bypassing of the formal rules that I was able to observe occurred not with the intention of subverting the PB process but rather to facilitate it in the face of its politicization). Another reason is that the political balance of power in post-crisis Buenos Aires remained extremely volatile until the September 2003 elections, and political intrigues meant that Schifrin had to make compromises that limited the speed and scope of the politicization of the PB process.

Possibly the most important bulwark against the politicization of the PB process was the particular nature of local politics in Buenos Aires, however. As Levitsky (2001: 30) has pointed out, political parties in Argentina can be conceived as 'informal mass parties', based on 'a dense collection of personal networks – operating out of unions, clubs, non-governmental organizations, and often activists' homes – that are often unconnected to (and autonomous from) the party bureaucracy'. These constitute the territorial base of traditional

political parties, but are highly independent and only loosely feder-
ated, except at a symbolic level, for example through the memory
of historical figures such as Evita Perón in the case of the Peronist
party (see Auyero 2001), or Hipólito Irigoyen for the Radicals.
This made the enterprise of systematically creating Frente Grande
party political networks through PB no straightforward matter, as it
inevitably involved engaging with and co-opting a variety of existing
local-level social forms, all of which had their own agendas and
interests that did not necessarily coincide with those of the Frente
Grande. Moreover, even when local grassroots associations or local
punteros and *punteras* (socio-political brokers) were well-disposed to
the Frente Grande, PB often had effects on the way they responded
to demands to mobilize and subvert it. The next section attempts
to depict ethnographically some of these processes specifically in
relation to the neighbourhood area of Abasto.

Participatory Budgeting in Abasto

The *área barrial* (neighbourhood area) of Abasto is a sub-unit of the
CGP no. 2 Sur (South) district, formally no. 1 of three sub-units
(see Map 9.1).[4] It straddles the Avenida Rivadavia, which historically
divides the more prosperous North from the impoverished South of
the city, and is an extremely heterogeneous neighbourhood, which
can be generally classified as socio-economically 'lower middle
class'. According to the 2001 GCBA census, the CGP no. 2 Sur
has a population of 190,000, equivalent to about 6 per cent of the
population of Buenos Aires.[5] My research involved attending several
PB meetings in Abasto, interviewing a range of participants and
GCBA officials, and carrying out a kerbside survey. I also spent time
in and around the CGP no. 2 Sur's administrative offices, which
were located in the *área barrial* no. 2.[6]

The most basic issue concerning any invited space is that those
being invited need to know about it. Knowledge about the PB process
in Buenos Aires was clearly extremely limited (though it should be
noted that my research was carried out during what was only the
second year of the process). An impromptu and unsystematic kerbside
survey conducted on 24 June 2003, during which I stopped and asked
103 men (54) and women (49) whether they had heard about the
PB process, elicited a positive tally of just 10.7 per cent (11 positive

Map 9.1   Buenos Aires CGPs, with detail of CGP no. 2 Sur

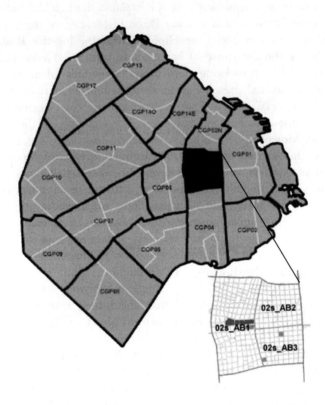

Source: GCBA, www.buenosaires.gov.ar/areas/hacienda/pp/areas.php?menu_id=11567.

replies). When I further asked how many had actually participated, just 1.9 per cent of respondents answered that they had (2 positive replies). To contextualize these figures, it is illuminating to compare them with data from the GCBA Statistics and Census Department's survey of knowledge about CGPs in Buenos Aires, which found that in 2003 only 36.4 per cent of the population within the CGP no. 2 Sur knew about the existence of their CGP, and that just 18.6 per cent had actually had any direct dealings with it.[7]

Such dismal figures are perhaps not surprising when one considers the PB process's shoestring budget. Certainly, there was very little advertising and few information campaigns. As a member of the PB Central Technical Coordination team remarked in an interview on 19 August 2003:

> Personally, I think that one of the greatest problems we've had has been with the minimal diffusion of information about the whole process.... This is something that can be seen in every neighbourhood, you find that the level of knowledge about PB that the average inhabitant has is really quite minimal. We're constantly trying to get more informa-tion out there, but there hasn't been a proper campaign or anything.... One of the things I really feel, and this is my personal opinion of course, is that for one reason or another we haven't properly exploited certain channels that, because they're in the government's hands, would be very easy to make use of in order to communicate effectively on a very large scale, for example by including something on PB in the information bulletins that all the kids in state schools receive at the beginning of the year to give to their parents... or also by advertising on the GCBA's radio station, or the new television station that it now has as well.... The radio in particular is particularly galling, as we've had almost no airtime at all on it, and what little that we've had has been because I know a lot of people there and I've passed on certain things to them informally.... Logically you'd want this kind of informing of the population to be formalized.

Considering the wider crisis context, the lack of funding for the PB process is not surprising. There is little doubt, though, that politics also played a role in this situation. Ibarra showed little interest in the PB process and seemed only to have sanctioned its implementation in order to gain Schifrin's political support. He was, however, clearly wary of Schifrin using PB to his own advantage, and several PB officials speculated that the low budget assigned to the process was a way for Ibarra to keep Schifrin in check.

At the same time, politicization was arguably one of the most effective means for mobilizing people to participate in the PB. Jorge Navarro, coordinator of the PB process in Buenos Aires and a close ally of Schifrin, admitted frankly in an on-the-record interview on 7 August 2003 that local Frente Grande political networks had been used to mobilize participation in the PB process in several CGPs. He maintained that PB inevitably had to be promoted through pre-existing networks due to the scarcity of funds, and that since the most easily mobilized and well-disposed ones were going to be

Frente Grande networks – particularly considering that PB was a
government initiative – this was a necessity. Such a justification makes
a good deal of sense, and has been similarly remarked on by Acharya
et al. (2004) in their study of the use of Partido dos Trabhaldores
(PT, Brazilian Workers' Party) networks in the implementation of PB
and deliberative policy councils in São Paulo, Brazil. The nature of
local-level politics in Argentina also arguably made it inevitable that
many of the channels for promoting PB and mobilizing participation
would overlap with party political networks, as the local community
organizations and associations that constituted the primary target
of any PB information and mobilization campaign were effectively
the same ones from which Argentinian political parties draw their
mobilizatory strength.

At the same time, the decentralized structure of party political
networks, and in particular the top-down chain that links macro-level
politicians to more localized *referentes* (local 'big men' or 'big women'
politicians), who are themselves in turn connected to micro-level
punteros and *punteras* who 'control' a local association and can turn
people out to vote, means that there is also considerable scope for
political demands from above to be subverted. This became apparent
at the Abasto final PB neighbourhood assembly that I attended on
13 June 2003, which was to decide on proposals to be put forward
for the 2004 municipal budget. It was held on a Friday evening in
a large school hall, and over 350 people attended, a high number
compared to other meetings I observed during my research. I recorded
in my field diary at the time that there were

> slightly more women than men – *c.* 60/40 split (?); predominance of older
> participants – *c.* 50 per cent over 55 years old, *c.* 30 per cent under 30
> years old, the rest 30–55 years old. There is a family atmosphere, with
> tango music playing in the background; much general conviviality and
> jovial exchanges between individuals who obviously know each other.

Both the debating and the voting proceeded in an orderly, although
often passionate, fashion. The assembly voted to prioritize health,
public works, education and socio-economic development projects,
which respectively included initiatives such as increasing the range
of services provided by the local health centre, putting in more
street lamps, setting up a neighbourhood apprenticeship scheme for
unemployed youths, and building a library. As people began to leave
once the results were announced, I approached a man in his late

forties, whom I had noticed following the proceedings intensely after having initially seemed rather nonchalant about them. I asked him how he had learnt about PB and why he had come:

> 'Well, actually I didn't really know much about it until tonight, I came because the woman over there told me to come', he replied, pointing to somebody across the room. 'She's done a lot of things for me and my family in the past, so when she asked me whether I could come, as she does from time to time, I of course said yes, and so here I am.'
>
> 'Why did she want you to come? Did she tell you how to vote?', I asked.
>
> 'Why, yes, she did, she told me to vote for this and that proposal, not to vote for this one, and she also told me to vote for this candidate for plenary delegate rather than that one.'
>
> 'And did you vote as she asked you to?'
>
> 'Well, for the delegate, yes, but not for the proposals. Normally I would have, but normally when she asks me to come to meetings like this, I just come, vote, and then leave as quickly as possible, because they can get really boring, you know. But you can't do that with this meeting, you have to sign up at the beginning or else you can't vote at the end, so I had to sit here through all three hours of tonight's meeting. But you know what? I heard a lot of really interesting things, I sat here and I listened to all the proposals, and thought to myself "there's some good ideas here", and so when it was time to vote, I didn't vote like she told me to, but for the proposals that I thought would be best for my neighbourhood.'

Such behaviour patterns on the part of those mobilized by *punteras* and *punteros* may not necessarily be common, but this exchange shows how even in an invited space subverted by politics there can still be scope for independent participation that arguably reverses the flow of subversion. To a large extent, the credit for this 'subverting of the subversion' can be attributed to the powerfully transformative process PB can often be for the individuals who participate in it. Certainly, this was something that also emerged – albeit in a different manner – from my subsequent interview on 24 June 2003 with Ana Balladares,[8] the *puntera* who had asked the person I had the exchange with to come to the PB assembly. When I questioned her on the matter, Ana readily told me that she had been mobilizing her networks in Abasto to ensure a high level of participation in the PB process since its inception, at the behest of a *referente* who was the dominant local Frente Grande politician, and who was connected in turn with various more macro-level politicians, including Ariel

Schifrin. In order to explain what she called her 'militancy', she began by telling me about her background.

She started by emphasizing that she had been 'a Peronist militant almost all my life, from the age of 16', although she was 'only able to join the party at the age of 18 in 1972'. She talked passionately about Evita Perón and the inspiration that her work in favour of 'the most humble and vulnerable class' constituted for her, and stated that 'even though I never got to know her because I was born three years after her death, I fell in love with that woman'. She also talked about Padre Carlos Mujica, a Catholic priest well known for his social work in the slums of Buenos Aires who was assassinated in 1974 by the right-wing 'Triple A' group, and explained how this radicalized her and led to her becoming a *Montonera* armed guerrilla during the military dictatorship that seized power in 1976. She was eventually caught and imprisoned for several months, and when she was released, escaped to Brazil, where she stayed until the restoration of democracy in 1983. On her return, Ana threw herself into mobilizing support for the Peronist party in Abasto, although doing so

> with a low profile, dealing with the social aspect of things, helping people in need... for example people who are on the verge of being expelled from their houses, I'd connect them with lawyers or friends who would be able to stop or extend the whole expulsion process, to buy some time to look for alternative social housing or something.

She then recounted the immense joy that she had felt when the Peronist party candidate Carlos Menem won the presidency in 1989, and how proud she had been to have 'contributed to this victory with my local territorial work'. She then went on to describe her progressive disillusion with Menem and his 'neoliberalism and corruption', until she felt that 'he did not represent Peronism any more', which in 1998 led her to 'break definitively with Peronism and close down my *unidad básica* (local unit)' in Abasto, although 'I kept my people'. Shortly after this 'low point in my life as a militant', she found a new focus, however:

> Near my house there was a Frente Grande locale, and one day I walked in with a friend who wanted to ask them a question but who didn't dare go alone by herself, so I went with her, and what drew my attention there was that there were photos of Evita, of Padre Mujica ... on the walls.... I said to myself 'what are my *compañeros* doing here, in this place,

this is very bizarre', and I began talking with one of the militants, who told me that they too had come from Peronism and that they too didn't think Menem represented Peronism any more, so they'd founded their own party to resist him.... I there and then decided to become a Frente Grande militant, and from then on worked my people for them.

Ana's militant activities soon came to include 'mobilizing my people' to ensure their participation in the PB process, which her *referente* was particularly anxious about, not only for political reasons but also because he had been an early and genuine convert to PB, involved in some of the limited pilot projects that were conducted in Buenos Aires during the late 1990s. Yet, while Ana to a large extent seemed to conform to her *referente*'s wishes, it became apparent that she also had her own agenda. 'For a long time', she told me,

> I'd been fighting to get a crèche set up in the neighbourhood.... There was only one crèche in the whole of Almagro, in Avenida Ramos Mejía. It was a municipal one, and had a waiting list of 150 kids, so another crèche was obviously something that was needed. The government wouldn't do anything, though, even when I found some unused land in the neigh-bourhood where it could be built.... When the PB process began in 2002, though, I thought to myself 'this may be an opportunity', and so I looked at how I could make it work.... I joined the socio-economic development commission, and worked to persuade everybody else that we should propose the crèche as our priority project and build it on this land.... We talked and talked between ourselves about it, and it ended up being a really great commission, because they all agreed with me, and the crèche became our commission's priority project.... I was sure we'd win, but then I heard that the education commission was propos-ing that a library be built on the land I'd found instead of the crèche, and so I began to fear that the crèche might not be voted as the overall neighbourhood priority.... To make sure that we'd win, I brought all my people to the final PB assembly and told everybody to vote for the socio-economic development commission, and that way we won!

Ana's response to the PB process might be considered more classically subversive than the actions of the people that she mobilized to come to the 2003 PB final assembly in Abasto, in so far as it subverted the spirit of the PB process. However, as Rubén Basignana, one of the CGP no. 2 Sur 2003 PB Provisional Council delegates, underscored during an interview conducted on 17 June 2003:

> It's human nature that people will try and push their own pet interests and project.... Even though I haven't travelled much, I don't know of any society where that doesn't happen, and it's certainly happened a

lot here during the past few years.... But the important thing is that I don't think that it's happened due to bad will or for selfish reasons. For example, somebody in my neighbourhood pushed very hard for a project to build a crèche in the neighbourhood, to the extent that she brought people to the assembly to vote for her project and make sure that it was chosen. But the crèche isn't being built for her, it's for the neighbourhood, you see? It's like a school; it's a necessity, especially in our neighbourhood where there are so many social problems.... So it's a good thing that we've now got this crèche, even if it was obtained through the negative political practices of the past.

Rubén in fact argued that ultimately such subversive practices didn't really matter because the PB process contained within it the seeds for a wholesale transformation of Argentinian politics and society:

> In the end, it doesn't really matter how the process works right now, because it's only the beginning. You have to see it as a tool, a fantastic tool that is completely different to the means for obtaining resources that we've known in the past, like clientelism, corruption, *asistencialismo* [social dependency], demagoguery, and all those terrible, terrible things.... It's a new means for us to make decisions, by participating.... Of course it's still being constructed, but I can already see that in ten years' time we're going to have a fabulous tool that will allow a new form of politics here in Argentina that will also act as an impediment to the bad habits of the past returning.... That's what I believe, that there are beautiful times ahead for Argentina, that after our journey through the worst darkness you can imagine during 1976[–83] and also the events of 19–20 December [2001], we're finally becoming a normal country again, as our president puts it. Wouldn't that be something, to be normal? We've been abnormal for much too long....

While Rubén's vision of the future evolution of Argentinian political culture might seem somewhat optimistic, there is one aspect of the PB process that definitely did seem to be having a significant and immediate impact. The process formally opened up institutional channels for direct communication with GCBA officials and bureaucrats, through local assemblies and thematic commissions, but most substantially through the city-wide plenary that was held after all the proposals had been received and examined by city officials. Many local neighbourhood inhabitants I talked to in fact seemed to have engaged in the PB process less as a form of bypassing politicians than as a means of accessing and positively influencing the government bureaucrats who dealt concretely with their problems. During a collective interview conducted on 22 June 2003 with six members of the self-styled Comisión de Vecinos de la plazoleta Moreno y Boedo (Moreno and Boedo streets neighbours' association), all of whom had participated in the 2002 city-wide plenary, they repeatedly praised 'how incredible an experience it was to be able to speak directly with the right people', because 'you normally have to wait forever to see anybody, and then they tell you, "no, I've got nothing to do with that" or something to that effect'. As one member of the group argued:

> It's a question of responsibility, what the PB does is make the civil servants responsible, because it gives us a forum where we can formulate precise demands and present them directly to them. They can't hide behind the politicians any more, because there's a direct connection between us and them now.

Conclusion

On the basis of the evidence presented in this chapter, it can be argued that the politicization of invited spaces of participation does not necessarily work solely in negative ways, as much of the theoretical literature suggests (see Hickey and Mohan 2005: 241–2). Certainly, PB in Buenos Aires would likely not have been implemented in the first place had it not been for its potential politicization, as its introduction was directly related to the fact that it was seen as a means of mobilizing political support networks in the city. This underlines the basic notion that the opening up of invited spaces of participation is a fundamentally political act, although in the case of PB in Buenos Aires it was arguably a contingent and somewhat 'unintentional' instance of democratization, something that goes against the grain of studies that have associated the introduction of participatory initiatives with programmatic politics (Acharya et al. 2004; Baiocchi 2003; Chavez and Goldfrank 2004; Heller 2001). At the same time, however, while the 'macro'-level political configurations surrounding the opening of invited spaces of participation are important, the ethnographic vignettes presented above of the PB process in Abasto suggest that what might be termed the 'micro'-level politics are also critical to consider. Indeed, it can be argued that whether political factors positively or negatively affect participatory initiatives will depend on the specific local political and social dynamics within which the distinct social actors involved and the participatory process itself are embedded.

This was manifest in the way in which the politicization of PB in
Buenos Aires led to better levels of mobilization in some areas of the
city such the CGP no. 2 Sur, but not in others, including the CGP
no. 2 Norte, for example. As one former participant in this latter
CGP explained to me in an email sent on 7 December 2004:

> There was so much deceitfulness, and so many disappointments due to
> all the politicking, that all the projects we wanted to set up and have
> included in the budget became secondary to certain people's political
> agendas.... It became so ugly, projects were being promoted by people
> simply in order to gain political support, and so of course people began
> to withdraw from the process ... even me. I've believed so much in it, I
> don't want to have anything more to do with PB; I feel as if I've wasted
> too much of my valuable time for nothing.... What's the use of having
> such a wonderful tool if you can't use it properly?

As Hickey and Mohan (2005: 250) have pointed out, the success
of participatory initiatives often depends on their being linked to a
broader political project and not opposing existing power relations.
The PB process in Abasto was clearly less conflictual than in the
CGP no. 2 Norte, at least partly because it did not challenge local
political configurations. Abasto had electoral affinities with the
governing Frente Grande party, while the CGP no. 2 Norte was a
more upper-middle-class and upper-class area that tended to vote
predominantly against the Frente Grande.

At the same time, there also existed in Abasto a very particular
constellation of competing actors, interests and practices that articulated together in such a way as to hold each other in check, thereby
permitting the emergence of an effective and representative PB
process, against the odds. Once again political factors are important in
understanding this, both at the level of specific individual trajectories
– as Ana Balladares's case demonstrates well – but also in terms of
the 'organized disorganization' (Levitsky 2001) of local-level politics
in Argentina. The decentralized mass of local associations and personal
relationships that constitute the basis of party politics in Argentina
inherently provided a counterpoint to any attempt by political
parties to assume control of the PB process. This afforded multiple
possibilities for independent behaviour, whether by neighbourhood
inhabitants, *punteras* or *referentes*. There were consequently almost
inevitably 'spaces of autonomy' within the politicized invited space of
participation that allowed for a localized 'subverting of the subversion'
of politicization. To a certain extent, this also occurred at a city-wide

level. As a member of the central PB Technical Coordination team explained in an interview on 19 August 2003:

> On the one hand you have the 'bad old ways' of politicking, while on the other hand you have a new project of participatory democracy that is supported by a broad spectrum of people, groups and organizations across the 51 neighbourhoods of Buenos Aires.... This makes it actually very difficult for the PB process to be hijacked completely, because it's something that would have to happen in 51 different points of the city, and to capture 51 areas is difficult for any political party. None of them has a presence in every neighbourhood, let alone a uniform one, and nor do any of them have enough competent cadres to attempt to capture the PB process properly. There are too many pre-existing groups, organizations and institutions in all of these areas that already display high levels of participation and militancy, for all sorts of reasons – including some really old and important ones – and that all have their own relationship with both the state and the PB process. Even if they only manage to ensure that the PB process continues without becoming too politicized in their own neighbourhood, this still means that political parties will lose, because there are too many of these small groups and organizations.

From this perspective, it can be argued that the real question about the dynamics of a politicized invited space of participation such as the Buenos Aires PB process concerns less the 'what' or 'how' of things than the 'why'. In particular, as a CGP no. 2 Sur employee asked in an interview conducted on 12 June 2003,

> Why are there all these different groups and individuals, some political, others not, some groups with a history of community activism, other groups with leaders? And why is it that they all want to participate, to be protagonists? That's the interesting issue to analyse – why do people, at some moment, get interested to become protagonists of something?

This is in many ways the fundamental question underlying the study of politics, and there are obviously different dimensions to its answer. One clearly lies in structural factors such as the 'crisis of representation' that the *Argentinazo* reflected, as well as the collapse of the Argentinian economy, in so far as desperate situations pull individuals out of the social torpor that (supposedly) characterizes the modern era (see Habermas 1987). Less contingent structural facets of Argentinian society can also be invoked, including the institutional vibrancy of its civil society (Jelin 2003), as well as the existence of political traditions that for many take on the form of veritable ways of life (Auyero 2001).

Another answer is related to factors that are more endogenous to the participatory process. As many of the interview extracts presented in this chapter reflect, during the course of my fieldwork I repeatedly heard how many Buenos Aires PB participants became enthused by, and converted to, the process and the empowerment it provided them, however they had came to be involved. Obviously, this was neither universal nor constant, and it was widely recognized that the process provided only a limited and imperfect form of empowerment, but often even those disillusioned by the process's politicization nevertheless saw it as a 'wonderful tool'. Indeed, I must include myself among the ranks of the converted, as I too came to be highly inspired by my real-life interaction with a process that I had previously only considered theoretically, and even rather cynically, in view of the way in which 'participation' and 'empowerment' have largely become vacuous 'buzzwords' within mainstream development discourse (see Cornwall and Brock 2005). However diluted these labels undoubtedly are, and however imperfectly they are put into practice, it is evident that the social processes to which they refer can nevertheless be powerfully transformative for those involved in them. As such, they can be conceived as radically political in nature, in so far as they are about the transformation of configurations of power and governance, and it is perhaps this political factor, more than any other, that we should not forget as we seek to harness the potential of spaces of change such as PB.

Notes

I am extremely grateful to a number of individuals for their assistance, including Sergio Borelli, Antolín Magallanes, Jorge Navarro and Ana Tittaferrante of the Secretaría de Descentralización y Participación Ciudadana (Secretariat for Decentralization and Citizen Participation), Rubén Basignana and Edith Szilvássy of the Consejo Provisorio del Presupuesto Participativo (Provisional Council of the Participatory Budget), Fernanda Clancy and María Súarez of the Centro de Gestión y Participación (Administration and Participation Centre) no. 2 Sur (South), and many, many participants in the Buenos Aires Participatory Budgeting process. Finally, I also want to thank Agustina Corica and Paula Giovagnoli for their research assistance, particularly in relation to the transcription of interviews. None of the above is responsible for any errors or inaccuracies in this text.

1. Elections were subsequently held in April 2003, and current President Néstor Kirchner was elected to a four-year term.

2. This included, for example, the *Plan Jefes y Jefas de Hogar Desocupados* (Plan for Unemployed Heads of Household), which distributed subsidies amounting to over US$500 million to 2 million households in 2002, and over US$600 million in 2003 (Galasso and Ravallion 2004: 367).

3. Further political factors subsequently led to the process's probably terminal decline from 2004 onwards. See Rodgers 2005 for details.

4. Most of my informants recognized 'Abasto' as having some socio-geographical significance – associating it in particular with a popular renovated market-place – but they also frequently complained that it was an entity that bore little relation to historic city neighbourhood divisions, and that it cut across the 'proper' neighbourhoods of Balvanera and Almagro.

5. See www.buenosaires.gov.ar/areas/hacienda/sis_estadistico/poblacion01.pdf (consulted 1 October 2005).

6. I also carried out similar research in the CGP no. 2 Norte, attended meetings in other CGPs, and interviewed a wide range of GCBA officials, academics and NGO activists generally involved in the PB process.

7. See www.buenosaires.gov.ar/areas/hacienda/sis_estadistico/nuevoinforme/ N139.pdf (consulted 1 October 2005).

8. Names of informants have been changed or omitted to protect their privacy.

References

Abers, R. (1996) 'From ideas to practice: the Partido dos Trabalhadores and participatory governance in Brazil', *Latin American Perspectives* 23(4): 35–53.

Abers, R. (1998) 'From clientelism to cooperation: local government, participatory policy, and civic organizing in Porto Alegre, Brazil', *Politics and Society* 26(4): 511–37.

Acharya, A., A. Gurza Lavalle and P. Houtzager (2004) 'Civil society representation in the participatory budget and deliberative councils of São Paulo, Brazil', *IDS Bulletin* 35(2): 40–48.

Auyero, J. (2001) *Poor People's Politics: Peronist Networks and the Legacy of Evita*, Durham NC: Duke University Press.

Baiocchi, G. (2001) Participation, activism, and politics: the Porto Alegre experiment and deliberative democratic theory', *Politics and Society* 29(1): 43–72.

Baiocchi, G. (2003) *Radicals in Power: The Workers' Party and Experiments with Urban Democracy in Brazil*, London: Zed Books.

Brock, K., A. Cornwall and J. Gaventa (2001) 'Power, knowledge and political spaces in the framing of poverty policy', IDS Working Paper No. 143, Institute of Development Studies, University of Sussex, Falmer.

Chavez, D., and B. Goldfrank (2004) *The Left in the City: Participatory Local Governments in Latin America*, London: Latin America Bureau.

Cooke, W., and U. Kothari, eds (2001) *Participation: The New Tyranny?*, London: Zed Books.

Cornwall, A. (2004) 'Introduction: new democratic spaces? The politics and dynamics of institutionalised participation', *IDS Bulletin* 35(2): 1–10.

Cornwall, A., and K. Brock (2005) 'What do buzzwords do for development policy? A critical look at "participation", "empowerment" and "poverty reduction"', *Third World Quarterly* 26(7): 1043–60.

Dinerstein, A. (2003) 'Que se vayan todos! Popular insurrection and the *asambleas barriales* in Argentina', *Bulletin of Latin American Research* 22(2): 187–200.

Fiszbein, A., P.I. Giovagnoli and I. Adúriz (2003) 'The Argentinian crisis and its impact on household welfare', *CEPAL Review* 79: 143–58.

Fung, A., and E.O. Wright, eds (2003) *Deepening Democracy: Institutional Innovations in Empowered Participatory Governance*, London: Verso.

Galasso, E., and M. Ravallion (2004) 'Social protection in a crisis: Argentina's Plan Jefes y Jefas', *World Bank Economic Review* 18(3): 367–99.

Gaventa, J. (2004) 'Towards participatory governance: assessing the transformative possibilities', in S. Hickey and G. Mohan (eds), *Participation: From Tyranny to Transformation*, London: Zed Books.

GCBA (Gobierno de la Ciudad Autónoma de Buenos Aire) (2003a) *Presupuesto Participativo: Una Realidad*, Buenos Aires: GCBA.

GCBA (Gobierno de la Ciudad Autónoma de Buenos Airess) (2003b) *Constitución de la Ciudad Autónoma de Buenos Aires*, Buenos Aires: Ediciones del País.

Genro, T., and U. De Souza (1997) *Orçamento Participativo: A Experiência de Porto Alegre*, São Paulo: Fundação Perseu Abramo.

Habermas, J. (1987) *The Theory of Communicative Action*, Volume 2: *Lifeworld and System – A Critique of Functionalist Reason*, Boston MA: Beacon Press.

Harriss, J., K. Stokke and O. Törnquist, eds (2005) *Politicising Democracy: Local Politics and Democratisation in Developing Countries*, London: Palgrave Macmillan.

Heller, P. (2001) 'Moving the state: the politics of democratic decentralization in Kerala, South Africa and Porto Alegre', *Politics and Society* 29(1): 131–63.

Hickey, S., and G. Mohan (2005) 'Relocating participation within a radical politics of development', *Development and Change* 36(2): 237–62.

Holston, J. (1999) 'Spaces of insurgent citizenship', in J. Holston, ed., *Cities and Citizenship*, Durham NC: Duke University Press.

Jelin, E. (2003) *Más allá de la Nación: Las Escalas Múltiples de los Movimientos Sociales*, Buenos Aires: Libros de Zorzal.

Kohli, A., and V. Shue (1994) 'State power and social forces: on political contention and accommodation in the Third World', in J. Migdal, A. Kohli and V. Shue, eds, *State Power and Social Forces: Domination and Transformation in the Third World*, New York: Cambridge University Press.

Levitsky, S. (2001) 'An "organized disorganisation": informal organisation and the persistence of local party structures in Argentine Peronism', *Journal of Latin American Studies* 33(1): 29–61.

López Levy, M. (2004) *We Are Millions: Neo-liberalism and New Forms of Political Action in Argentina*, London: Latin America Bureau.

Manzetti, L. (2002) 'The Argentine implosion', North–South Agenda Working Paper No. 59, Miami: North–South Center.

Navarro, J. (2005) 'Presupuesto participativo en la ciudad de Buenos Aires', in R. Romero, ed., *Democracia Participativa: Una Utopía en Marcha*, Buenos Aires: Ediciones Cooperativas.

Rodgers, D. (2005) 'Unintentional democratisation? The Argentinazo and the politics of participatory budgeting in Buenos Aires, 2001–2004', Crisis States Programme Working Paper No. 61, London: Crisis States Research Centre.

Tedesco, L. (2002) 'Argentina's turmoil: the politics of informality and the roots of economic meltdown', *Cambridge Review of International Affairs* 15(3): 469–81.

Participation, Mutation and Political Transition: New Democratic Spaces in Peri-urban Angola

Sandra Roque and Alex Shankland

This chapter examines participation spaces in peri-urban Luanda, Angola – a context very different from those that have originated most recent studies in this field and which presents a series of apparently highly adverse conditions for the development of citizen participation. Sometimes labelled a 'fragile' or 'failed' state, Angola could more correctly be described as a state that is failing its people. It has a tradition of centralized and authoritarian rule stretching back through decades of single-party government and civil war to the centuries of Portuguese domination and colonization. This tradition has remained powerful despite the shift towards economic liberalization and formal multi-party democracy since 1991. Angola is sub-Saharan Africa's second-largest oil producer, with a GDP per capita 29 per cent above the continent's average; nevertheless, its Human Development Index is among the worst in the world, with the country rated 166th out of 177 nations (UNDP 2004).[1] With the end of the civil war in 2002, attention has begun to shift to the role of governance issues in perpetuating this situation, and in particular to the link between limited participation and accountability and lack of social justice.

This chapter argues, however, that significant 'invisible' processes of democratization may be under way – including the emergence of new leaders at the local level and shifts in citizens' expectations of their interactions with government. It examines the role of NGO-sponsored participation processes in contributing to this trend in the capital, Luanda, through case studies drawn from the Luanda

Urban Poverty Programme (LUPP). The analysis argues that while the 'invited spaces' created by these NGOs may begin as conventional participation-in-development models, in the particular social and political context of Luanda they mutate into other forms of participation. These forms reflect the interests, agency and strategies of local actors, their encounters with and adaptation to a changing context, and the release of repressed political energy which follows the opening up of new participation spaces in a setting long characterized by lack of responsiveness. The chapter concludes by examining the challenges for NGOs promoting new participation spaces in contexts like Luanda, and the potential wider application of the lessons learned. In particular, it argues that there is a need to pay greater attention to the accountability implications of new spaces if the emerging leadership that they foster is not simply to reproduce the authoritarian practices of the old, while recognizing that even when it has autocratic or elitist elements, this leadership may still play an essential part in steps towards broader participation.

New Democratic Spaces in Adverse Contexts

Recent writing on citizenship and participation has increasingly come to focus on the arenas within which new social and political relations are constructed. Some of these 'new democratic spaces' (Cornwall 2004) have been described as sites of 'deliberative democracy' or even 'empowered participatory governance' (Fung and Wright 2003), where the exercise of reasoned debate between political equals in public space leads to the emergence of consensus and binding decisions. In the development field, there has been a proliferation of participation spaces, often as a result of pressure from multilateral, bilateral or non-governmental development agencies for whom the setting up of user committees or stakeholder fora has become the default means of signalling commitment to participation, citizenship and accountability. At the same time, governance innovations developed in particular parts of the global 'South', such as participatory budgeting or citizen report cards, are being exported both elsewhere in the 'South' and to parts of the 'North'. Thus, institutions and practices originating from particular sets of conditions are increasingly appearing in radically different settings, many of which are unpromising or even highly adverse.

Most discussions of the new democratic spaces have focused on the conditions that enable their success, with authors variously emphasizing strong associative networks, low levels of inequality, social traditions of conflict resolution through public debate, enabling legal frameworks and pro-poor political parties. While some studies have examined the implications of unfavourable contextual factors and the role of different enabling conditions in overcoming them,[2] few have attempted an examination of the nature and potential of participatory spaces in settings where few of these conditions are present, or even none. Potentially adverse settings include countries and regions with fragmented societies, high levels of inequality, restrictive legal frameworks, a highly authoritarian political culture and a history of armed conflict. All of these conditions apply to Angola.

In such settings, it is common to find the (often unspoken but nonetheless powerful) assumption that the micro-level changes that may lead to 'empowered participatory governance' are not even worth looking for, since local-level participation is largely meaningless without governance reforms focusing on macro-level political institutions. As a country emerging from one of the world's longest-running and most destructive civil wars, Angola is a prime target for what Llamazares calls the 'emerging consensus' of the 'growing international post-war peacebuilding community', according to whose prescriptions 'the political-constitutional deficit during the initial phase is addressed by transitional governing measures, in the medium term by the organizing of a crucial second election, and finally the consolidation of good governance and civil society' (2005: 15). Thus, micro-level democratization is relegated in the dominant peace-building discourse to the 'final' stage of democratic reconstruction, leading to neglect of the potentially vital contribution which it may make to ensuring the depth and durability of the transition to peace.

This discourse contrasts with the evidence that donor-sponsored proliferation of participation spaces is increasingly extending to post-conflict societies such as Angola. Although humanitarian relief, demobilization support and infrastructure-rehabilitation assistance continue to dominate aid portfolios in Angola, donor interventions to promote the consolidation of good governance and civil society have mushroomed since the end of the war. This shift has occurred despite the fact that the transitional governing measures and elections prescribed by the dominant peace-building discourse are either absent or uncertain.[3] The new spaces, which include networks of groups mobilized for collective action and fora for citizen–state engagement, are thus emerging in a context where the democratic 'rules of the game' have yet to be clearly established. This lack of clarity is a common feature of countries in post-conflict and/or post-authoritarian transition, but it is one whose implications are often given insufficient consideration by both academics and donors.

Donor 'democracy-building' interventions in Angola have largely followed the logic described for Africa in general by Robinson and Friedman (2005), who draw attention to the shift in priorities since the 1990s from political conditionality based on elections towards investment in civil society as a catalyst of democratization. The World Bank, for example, describes one of the aims of its funding for the Fundo de Apoio Social (FAS) social fund programme as being 'to support a governance system in which local governments and communities may gradually become mutually accountable' (World Bank 2004: 1), and the UK Department for International Development (DFID) Angola strategy aims to promote 'a political system which allows all people to influence state policy and practice' by supporting 'spaces for dialogue' and 'state citizen engagement' (Jobes 2004: 2). Donors are thus promoting both citizen mobilization and new democratic spaces in Angola in terms that are virtually identical to those used in far less adverse contexts.

In addition to institutional fluidity and lack of clarity on the democratic 'rules of the game', a further factor of transitional contexts such as Angola's is the identities of the institutions that are actually creating 'new democratic spaces'. While the shift in discourse in recent years towards a focus on participation in governance rather than participation in projects (Gaventa and Valderrama 1999) has generated an assumption that today's participation spaces are created by governments rather than NGOs, it is important to remember that where government has been unable or unwilling to introduce the necessary reforms, NGOs continue to play a key role in the creation of participation spaces. While some NGOs have an explicit 'participatory governance' agenda, others may view these spaces above all as sites for the mobilization of local resources for service provision. Even where this is the case, some of the spaces created can come to play a governance role – and thus have wider political significance – despite their origins outside conventional governance-reform processes.

The nature of this role, and its precise implications for processes of democratization, will ultimately be shaped by the complex interplay between the interests and agendas of government, donors, NGOs and citizen groups both at the policy level and on the ground. The scope for agency is broadest where the balance of power does not overwhelmingly favour one group; at the national level in Angola, for example, while oil and diamond revenues ensure that the government is far less donor-dependent than those of many other poor African states, the need for donors' support in accessing international credit markets ensures that it is not completely insulated from the pressure they may seek to apply (DFID 2005a: 15). At the grassroots level, international NGOs' ability to mobilize financial and technical resources interacts with the political power of local government representatives and the capacity of citizens to exploit new opportunities to further their individual or collective political and livelihood strategies. This capacity for agency on the part of some grassroots actors is further increased when the context – as in Angola – is one of unclear and shifting institutional roles and rules.

Angola: A Changing Social and Political Context

Recent and uncertain democracy

The history of the state in Angola has been marked by strong control over society, centralization and authoritarian practices. After a long period of colonial rule by Portugal, which had itself been ruled by a dictatorship since 1926, Independence was proclaimed in 1975 by the Movimento Popular pela Libertação de Angola (MPLA), one of the three Angolan liberation movements. This political movement was influenced by Marxist–Leninist ideals and founded a strong one-party state, which was highly centralized and made no allowance for autonomy on the part of organized social groups and political organizations.

Although the periods just before and after independence saw the emergence and significant activity of different civic and political organizations, the Angolan government gradually imposed control over this social space (Pestana 2003). The need for a strong state was justified by the government and perceived by part of society as necessary to confront increasing threats, both external, related to the cold war at the time and the political geography of Southern Africa,[4] and internal, linked mostly to conflicting political visions and ideologies of Angolan political elites (Hodges 2002).[5] With the exception of brief periods of peace just after Independence and following peace agreements in the 1990s, Angola lived at war until 2002.

In 1991, with the end of the cold war, under the weight of a growing economic crisis and following the signature of the Bicesse Peace Agreement with União Nacional para a Independência Total de Angola (UNITA), the Angolan government abandoned all references to Marxist–Leninist ideology and changed the country's constitution, allowing for the institution of a multi-party political system and a formally democratic state. These changes allowed multi-party elections to be held in 1992, but, after UNITA refused to accept the outcome of these elections, civil war broke out again. The war ended in 2002 with the military defeat of UNITA. As no other political force emerged during the 1990s there is currently no real opposition to the MPLA.

While the current strong position of the MPLA would allow those in power to maintain the political status quo, it is undeniable that Angola is changing. Strategies are being developed for macroeconomic recovery and infrastructure reconstruction, a Poverty Reduction Strategy Paper (PRSP) has been produced, and legislation has been passed to provide for national parliamentary and presidential elections in 2006. New policy frameworks are being discussed, albeit largely within a closed circle of policymakers. These include provision for the decentralization of state administration, which could potentially play a crucial role in legitimating and institutionalizing new democratic spaces at the local level. However, the current decentralization process has for the moment only reached provincial level, where it has led to greater concentration of power in the hands of Provincial Governors, who thus have scope to behave as 'decentralized despots' (see Mamdani 1996). The final shape of provisions for decentralization to the municipal and *comuna* (sub-municipal) level remains unclear, but the government's formal recognition that such provisions are on its agenda has created political space for experimentation with local participation initiatives in a number of municipalities around the country.[6]

At the same time, the easing of political repression and media censorship – above all in the capital, Luanda – has increased the scope for civic associations' advocacy initiatives and the visibility of alternative perspectives on policy issues. Ordinary Angolans are making plans to (re)build their lives, and new actors are beginning to emerge, mobilizing local and donor resources for service provision and occupying the emerging spaces outside the institutions of 'formal democracy' that provide some opportunities for citizen voice and the beginnings of democratic debate.

Luanda: between the modern capital and the musseques

The population of Luanda has grown hugely since independence, as a result of migration linked to the return of Angolan refugees from the former Zaire (now Democratic Republic of Congo), the collapse of the rural economy, and the war. Most of these new residents settled in the peri-urban areas, increasing the population density of Luanda's *musseques*, the informal settlements surrounding the formal 'cement city' and occupied by the poorer inhabitants of the capital. No one really knows how many people live in the city, but current estimates suggest a total population of over 4 million, between two-thirds and three-quarters of whom may live in the *musseques*. This population growth has not been accompanied by expansion of the supply of public services, leaving most *musseque* residents largely dependent on self-provisioning. The pressures faced by poor households are enormous, and, given the decline in the formal private sector and the low salaries in the public sector, most households depend on the informal sector to survive.

The consequences of many years of neglect and little or no investment are evident even in the 'cement city': it has crumbling infrastructure, bad roads and piles of uncollected rubbish. After the end of the war, the authorities seem to have decided that this situation was no longer tolerable, but their approach to resolving Luanda's huge problems demonstrated the Angolan government's continued reliance on centralized, command-and-control approaches. In 2004, the president dismissed the provincial government and nominated a group of three officials (known as the *troïka*) to administer the capital. They were tasked with solving Luanda's multiplicity of problems within a six-month mandate. This decision was highly controversial: though this commitment to decisive intervention was welcomed by many, these three officials were known to have an authoritarian governing style. After its mandate was renewed by another six months, the *troïka* was dissolved at the end of 2004 and Luanda's provincial government was re-established. The capital's problems remain as complex and deeply rooted as ever.

Despite this erratic approach to its governance, Luanda is chang-ing. Major road works and construction of new residential areas are under way. However, there seems to be no clear urban policy. Recent violent evictions in *musseques* and the dismantling of street markets where informal traders operate seem to indicate that the vision underlying the current changes points to (re)building a modern city where the *musseque* is seen as marginal. The *musseques* are perceived by many Angolan policymakers and part of the elite as a temporary phenomenon whose huge growth was due to the war and whose size will gradually decline with the return of war-displaced people to their areas of origin, the development of the country and the growth of the modern city. However, the *musseques* continue to grow in the post-war period largely due to in-city migration and natural growth (Development Workshop 2003).

Collective Action and Participation Spaces in Luanda's *Musseques*

Existing participation spaces

Luanda's *musseques* are generally heterogeneous, as their population has grown as a result of massive war-associated migration, which at different moments involved people from a wide variety of regions in the country, including both rural and urban areas. Such hetero-geneity combines with very harsh living conditions to hinder the establishment of extensive social networks (Robson and Roque 2001). In this environment, churches provide one of the important spaces where people can meet, socialize, be integrated into social networks and participate in organized activities for the benefit of the church or particular social groups.

Small informal mutual aid groups also exist in the *musseques*. In most cases these groups are composed of friends or people who know each other very well. One of the most common types of group is known in Luanda as *kixikila,* where a system of reciprocal loaning and pooled savings brings together a few individuals. Many micro-finance systems set up by NGOs seek to draw upon social relationships constructed within these networks. At a slightly larger scale, some local organized groups have been promoted by national or international NGOs, frequently with a view to helping manage specific social services (water, schools, etc.). Very often the vision put forward by NGOs for the creation of these groups also emphasizes the strengthening of local institutions such as *kixikila*, and the promotion of local capacity for mutual aid.

After the new Constitution of 1991 entrenched a right to freedom of association, numerous independent associations or micro-NGOs were created, many of them based in the *musseques*. Functioning principally as 'non-profit social enterprises' driven by 'public service contracting' (Sogge and Thaw 2003: 11), most of these organizations are highly dependent on external donor funding and do not in general claim to represent particular social groups. In the *musseques*, they are often headed by relatively well-educated men, many of whom were previously employed in the formal sector and often play a leadership role in their communities. However, little is known about the internal practices of these organizations and their relationships with the communities with which they work.

Finally, the Comissões de Moradores (CMs, literally 'residents' committees') theoretically represent a participation space for *musseque* residents. Created by the government after independence, CMs are supposed to represent the residents of a certain area in dealings with the local administration. In practice, CM members have often been appointed by local administrators with little or no consultation. In most cases, CM members perceive themselves, and are perceived by residents, as serving the interests of the administration. Their status and role in the neighbourhoods have nevertheless changed over time. They lost much of their controlling power with political liberalization, and currently their role in the *musseques* is mostly related to land use allocation and mediation of minor neighbourhood conflicts. However, their strong relationship with the administration continues, and in many cases they represent a resource on which the holders of political power can draw for mobilization in the *musseques*, above all in the run-up to elections.

LUPP's vision for mobilization and participation spaces

The Luanda Urban Poverty Programme (LUPP), which began in 1999, has projects located in *musseques* spread over four different municipalities: Kilamba Kiaxi, Cazenga, Sambizanga and Cacuaco. LUPP is one of the few development programmes working in Angolan peri-urban areas, as most of the NGOs and development agencies have concentrated their operations in rural zones, in line with the donors' emphasis on relief and reconstruction work in those areas most directly affected by the war. While the programme initially prioritized poverty reduction through livelihoods support and development of infrastructure for service delivery, it has since 2003 changed its scope. Although LUPP continues working on livelihoods and service delivery, it increasingly seeks to draw upon its projects' accumulated experience to influence policy and practice for urban development and poverty reduction in Luanda. In 2005, a review of the programme emphasized its increasing focus on 'strategic goals of empowerment and good governance through participatory development' (DFID 2005b: 3).

In line with this change in emphasis, a significant share of LUPP's effort has been channelled into fostering social organization in the *musseques*, and facilitating engagement between local organized groups and state institutions. LUPP has thus become a key player in encouraging the emergence of a variety of local groupings and 'new democratic spaces' in the *musseques*. While many of these groups are intended to develop the capacity to provide and manage services for *musseque* residents, they are also expected to represent local communities in dealing with state institutions, to defend their rights and to promote broader social change towards a more equitable, democratic and tolerant society. By encouraging greater participation of *musseque* residents in the policy realm, LUPP has thus introduced a more political dimension to the programme's action and given it a democracy-building agenda, expressed in LUPP documents as emphasizing 'participatory governance' and the promotion of 'constructive engagement between government and civil society' (Baskin 2003: 3).

Participation in the musseques: two NGO-initiated experiences

Among the groups and spaces created and/or supported by LUPP are local associations, alliances of local NGOs, organized community groups for delivery of services such as water, childcare and micro-finance, local groups for urban micro-planning and municipal fora and councils for local development. Our analysis here focuses on two specific experiences: the process of federation of local Water Committees to create Associations of Water Committees (ACAs); and the process of social and political mobilization in Kilamba

Kiaxi municipality that led to the constitution of the Kilamba Kiaxi Development Forum (KKDF). The KKDF represents one of the few experiences in Angola of a local municipal forum bringing together representatives of the administration, members of various local organizations and individual residents. ACAs provide an example of a membership-based organization engaging with the state on specific issues, while also sharing many of the features of local civic organizations such as those that take part in the KKDF.

The Associations of Water Committees (ACAs)

Water distribution is one of the areas on which LUPP has been focusing since it started, as access to water has been a source of great difficulty for residents in many of Luanda's *musseques*. In order to improve water management LUPP has created Water Committees: neighbourhood-based organized groups with two members elected by local residents to manage water standposts. Their duties include organizing water distribution and collecting payment for water from residents, keeping the area clean and carrying out maintenance of the standpost.

In response to the difficulties experienced by the Water Committees in dealing with state institutions, in particular the Provincial Water Company (EPAL) and the local administration, LUPP and the most active members of the Water Committees decided to federate the committees in order to increase their negotiating power. Two Associations of Water Committees (ACAs) were then created with support from LUPP. These ACAs have been legally registered and have formal democratic structures and rules, including an elected leadership, an Executive Body and provision for regular general assemblies.

However, ACAs have also been expected to take on functions that go beyond representation: they have been charged with monitoring and supervising the Water Committees. As a result, ACAs' Executive Bodies are now overseeing the whole process involved in local water distribution: they direct the establishment of new standposts, organize and lead the constitution of new Water Committees, monitor the functioning of the standposts, collect payments from the Water Committees and distribute the money between the different actors involved (Water Committees, ACAs, local administration and EPAL). In their representational role, ACAs have become the interface between Water Committees and the authorities: they have now been recognized by both the local administration and EPAL as the single interlocutor for water-related matters in their neighbourhoods.

In addition, in line with LUPP's civil society-building vision for locally organized groups, ACAs have been encouraged by the programme to become local development actors, receiving training in project design, leadership and management. ACAs themselves are also seeking to widen their remit beyond water-related matters. They have begun to develop activities in other areas such as waste collection, health and civic education, and have developed project proposals to submit to other aid donors. ACAs have also joined NGO alliances facilitated by LUPP, and some of their members take part in discussions on urban development and policy at the local level. In reality, ACAs seem to be seeking to become what the members of their Executive Bodies perceive as 'a local NGO': a group of people with leadership capacity, with the desire to help bring about improvements in their neighbourhoods, and with the skills to adopt and use the discourse and methodological tools of the 'development industry' to access wider social contacts, training, funds and new livelihood opportunities.

Local organization in Kilamba Kiaxi: residents' associations, local NGOs and the Kilamba Kiaxi Development Forum (KKDF)

The beginnings of the KKDF The embryo of the Kilamba Kiaxi Development Forum was a Water and Sanitation Forum created by LUPP that included programme staff, EPAL and other organizations involved in water distribution in the municipality. However, the Kilamba Kiaxi municipal administration did not take part in that forum. Wishing to move beyond water and sanitation issues and acknowledging the importance of the municipal government in local development, LUPP created the KKDF in 2001. The forum was intended by the Programme to provide a place where different social and development actors could meet to discuss, coordinate and integrate local development issues and activities as well as help to build a culture of engagement between the community and the government. Although the local administration was formally part of KKDF and the forum was jointly launched by LUPP and the administration, its initial participation was hesitant.

According to LUPP's vision during the initial stages of the process, it was important to organize Kilamba Kiaxi's communities to contest the official vision for future urban development – one that excluded the *musseques* and their population. It was seen as necessary to organize local residents so that they could construct a common voice to deal with the authorities. This process centred on two major activities: the creation of area-based residents' organizations and the enhancement of local NGOs' role in the municipality. The attitude of the Kilamba Kiaxi municipal administration reflected an Angolan tradition of state administration in which civil servants feel accountable above all to the higher levels of the state hierarchy and very little to those to whom they are supposed to provide services. There is also evidence that local administrators tend to avoid open dialogue with local residents for fear of being confronted with problems for which they lack the technical capacity, the financial means or the political will to resolve. The country was also still at war in 2001 and the government did not trust independent political (or potentially political) initiatives.

Organizing local residents: the creation of ODAs The Area-Based Development Organizations (Organizações para o Desenvolvimento das Áreas, ODAs) were created to articulate and represent what LUPP described as the 'genuine vision' of the residents of a particular geographical area. As a result, they were purposefully constituted as parallel structures to the Comissões de Moradores. The CMs were seen as being primarily at the service of the administration and the MPLA and, consequently, as unaccountable to local residents. The constitution of ODAs was facilitated using LUPP's own methodology and promoted at the initial stage the inclusion of different social groups within a specific geographical area (women, men, children, disabled people, etc.), who subsequently elected local leaders to form the ODAs. An ODA has an average of thirty members, two-thirds of whom are men. The members of the organization's elected leadership body are intended to serve as the representatives of a specific geographical constituency, with the ability to present and defend their constituents' vision and plan in fora such as the KKDF.

ODAs received training from LUPP that was especially oriented towards the organization of urban services. There are approximately forty ODAs in Kilamba Kiaxi, twenty of which are considered by LUPP to be active. As intended by LUPP, the process for the creation of new ODAs was handed over to existing ODAs that had already been trained for this purpose: the expectation was that this process would generate a 'local urban movement'.

Reinforcing the role of local NGOs As in other neighbourhoods in Luanda, several local NGOs already existed in Kilamba Kiaxi Municipality. Many of these organizations were formally constituted as membership-based organizations, but in reality were barely active. As noted earlier, these organizations tend to function as social service contractors and are strongly dependent on donor funding. In line with its objective of enhancing local organizations' role in the municipality, LUPP trained many of these NGOs in urban development issues and tools for development interventions (project design and management, gender analysis, etc.). These NGOs are often involved in the implementation of activities that have been prioritized by ODAs and funded by LUPP.

In addition, following the same logic as with the Water Committees and ACAs, LUPP facilitated the creation of a local NGO Alliance in order to strengthen their voice when dealing with official authorities and reinforce their capacity for intervention in the municipality. As absence of independent financial resources constitutes a major obstacle to the continued existence of such organizations, LUPP funded a small computer services centre to be managed by the Alliance, which was intended to generate resources for its activities.

Local organizations and the KKDF today: building a stronger engagement with the state

After almost four years of existence, the process of local organization and mobilization in Kilamba Kiaxi has evolved. One of the major changes is the role currently played by the municipal administration. Although the municipal administration's engagement with the forum was initially hesitant, the initiative mobilized a massive level of participation from the local population and organizations. The process also attracted a few prominent Angolan politicians belonging to the government and MPLA, who informally approved the initiative and gave it some external legitimacy. It is important to note that the formal presence of decentralization on the Angolan policy agenda since 2000 gave room for these politicians to be openly supportive of the forum. LUPP's attitude in relation to the municipal administration also changed, leading one of their managers to state that '[while LUPP had] focused considerable energies in building capacity through local NGOs and [ODAs] it soon became apparent that for an effective participatory process to take root strong local government intervention was required' (Baskin 2003: 7).

Finally, with the end of the war in February 2002, the conditions were created for a rapprochement between local organizations and LUPP, on the one hand, and the municipal administration, on the other. A stronger participation of the local administration in the process gave greater legitimacy to the KKDF and reinforced its purpose of providing a space for engagement between Kilamba Kiaxi residents, their representatives and the municipal authorities. At the time, this was an innovative experience in a political environment where local authorities are not generally used to dialoguing with local residents.

Currently, KKDF sessions are chaired by the municipal administrator. Discussions at the forum are based on issues brought in by local NGOs and residents' representatives, in particular ODAs. The forum is also developing its organizational structure and becoming institutionalized: it has established two technical committees composed of members of the administration and leaders of local organizations such as the NGO Alliance and churches. These committees are still learning to engage with and propose solutions to complex urban management problems. They are also faced with a lack of financial support to implement their decisions. LUPP continues to play a major part in organizing the forum and fostering the process in general.

The KKDF is intended to provide the site for the production of a municipal development plan, but, in the absence of financial resources to formulate it and implement recommendations, it continues to function principally as a discussion space rather than a decision-making body. A municipal fund, bringing together small grants from NGOs and other donors, has been created with a board including representatives of LUPP, the municipal administration and the ODAs. However, these are still small-scale resources that do not include government funds held at the provincial level, and cannot fund the full implementation of a municipal development plan. Despite these limitations, the KKDF experience has become widely known, and it is credited with ensuring that Kilamba Kiaxi was selected to be one of the few municipalities to implement the Angolan municipal decentralization pilot project currently being prepared by the government with UNDP and World Bank support.

Participation and Change:
The Expected and the Unexpected

From community development to democracy-building?

LUPP's founding objective was to ensure improved livelihoods and access to services for marginalized peri-urban communities in Luanda, and this has indeed been one of the major results of its activities. This has been achieved through a strategy involving the creation or reinforcement of local organizations. The emergence of ACAs, for example, has allowed LUPP to hand over the coordination of the different Water Committees and the supervision of their activities to a local collective actor, a process that has gone hand in hand with improved local water management. The activities of some ODAs have also generated improvements in service delivery: for example, the existence of an ODA in the local market has had a significant impact on the market's rubbish collection and sanitation. The coordination through the KKDF of ODAs, NGOs and other local actors such as churches has also helped raise resources in the municipality to build and manage some new local schools.

Beyond their immediate impacts on services, there is evidence that LUPP's activities are also contributing to the broader democracy-building or 'participatory governance' agenda that the programme has come to espouse. Here, though, its impact is often manifested in unexpected ways. One example is the increasingly visible presence in LUPP-created spaces of members of the CMs – institutions initially regarded by parts of the programme (notably the ODA-based mobilization project in Kilamba Kiaxi) with suspicion and even hostility. That these spaces have come to be perceived as settings where meaningful things happen is signalled by the migration of CM members not only to the Water Committees and ACAs, but also to the ODAs, which initially set out to exclude them. The presence of CM members does not necessarily mean that ODAs and Water Committees have imported the hierarchical relationship that CMs have in relation to the local administration. There are signs that the CMs themselves are beginning to change, with some leaders acquiring a reputation as good representatives of residents' views and demonstrating significant mobilization power. A wider pattern seems to be emerging of leaders of the CMs trying to position themselves in a changing political environment.

More broadly, the new spaces promoted by LUPP have provided opportunities for citizens to deliberate on issues of common concern, some of which are the focus of ongoing policy debate. As Robinson and Friedman point out, 'even where they do not exert policy influence, the role of civil society in providing citizens with an independent sphere of association in which they can participate and deliberate priorities is an important democratic function in its own right' (2005: 29). It may be ACAs' leaders rather than their members who enjoy greater proximity to state institutions, but previously this open access to information and opportunity for influence was available to no citizens at all. KKDF meetings may fall short of the ideal of deliberative democracy – women are present but largely silent, discussions are dominated by the leaders of better-established organizations, and there are no mechanisms to ensure that the decisions taken are actually implemented – but the forum nevertheless provides a space where a larger number and much greater diversity of people can gain a voice in the definition of local priorities than was the case with any pre-existing institution.

Towards broader institutional change?

For the KKDF, however, if financial resources are not available for the design of a full Municipal Development Plan and the implementation of activities that result in clear improvements in Kilamba Kiaxi, there is a risk that the forum will lead to frustration, disenchantment and demobilization. Much depends on the future of the decentralization project for which Kilamba Kiaxi has been selected as a pilot site. However, the future of the decentralization process remains unclear and there are no indications that it will move forward before the elections in 2006. A recent World Bank document notes that, despite some promising signs, 'there are many challenges ahead to ensure that a sound institutional basis as well as an effective fiscal framework and legislation exist for decentralization and local development' (World Bank 2004: 5). The extent to which Kilamba Kiaxi can serve as a model for other municipalities in Angola depends, in turn, on whether and how the pilot project will feed into the nationwide decentralization process.[7]

The contradictions and impasses created by the stalling of the national decentralization process are evident in other ways in Kilamba Kiaxi. In particular, the lack of clarity over the emerging rules of the game has provided scope for more explicit divergence between the visions of LUPP and the municipal administration over the KKDF's future institutional role. While LUPP expects the forum to provide a space for construction of 'a shared vision and consensus with regard to future growth' (Baskins 2003: 9) and a potential site for construction of a participatory Municipal Development Plan, at a forum meeting held in June 2005 the municipal administrator identified the KKDF as the place to discuss 'micro-issues' and 'community problems', whereas 'macro-issues of the municipality' were to be discussed in the municipal council. As defined in the Angolan legislation, municipal councils are classic 'invited spaces': they are meetings of the municipal government which may be attended by specific individuals and organizations at the invitation of the Administrator 'when he judges this to be necessary' (República de Angola 1999). Without the legitimacy of a decentralization policy framework which endorses the forum model, there is thus the risk that the KKDF will be seen as a space to discuss what may be perceived as 'minor issues' – such as waste collection or neighbourhood security – while 'important projects' requiring significant investment are discussed in the municipal council.

Changing state–citizen relations?

In Kilamba Kiaxi, although political support from the local administrator does currently exist, the lack of financial resources and a legal framework to give legitimacy to the process and establish new rules and procedures has resulted in an absence of incentives for civil servants in the local administration to change their attitudes and behaviour. LUPP staff describe a wide gap between the expectations of local organizations and residents who (partly as a result of training and support from the programme) demand more participatory and responsive governance, and the response from local administration officials. The quality of service delivery in the administration remains little improved, and officials largely continue to maintain the same unaccountable and sometimes dismissive treatment of local residents.

Pressure for change may, however, be emerging from below. In addition to their role in improving service delivery, the variety of organizations created or encouraged by LUPP have also provided a wide range of social spaces where people can meet and discuss matters relating to their neighbourhood, in a context where such spaces were previously almost non-existent. This seems, in turn, to be contributing to a (still tentative but nonetheless significant) growth of autonomous action by citizens seeking to claim their rights, with members of LUPP-supported groups approaching local authorities to complain of abusive behaviour by officials or question decisions that harm their livelihoods, such as market closures.

New leaders and new forms of leadership?

These new local organizational structures have also allowed for the mushrooming of a range of new leaders in the *musseques*: a set of people who have initiative, who wish to take on responsibilities and to be active in the public sphere. Most of the leaders of the NGO Alliances, ACAs and ODAs are men, belong to the relatively privileged *musseque* middle class, are reasonably well-educated and have some command of 'policy-speak'. Many were already perceived as leaders in their communities. What these new organizational structures have provided is a public sphere where they can express themselves and extend their influence beyond their own immediate localities.

While the strengthening of leadership can be an extremely valuable asset in building local organizations, the impact on broader processes of democratization depends on the quality of this leadership. Authoritarian leadership styles are not likely to ensure that organizations express the views of their constituents. Many of the organizations promoted by LUPP are membership-based organizations with the potential to express the voice of a significant number of people and thereby to play an important role in the democratization of political life. A key element in fulfilling this role involves developing internal democratic practices (Robinson and Friedman 2005), including robust accountability mechanisms – especially in a country such as Angola, with its long history of leadership models portraying people in power as bearers of rights without obligations.

Internal accountability mechanisms are not always strong in LUPP-supported groups. The different functions assumed by the ACAs, for example, seem to be generating contradictions in their relationship with their constituencies. ACAs are formally accountable to a General Assembly of the Water Committees they represent, whose members are in turn accountable to the local residents of specific areas and are subject to re-election every year. However, ACAs are also expected to supervise the Water Committees, inverting their accountability relations. In practice, the Committees and their membership base have little power to hold ACAs accountable, as is evidenced by one ACA's expressed intention to retain Water Committee representatives who had been voted out by their own neighbourhood assemblies. This decision appears to have been motivated by the desire to become a consolidated organization, with a stable membership.

New directions for local organizations?

The incident described above reflects an apparent mutation in ACAs' missions, from 'representative associations' to 'local NGOs' whose primary function is service delivery in a wide range of sectors. This requires ACAs to become independent from their membership base, breaking the chain of accountability initially established to support their representative function and placing in question the legitimacy of their supervisory function. The scope for such 'mutations' derives both from the new and experimental nature of the structures promoted by LUPP and from the wider lack of clarity on organizational models and political/institutional rules of the game that characterizes Angola's confused and hesitant democratic transition. While this may lead local organizations away from the institutional roles originally envisaged for them, it demonstrates the importance of the agency exercised by such grassroots groups as they pursue evolving agendas and respond to the opportunities and constraints presented by the context in which they are operating.

Mutation into a 'non-profit social enterprise' type of organization is a path that may be chosen by many membership-based organizations – including structures such as ODAs – in a social context like Angola's where livelihood opportunities for people living in the *musseques* are scarce and working on service delivery combines contributing to the community and gaining political capital with the possibility of generating an income. While this type of organization can undoubtedly make a positive contribution to their communities, their political role in building democracy in Angola will depend on the extent to which their activities are grounded on strong internal democratic practices – and the scope for establishing alternative mechanisms to fulfil the representative roles which they may be leaving behind.

Lessons and Implications

The literature on empowered participatory governance assumes that while contexts may be favourable or unfavourable, they are largely static. The rules of the political game have already crystallized, and changes arise from the emergence of new actors (left political parties, social movements) rather than any fluidity or indefinition in the system itself. In countries immersed in the messy transitions that characterize most post-authoritarian and/or post-conflict settings, this assumption does not apply. This makes it all the more important to avoid generalizations and seek to understand the specific social and political dynamics of transitional contexts and their implications for emerging 'new democratic spaces'. As a recent review of post-conflict governance interventions notes, 'understanding, and intervening in, the dynamics of states where all is not well, where the social and institutional fabric has been shredded and violence has erupted, call for a careful combination of the general (and generalizable) and the situation-specific' (Brinkerhoff 2005: 12).

Angola is currently engaged in just such a complex transition, characterized by the coexistence of authoritarian political practice and a command-and-control bureaucracy with a formally democratic institutional framework, and of a heavily centralized political culture with the emergence of a host of new local political actors and spaces. The evidence from Luanda suggests that contexts where the political and institutional rules are unclear, inappropriate, or both, encourage new actors and spaces to mutate as they develop. This may occasionally have negative consequences – such as the hijacking of plural spaces by narrow interests or the reproduction of authoritarian leadership styles – but it also permits adaptation that enables these structures to respond to the demands and opportunities of their particular contexts in ways which may be more effective than preprogrammed models. The shifting roles that accompany such processes of adaptation may be confusing and sometimes contradictory, but they are also part of a vitally necessary process of democratic experimentation. The outcomes of this process will be crucially determined by the agency of a multiplicity of actors – often operating at cross-purposes – at both policy and grassroots levels. The dominant post-conflict peace-building discourse assumes a neatly sequential model of top-down transformation, in which micro-level democratization is relegated to the final stage. The evidence from Luanda suggests that while consolidating an enabling macro-framework (whether for decentralization or for elections) is essential, in practice democratization does not wait for this framework to be in place. Instead, whatever emerging spaces exist will provide an outlet for long-repressed political energy. With this in mind, we argue for recognition of the reality that establishing rules that are both locally appropriate and politically legitimate will necessarily require a long and messy period of negotiation between old and emerging actors in both old and emerging spaces. Establishing links between local experimentation in 'new democratic spaces' and macro-level processes of political change is a fundamental element in ensuring that such messy transitions are ultimately meaningful and successful.

NGOs, as sponsors of new spaces and providers of resources that new actors can use to build a social and political base, potentially play a key role in this process. Given the relative significance of their inputs in a very resource-scarce context, NGO projects such as those discussed in this chapter are *de facto* governance interventions whether or not they play explicit attention to the nature of relationships with the state and the political process. NGOs' approach to mobilization and institutional design therefore needs to move beyond conventional concerns, and begin to focus on the wider political effects of interventions as much as on their immediate poverty-reduction impact. Our suggestion is that a key starting point for this process is an emphasis on the role of accountability in new structures. Whether in holding the state and other powerful actors (including NGOs themselves) to account, or in developing more transparent and accountable leadership practices within the institutions themselves, this will help to bridge the gap between ad hoc, project-based interventions and wider processes of social and political democratization.

Notes

This chapter is based on the authors' work in Angola and elsewhere over a number of years, but draws specifically on a series of consultancy studies carried out between September 2003 and December 2004 for the Luanda Urban Poverty Programme (LUPP), a joint initiative of Save the Children UK (SCUK), CARE and Development Workshop (DW) in partnership with One World Action (OWA), funded by the UK Department for International Development (DFID). We are very grateful to everyone from the communities and the project teams who contributed their reflections, and to LUPP and DFID for their permission to use the material on which part of this chapter draws. In particular we would like to thank Kate Ashton, Allan Cain, Ken Caplan, Susan Grant, Katja Jobes, Martin Johnston, Daniel Miji, Fernando Pacheco and our Citizenship DRC 'Spaces for Change' group colleagues for thoughtful comments on earlier drafts of this chapter.

1. Angola is currently the second largest oil producer in Africa (after Nigeria), with a production of 900,000 barrels per day (expected to reach 2.2 million barrels by 2008); in 2000 the country accounted for 15 per cent of the world's diamond production (Hodges 2004). However, the country's estimated life expectancy at birth is 7 per cent below the average for sub-Saharan African countries and its estimated adult illiteracy rate is 50.6 per cent higher (Republic of Angola 2003).

2. This is the case, for example, with the literature on unfavourable contextual factors and enabling conditions in Brazil, discussed in Coelho et al. 2002.

3. Attempts to form a national unity government were abandoned after the failure of peace accords during the 1990s, while local, parliamentary and presidential elections have been repeatedly postponed and are now due to take place in 2006 (see below).

4. Angola was at war with apartheid South Africa until 1990.

5. These were mainly divided along the three principal liberation movements: MPLA, UNITA and FNLA (Frente Nacional para a Libertação de Angola).

6. The authors would like to thank Fernando Pacheco for his insights into the decentralization process in Angola.

7. LUPP has recognized the importance of this issue, and is currently seeking to implement an influencing strategy which links its micro-level interventions with broader policy debates.

References

Brinkerhoff, D. (2005) 'Rebuilding governance in failed states and post-conflict societies: core concepts and cross-cutting themes', *Public Administration and Development* 25(1): 3–14.

Coelho, V.S., I.A. de Andrade and M. Cifuentes (2002) 'Deliberative fora and the democratisation of social policies in Brazil', *IDS Bulletin* 33(2).

Cornwall, A. (2004) 'New democratic spaces? The politics and dynamics of institutionalised participation' *IDS Bulletin* 33(2).

DFID (Department for International Development) (2005a) *Why We Need To Work More Effectively in Fragile States*, London: DFID.

DFID (Department for International Development) (2005b) *Luanda Urban Poverty Programme II Output to Purpose Review Report*, London: DFID, June, mimeo.

Development Workshop & Centre for Environment and Human Settlements (2003), 'The opportunity and constraints of appropriate urban land management for economic and social development in Angola', Luanda.

Fung, A., and E.O. Wright (2003) *Deepening Democracy: Institutional Innovations in Empowered Participatory Governance*, London: Verso.

Gaventa, J., and C. Valderrama (1999) 'Strengthening participation in local governance', background note prepared for Institute of Development Studies workshop, University of Sussex, Falmer, June.

Hodges, T. (2002) *Angola – Do Afro-Stalinismo ao Capitalismo Selvagem*, Lisbon: Principia.

Hodges, T. (2004) 'The role of resource management in building sustainable peace', in G. Meijer, ed., *From Military Peace to Social Justice? The Angolan Peace Process*, Accord Series, No. 15, London: Conciliation Resources.

Jobes, K. (2004) 'DFID's Angola Strategy', seminar presentation at Institute of Development Studies, University of Sussex, Falmer, November.

Llamazares, M. (2005) 'Post-war peacebuilding reviewed: a critical exploration of generic approaches to post-war reconstruction', *CCR Working Paper* 14.

Mamdani, M. (1996) *Citizens and Subjects; Contemporary Africa and the Legacy of Late Colonialism*, Princeton: Princeton University Press.

Pestana, N. (2003) 'As dinâmicas da sociedade civil em Angola', *CEA–ISCTE Occasional Paper* 7.

Sogge, D., and D. Thaw (2003) 'Ibis programming and civil society support – review report', Luanda: Ibis.

Republic of Angola (1999) *Decreto-Lei No. 17/9,* Diário da República, I Série 44, 29 October.

Republic of Angola (2003) *Estratégia de combate à pobreza – reinserção social, reabilitação e reconstrução e estabilização económica*, Ministry of Urban Planning, Luanda.

Robinson, M. and S. Friedman (2005) 'Civil society, democratisation and foreign aid in Africa', IDS Discussion Paper No. 383.

Baskin, J. (2003) 'Working towards good governance – a discussion paper', draft, Luanda: The LURE Project, June.

Robson, P., and S. Roque (2001) 'Here in the city there is nothing left over for lending a hand', *Development Workshop Occasional Paper* 2, Guelph.

UNDP (United Nations Development Programme) (2004) *Human Development Report 2004: Cultural Liberty in Today's Diverse World*, New York: UNDP.

World Bank (2004) 'Aide Mémoire: Third Social Action Fund Project (FAS III) 2nd Implementation Support Mission', draft, Washington DC: World Bank, December.

Citizen Participation in South Africa: Land Struggles and HIV/AIDS Activism

Bettina von Lieres

In recent years new democratic spaces for citizen participation have proliferated in South Africa. These range from 'invited' spaces created by the government to spaces created by poor people themselves. Whereas the former are often set up in response to legal guarantees for citizen participation, the latter are initiated in response to the failure of the government to deliver services or fulfil promises, and to include citizens in decision-making. These grassroots initiatives create new interfaces between marginalized people and the institutions that affect their lives, particularly those of the state, and it is on these initiatives that I focus. This chapter discusses two cases of grassroots citizenship engagement in South Africa's health and land sectors: the AIDS/HIV Treatment Action Campaign (TAC), and citizen engagement around land politics. I argue that while there are some similarities between these two cases in the ways in which poor people are creating new spaces for engagement, there are also distinct differences. In both sectors, citizens and their organizations and allies are attempting to create a new set of intermediary institutions and/or practices of engagement distinct from the state and public spheres. However, there are also important variations in the ways in which these citizen engagements are creating new democratic capacity for poor people. In the field of AIDS/HIV activism there have been significant successes in forging new spaces for citizen engagement across the citizen society/state boundary, and in creating a viable social movement capable of engaging the state both nationally and locally. There is evidence of new formal and informal intermediary spaces in which activist organizations and their marginalized constituency engage (collaboratively and critically) with the local state. In the land arena, by contrast, citizen participation is sporadic and situated in largely adversarial, short-term confrontations with the state. While the recent emergence of the Landless People's Movement (LPM) signals the potential of a rural social movement with the capacity to generate new spaces for citizen participation from below, the marked failure of the state to reach into rural areas and to facilitate new institutional spaces for citizen participation means that there is little or no citizen engagement with local state structures, few alliances between the state, NGOs and local social movements, and a marked absence of new spaces for citizen participation.

This chapter explores reasons for these differences in forms of citizen participation in the HIV/AIDS arena and in the land sector. I show how they provide contrasting examples of the ways in which the creation of new democratic spaces in post-apartheid South Africa are framed within old attitudes, practices and expectations. I also show how both these cases raise important questions around the problem of marginalized communities and democratic inclusion. Both involve extremely marginalized groups, whose legal citizenship is not supported by experiences of actual inclusion in the political, economic and social life of post-apartheid society. The two cases raise questions around the construction of intermediary forms of citizen participation in a context where there is a historical absence of institutions and spaces mediating the relation between state and civil society, as a result of the state's authoritarianism during and before the apartheid regime.

Where historically marginalized groups have had little or no access to formal democratic spaces of the public sphere at the general and intermediary levels, there may be no political culture of engaging with the state to achieve one's goals. As a consequence of this, organizations and social movements representing marginalized communities often struggle to galvanize support for longer-term, effective engagement with the state, in the face of their members' uncertainties about their entitlements vis-à-vis the state. Where engagements do occur, there is often evidence of a culture of 'non-bindingness' in local decision-making spaces – an unwillingness to commit to and accept joint decisions and agreements with other stakeholders. This, in turn, has its roots in historical experiences of engaging with the state as deeply risky and conflictual processes, disconnected from legitimate outcomes, and involving the continual unsettling of established agreements and procedures. In contexts where marginalized groups experience a high level of exclusion from mainstream political and economic processes, engagements with the state often depend on the ways in which citizens' expectations are shaped by pre-existing and contextual relations of power.

Citizen Engagement in the Land Sector

In many analyses of post-apartheid South Africa, the challenge for citizen participation is not to initiate democracy, but instead to 'deepen' it. This view holds that while there is much evidence in South Africa of discourses of participation and active citizenship that build on traditions of liberal democracy, there is also growing evidence of a widening gap between legal assurances for participation and the actual inclusion of poor citizens in democratic participation.

Among the key obstacles to greater citizen participation in the land sector are structural poverty and inequality. More than 70 per cent of the country's poorest people reside in rural areas, and more than 70 per cent of all rural people are poor (Aliber 2003). Rural poverty is due to the land dispossession and migrant labour systems initiated during the colonial era, and refined under apartheid rule. Between 1960 and 1983 more than 3.5 million people lost land and homes through forced removals of one kind or another (Cousins 2004).

In line with the constitution, post-apartheid South Africa's current land policy has three distinct components: a land redistribution programme, aimed at broadening access to land among the country's black majority; a land restitution programme to restore land or provide alternative compensation to those dispossessed as a result of racially discriminatory laws and practices since 1913; and a tenure reform programme to secure the rights of people living under insecure arrangements on land owned by others, including the state (in communal areas) and private landowners (Cousins 2004). On the whole, land reform has been limited, with less than 2.3 per cent of agricultural land transferred at the end of 2002 under the combined redistribution and restitution programmes since 1994 (Greenberg 2004: 9). The land tenure programme is mired in controversy over the role of traditional authorities and its role in communal tenure regimes (Cousins and Claasens 2005: 16).

In post-apartheid South Africa rural citizens are bearers of rights which involve little, if any, meaningful involvement in local decision-making processes. The majority of rural citizens are either poorly paid and insecure farm workers, labour tenants or unemployed 'farm dwellers'. While there was certainly no attempt by the apartheid state to develop citizen capacity for engagement (rural government was in the hands of appointed chiefs and completely excluded rural communities), the current situation is not dramatically different. The introduction of democracy in 1994 released many expectations for new forms of citizen participation in rural areas. However, for labour tenants and farm workers post-apartheid democracy has meant little more than 'the formal extension of minimum labour standards and formal protection against arbitrary eviction' (Greenberg 2004: 10). Weak rural state structures have offered little protection against abuses of power by farm owners against tenants and farm workers, and rural citizens have been offered few new opportunities for meaningful political participation.

The state's inability to reach into rural areas is, at least in part, due to the way in which traditional leaders and authorities are redefining local government in these areas. Koelble points out that 'there is a certain irony in the fact that the professed instruments for weakening the tribal authorities – the Municipal Structures Act of 1998 and the Municipal Systems Act of 1999 – have become instruments for the re-assertion of chiefly power' (Koelble 2005: 7). Since 1999 the number of municipalities went down from 850 to 284; at the same time as the actual area covered by local government structures increased dramatically with the inclusion of former Bantustan territories. Traditional leaders occupy 20 per cent of the seats in the municipal government; according to the new local government legislation they are to be consulted by the elected officials on matters pertaining to development. As Koelble observes, 'this form of representation goes far beyond the restricted and vague role given to tribal authorities in the constitution' (Koelble 2005: 8). In addition, the Communal Land Rights Act of 2004 gives traditional leaders the right to distribute communal lands and control its usage (Ntsebeza 2004). Against this background, and in the context of an absent local state, traditional leaders are reasserting their power in rural areas. Citizen participation can be severely circumscribed by the cultural and political power traditional leaders wield in their communities.

In addition to the state's inability to set up effective local government in rural areas, state planning for greater inclusion has been limited to technocratic exercises where participation amounts to little more than consultation or information sessions by the state. One of the few institutional innovations for ordinary rural citizens, the Communal Property Associations (CPAs), established in 1996, aimed to facilitate active engagement of the very modest number of beneficiaries of land restitution and redistribution programmes in decisions around tenure and management of communal assets. They were designed as an alternative to trusts, which had given too much power to appointed trustees, but even this one innovative form is now generally considered to have failed to achieve both its democratic and its productive goals. The reasons for the collapse of the CPAs are numerous. Cousins writes that

> constitutions have been poorly drafted and often misunderstood by members, and the rights of members (especially in relation to land and resource use) are often ill-defined. In some cases traditional leaders have contested the authority of elected trustees, and in others elites have captured the benefits of ownership. (Cousins 2005: 14)

Conflicts over different interpretations of entitlements and the bindingness of decisions have led to the collapse of some of the CPAs.

Since 1999 there have been few opportunities for civil society groups to engage directly with policymakers. After 1999, in particular, 'the new emphasis in redistribution policy on de-racializing commercial agriculture and creating opportunities for emergent farmers, rather than on reducing poverty and enhancing the livelihood opportunities of the poor and marginalized, provoked a great deal of negative comment, but little sustained mobilisation, from civil society' (Cousins 1994). Today, most opportunities for citizen engagement take place in short-term 'project' spaces, with few opportunities for engagement in democratic, multi-stakeholder spaces.

Despite failures to implement new forms of citizen participation, there are multiple discourses and practices of citizenship in South Africa's land sector. NGOs, the state, donor agencies and emerging rural organizations engage in dialogue around issues of law and policymaking, and participation. Cousins (2004) points out that

> discourses of popular participation, accountability and socio-economic rights have contended with *realpolitik* considerations of stakeholder negotiation and bargaining; notions of 'continuing struggle' and popular

mobilization have been cut across by emerging discourses of 'lobbying and advocacy' to influence policy. Concerns to build the capacity of rural people to claim their rights and decide on their own futures have battled with approaches to project planning that involve consultation with 'beneficiaries'.

Where discourses and practices of participation are promoted by the state, they are often limited to formal 'consultations' and information sessions by the government.

Since 1998, one of the key stumbling blocks in the development of new forms of citizen engagement has been disagreements around the identity and definitions of 'citizens' in the land sector. An example of this is to be found in the area of tenure reform policy and activism. The major focus of attention in the state's land tenure reform policy has been a series of negotiations between various state and non-state stakeholders around a new law to provide improved security of tenure in communal systems. Land tenure policies have been largely framed within a 'market-assisted' approach to land acquisition and redistribution: there has been a shift from seeing rural community members as 'active agents within local struggles', whose efforts to 'mobilize and organize' should be supported, to portraying them as 'beneficiaries' or 'clients' with varying needs or demands for land that the government should play a part in 'facilitating'.

As a result, the state has become the locus of key decision-making on land, even when it consults stakeholders, or outsources functions to providers (Cousins 2004). Lack of consultation between citizen organizations and the state has led to the development of highly adversarial relationships between the parties. Cousins points out that one partial exception is the working relationship between a National Land Committee (NLC) affiliate, the Border Rural Committee, and the Commission on the Restitution of Land Rights, with the acceptance of restitution claims for land lost through 'betterment' (land use) planning in the former 'homelands' during the apartheid era (Cousins 2004).

Recent developments may point to the emergence of more active forms of citizen engagement, capable of engaging with the state. In 2001 the Landless People's Movement (LPM), supported by the NLC, a broad social movement representing rural and urban residents, was formed to challenge the government on the inadequacies of its land reform programme. Since its formation the LPM has begun to construct an identity around multiple demands (access to basic services, freedom of movement and freedom to stay in one place, participation by people in decisions affecting their own lives) and the issue of landlessness. The LPM grew out of a series of efforts by rural NGOs like the NLC to construct a rural social movement. Among the LPM's precursors were the Rural Development Initiative (RDI), a coalition of rural NGOs and CBOs with a broad-based rural character created in 1998, and a joint initiative between the Rural Development Services Network (RDSN) and the South African Municipal Services Workers' Union (SAMWU) to form a national grassroots movement around rural water provision based on the demand of 50 litres free per person per day (Greenberg 2004: 16).

The LPM mobilizes rural and urban marginalized people. It has engaged in a series of high-profile mobilizations and land occupations involving large numbers of its members. While there are a number of internal tensions in the movement around the issue of how to engage with the state (with some NGOs seeking a continuation of critical engagement with the state, and others advocating a more antagonistic relationship), the movement can be seen as already having had a significant impact on state–citizen relations since its inception. The state has responded to the LPM with a 'mixture of reform and repression', while other national stakeholders have become 'more vocal about their opinions on land distribution' (Greenberg 2004: 31). The Congress of South African Trade Unions (COSATU) and the South African Communist Party (SACP) have supported the LPM's call for a land summit. In addition, business leaders have also begun to call for the implementation of the government's land programme.

On the whole, citizen participation in the land sector decision-making highlights that the state has shown little interest in or capacity for investing resources, energy or time in building new spaces for effective citizen representation and participation in the conception and design of public programmes or of new policies, rules and regulations. The opening up of legal democratic frameworks has not automatically guaranteed effective democratic self-representation by marginalized rural groups. Most engagements by citizens have been mediated by pre-existing practices of political engagement of NGOs or by traditional authorities. As yet, there is little evidence of 'middle space' engagement, situations in which rural citizens are engaging on their own terms with the local state in an attempt to achieve their goals, forge new relationships with state actors and traditional authorities, influence new policies or demand new ways of delivering services.

New Democratic Spaces and Political Context in South Africa: The Treatment Action Campaign (TAC)

Recent developments in the health sector and AIDS activism also highlight complex dynamics of inclusion that result from attempts to foster greater democratic participation among the urban poor in new democratic spaces. As in the land sector, these dynamics result from the state's failure adequately to provide space for greater citizen engagement. However, in contrast with the latter, a strong social movement has forged new spaces for sustained citizen engagement at the intersection between civil society and the state.

The TAC is attempting to build a middle-level citizenship through its own involvement in intermediary state-run institutions, as well as a variety of more informal spaces. In its attempt to mobilize support, it is increasingly struggling for the opening up and democratization of intermediary local state institutions such as schools and clinics. For instance, the TAC-supported Médecins Sans Frontières (MSF) AIDS treatment units in Khayelitsha and Lusikisiki are located within state clinics. In this sense, TAC and MSF are engaged in attempts to disseminate the politics of rights and health citizenship into the middle-level institutional fabric of society. The aim of these initiatives has been to transform practices in these institutions, to bring them closer to the people, and to transform them into spaces that mediate state–citizen relations. TAC's regional offices and local branches also work closely with CBOs in their area so that they are able to create links with state-run local clinics. The organization trains AIDS councillors and treatment literacy practitioners (TLPs), as well as carrying out audits of clinics and hospitals that are running Prevention of Mother-to-Child Transmission (PMTCT) and Anti-Retroviral (ARV) programmes.[1] As well as engaging in the middle ground between state and the public sphere, TAC's local branches also engage in grassroots social mobilization efforts in highly localized spaces. In August 2002, TAC launched a campaign to have the local clinic in Nyanga, one of the more impoverished sections of Cape Town's townships, opened for five, instead of two, days a week. TAC activists recognize that these local spaces are not transient, and that they provide important sites for engagement with the local state.

The organization is an example of a new social movement that has constructed its own arena of action in multiple spaces. Its strength as a social movement lies in its capacity to mobilize the poor in a variety of spaces, ranging from institutions that serve as an interface between people and governmental authorities, to more transient methods such as one-off campaigns aimed at opening up deliberation over policies. Future challenges for the organization lie in consolidating past gains among its members and the broader South African society. These challenges are becoming particularly evident as ARV programmes are launched in rural areas characterized by chronic poverty and marginalization, and where there has been little AIDS activism and social mobilization. It is in these large, remote, and under-serviced areas, many of them in the former Bantustans, that the socio-cultural and political obstacles to AIDS treatment are most pronounced.

It is here that TAC's brand of AIDS activism and social mobiliza- tion could make the difference between life and death, but may be most difficult to mount and sustain. It is in these rural areas that TAC's tried and tested methods of political mobilization and engagement could face their biggest challenges. As in the land sector, it is here that the absence of intermediary and 'middle space' institutions and practices provides ongoing space for dynamics of power and exclusion. In urban areas, however, diverse TAC activities and interventions have contributed to creating new political spaces for engagement at local and national levels. TAC's campaigns cut across institutional and non-institutional spaces at the intermediary level between the state and other more structured public spaces. They are capable of generating multiple kinds of relations to the state. As a result of TAC's contestation within multiple sites and across the state/civil society boundary, ordinary citizens have been able to build their political capabilities for democratic engagement. Alongside TAC's effective use of courts, the media, the Internet, email, and transnational advocacy networks, a crucial aspect of TAC's work has been its recruitment of large numbers of mostly young and unemployed black women into its ranks. TAC's interventions in these multiple spaces have allowed its membership to move from the margins into effective citizen engagement. The challenge for the future lies in translating these forms of engagement into longer-term 'middle space' institutions capable of mediating the relation between the state and its people.

Marginalized Citizens and the Problem of Participation

Both of these cases raise important challenges for the problem of citizen engagement among marginalized groups. They illuminate how specific political and power dynamics affect processes of democratization, and the multiple ways in which power is negotiated across the state/civil society divide and across the boundaries of the public sphere.

In the land sector, social movements find it hard to mobilize beyond a small core of activists. Higher structural poverty is clearly a key barrier to citizen participation in the land sector. However, there are other obstacles to democracy too. Some of these have to do with the way in which the state is holding on to state-centred definitions of citizenship, the complex dynamics of mobilization, the organization of rural peoples themselves, and the difficulties of engaging citizens in a sector that is more varied and fragmented than its urban complement. Where engagement does take place, traditional power dynamics, inadequate local capacity to run these engagements, and the lack of organized political constituencies in rural areas often limit its democratic potential.

Post-apartheid citizenship politics in the land sector has produced many struggles over definitions around rights and obligations among those in charge of state departments, NGOs and donor agencies, but few new democratic institutions for citizens on the ground. The lack of organized local rural social movements, and the absence of a layer of intermediary institutions, have meant that citizen engagement remains restricted to involvements in 'projects'. These are often short-term, expert-driven, and linked intermittently to wider social mobilizations. Rural citizens have few opportunities to practise democratic citizenship, and to represent themselves. It is often only after crossing the threshold of self-representation and identification that the marginalized can make effective claims for greater inclusion. However, the condition of marginalization itself hinders easy access to the institutions and practices of participation and representation, especially in political arenas where there are few institutions mediating the relation between state and civil society. In the land sector these barriers to inclusive citizenship are further entrenched by the role that traditional authorities potentially play in promoting anti-democratic local practices.

This raises a series of questions about forms of participation among marginalized groups in contexts where there is a marked absence of institutions for citizen participation. Any approach to citizen participation among marginalized peoples must confront the deeper problems of how people who are excluded are to develop a sense of their own participation as worthwhile and effective in a context marked by complex dynamics of power and participation. New democratic arenas are often transplanted onto institutional landscapes in which historical patterns of political engagement can potentially weaken new forms of participation.

Disparities between the official democratic discourses on political rights and citizenship, and political realities on the ground, often have the effect of alienating marginalized groups from the public sphere as they are forced into informal and hidden social and economic practices by the state's unwillingness to recognize these very real conditions, and as a result its inability to govern them. This can result in a wider politics of disengagement from the state and a situation where the ordinary person becomes more and more alienated from public institutions because these institutions seem increasingly remote and unresponsive to their needs. This, in turn, speaks to the importance of illuminating how specific political and power dynamics affect the process of democratization, and to consider the multiple ways in which power is negotiated across the state/civil society divide and across the boundaries of the public sphere.

In contexts where marginalized groups eschew participation in state-created spaces and initiatives, a different kind of potential for engagement exists, one that is rooted in episodic engagements in a variety of non-institutional and state-run spaces, and across state/civil society/public sphere boundaries. TAC, for example, has used a variety of ways to mobilize its constituency (Robins and von Lieres 2004). The case of the TAC highlights the fact that in many Southern contexts citizens' political lives and identities are not necessarily framed by the bifurcated model of civil society and state. In the health sector, this organization provides an example of practices that cut across institutional and non-institutional spaces, and that are capable of generating multiple relations to the state. As a result of its contestation within multiple sites, TAC can be seen to be enabling ordinary citizens to build their political capabilities for democratic engagement. TAC's interventions in these multiple spaces have allowed its membership to emerge from the margins of the political system.

The case of TAC challenges those perspectives that posit the concepts of 'civil society' and the 'public sphere' as cornerstones of participation and citizenship theories. In a recent article, Acharya et al. (2004: 40–41) rightly argue that the civil-society perspective, shared by the literatures on civil society, deliberative democracy and empowered participation,

> holds the assumption that it is relatively unproblematic for individual or collective actors to reach and use institutional arrangements for citizen participation. The core of the perspective is a dichotomous reading of the relations between state (authoritarian), which for some includes political parties, and society (democratic). The conviction [is] that authentic civil society actors are a democratizing and rationalizing force of public action because of their deliberative logic (versus interest-based), decentralized nature and rootedness in the social life of local communities and autonomy (for most people, from the spheres of the state, political parties and interest groups politics). These features, it is believed, give civil society a particular democratizing logic that contrasts favourably to that of the interest-based logic of representative bodies, the techno-bureaucratic logic of state agencies and the exclusionary logic of the market. It is an article of faith in the civil society perspective that citizen participation increases the opportunity to influence policies for lower income and other excluded populations, whose interests are marginalized in the classic representative institutions.

The authors argue for a 'polity' perspective in which 'participation is a contingent outcome, produced as collective actors (civil society, state and other) negotiate relations in a pre-existing institutional terrain that constrains and facilitates particular kinds of action' (Acharya et al. 2004: 42).

The arguments of Acharya et al. are extremely useful in understanding some of the specific challenges of democratization in South Africa, where new democratic spaces are being created in the context of older patterns of local and traditional institutions over which new democratic institutions are being laid. In post-apartheid South Africa there is growing evidence of a widening gap between legal assurances for participation and the actual inclusion of marginalized people in democratic participation. The state shows little interest in investing resources, energy or time in supporting effective citizen representation in the conception and design of public programmes or of new policies, rules and regulations. Marginalized peoples themselves are often unable to organize themselves to participate in public policy debates and other wider forms of democratic engagement. The opening up of new democratic institutions and spaces does not automatically guarantee democratic self-representation by marginalized groups.

Conclusion

New sites of participation among marginalized peoples in post-apartheid South Africa may be long-term, stable spaces that poor people fashion for themselves and through which they engage with the state (in the case of the TAC) or they may be one-off adversarial spaces in which they gain a sense of the legitimacy of their concerns (in the case of the land sector). Although these latter forms of participation may be short-lived, and seem to have little long-term effect, they nonetheless potentially provide their members with opportunities to engage simultaneously in a variety of participatory spaces that cut across institutional and non-institutional spaces, and allow for the articulation of new forms of citizenship from below. They also, however, reaffirm the important role of democratic local state structures in facilitating new spaces for citizen participation from below. The real challenge for democracy in South Africa lies in building a strong 'middle space' politics, one in which urban and rural citizens engage actively with the state in defining the new democratic landscape. It is here that the real potential for deeper forms of democratic inclusion among South Africa's marginalized lie.

Note

1. Thanks to Steven Robins for the information on MSF–TAC collaborations.

References

Aliber, M. (2003) 'Chronic poverty in South Africa: incidence, causes and policies', *World Development* 31(3).

Acharya, A., A. Gurza Lavalle and P.P. Houtzager (2004) 'Civil society representation in the participatory budget and deliberative councils of São Paulo, Brazil', *IDS Bulletin* 35(2), April.

Cousins, B. (2004) 'Grounding democracy: the politics of land in post-apartheid South Africa', *Supplement to the Mail & Guardian*, 26 November.

Cousins, B. (2005) 'Agrarian reform and the "two economies": transforming South Africa's countryside', Programme for Land and Agrarian Studies, School of Government, University of the Western Cape, draft; reprinted in R. Hall and

L. Ntsebeza, eds, *The Land Question in South Africa: the Challenge of Transformation and Redistribution*, Cape Town: HSRC Press, 2006.

Cousins, B., and A. Claasens (2005) 'Communal land rights and democracy in post-apartheid South Africa', in P. Jones and K. Stokke, eds, *Democratizing Development: The Politics of Socio-Economic Rights in South Africa*, Leiden and Boston: Martinus Nijhoff.

Greenberg, D. (2004) 'The Landless People's Movement and the failure of post-apartheid land reform', case study for the UKZN project Globalization, Marginalization and New Social Movements in Post-Apartheid South Africa, University of Kwazulu–Natal.

Koelble, T. (2005) 'Democracy, traditional leadership and the international economy of South Africa', Centre for Social Science Research (CSSR) Working Paper 114, University of Cape Town.

Ntsebeza, L. (2004) 'Rural governance and citizenship in post-apartheid South Africa', in J. Daniel, R. Southall and J. Lutchman, eds, *State of the Nation: South Africa 2004–2005*, Cape Town: HSRC Press.

Robins, S., and B. von Lieres (2004) 'AIDS activism and globalization from below: occupying new spaces of citizenship in post-apartheid South Africa', *IDS Bulletin* 35(2).

Whose Spaces? Contestations and Negotiations in Health and Community Regeneration Fora in the UK

Marian Barnes

Public participation in public policy in the UK has had an increasingly high profile since the election of the New Labour government in 1997. Many of the practical initiatives operating at local level have histories which pre-date 1997, and the characteristics of these initiatives reflect earlier attempts by government to change the nature of the relationship between government, public services and 'the public'. For example, the conceptualization of the public as consumers of services remains evident in initiatives such as 'Best Value' in which the public are consulted about the performance of their local authorities. But under New Labour the discourse of citizen participation has become a central feature not only of policymaking and service delivery but also of attempts to create active, responsible citizens, and to achieve democratic renewal.

Substantial claims are made for what public participation can deliver. An analysis of official documents from the Department of Health (responsible for health services delivered via National Health Service (NHS) agencies at local level, and social care services delivered by local government), from the Office of the Deputy Prime Minister (responsible for local government and urban regeneration) and, most recently, from the Home Office (responsible not only for crime and criminal justice policies but also for immigration services and what has become known as 'civil renewal') reveals a wide range of purposes and aspirations for public participation. These include (Barnes et al. 2004a):

- improving the quality and responsiveness of public services;
- improving the legitimacy of decision-making;
- enabling services to be designed and delivered by community organizations and/or 'local people';
- revitalizing democracy;
- creating more responsible citizens;
- generating 'positive freedom', civic virtues, mutuality and trust;
- building community capacity;
- increasing social cohesion and improving social order;
- creating healthier citizens;
- reducing social exclusion;
- building individual skills and capacity.

Thus concerns about the nature of public services, the policymaking process, about social relationships, inequality and injustice are driving official imperatives towards increased public involvement. But the study on which this chapter is based revealed that the origins of such activities also derive from:

- supranational institutions and initiatives, e.g. the European Social Fund and the Rio environmental summit;
- local government initiatives for decentralization and devolution;
- service-specific initiatives, for example in relation to maternity and mental health services;
- initiatives deriving from autonomous actions among local communities, communities of identity and from within user groups.

It is not possible to understand the characteristics and impact of public participation in the UK solely by looking at official initiatives and the invited spaces to which they have given rise. One characteristic of the current situation is that it is increasingly difficult to make a clear distinction between officially sponsored participation and autonomous action. Groups claiming a right to be heard in the policy process are being offered opportunities to take part alongside public officials and politicians, and it is here that the concept of 'partnership' has assumed a particular significance – albeit one that is highly contested (Barnes et al. 1999).

In this chapter, I discuss two examples that illustrate the tensions which arise when autonomous groups enter 'invited spaces'.[1] I consider the way in which people come to take part in such initiatives, and the type of dialogue that takes place within them. I relate this to the opportunities and constraints deriving from the particular institutional and political context in which they develop and suggest that these, plus unequal power relationships, limit the potential for change. I discuss these examples by reference to theories of deliberative democracy and social movement theory. I write from the perspective of an academic researcher who has also been directly involved as an ally in the development and support of participatory initiatives. In particular I have been involved in initiatives which have sought to give voice to those often considered incompetent, by virtue of age or impairment, to take part (Barnes and Bowl 2001; Barnes and Bennett 1998).

These two case studies were part of a study of public participation in two English cities (Barnes et al. 2004b). This involved mapping participation initiatives using a snowball technique, starting with contacts in the local authorities, local health service organizations and voluntary- and community-sector contacts. Detailed case studies were conducted of seventeen initiatives. Data collection included observations, interviews with both citizens and the officials with whom they were in dialogue, and with local officials who had strategic responsibilities for public participation. Since we negotiated access on the basis of anonymity, the names of interviewees and their locations are not revealed.

Mobilization, Identity Building and Deliberation

Theorists of social movements have advanced different explanations of why people take part in collective action. For example, Tarrow (1994) highlights the importance of 'opportunity structures' that frame the way in which social movement activists mobilize membership and construct strategies for action. The policy context outlined above offers a particular opportunity structure within which those engaged in collective action can recruit members. Specific policy initiatives (such as neighbourhood renewal, and patient and public involvement in the NHS) and the different discourses underpinning them (see Barnes et al. forthcoming) have been influential in shaping the forms of action in which activists in a variety of social movements in the UK have become engaged, including disability activists, and those engaged in urban, environmental, poverty and public health movements.

These opportunities also pose constraints. Many forms of deliberative practice through which public participation is being encouraged are designed to engage a cross section of citizens to deliberate to consensus (Bobbio 2003). Often the officials designing such practices deliberately seek to engage those who are not already mobilized and question the authority of disabled people, local residents or others engaged in collective action to represent the views of 'ordinary citizens' – even though existing organization can provide a structure through which such representation can occur (Barnes et al. 1999). Practices based in theories of deliberative democracy also tend to privilege forms of exchange based in reasoned argument, forms more akin to dialogic processes familiar to public service managers and professionals than to many of the discursive styles adopted within social movements. As Young (2000) has argued, such practices can be exclusionary, rendering illegitimate discursive styles employing the use of narrative and rhetoric and failing to recognize the significance of 'greeting' as a means of demonstrating recognition and respect. Fraser (1997: 81) has argued the importance of alternative 'discursive arenas' in which different publics can generate alternative discourses which may challenge the notion of a 'common good' and which, she argues, 'better promote the ideal of participatory parity than does a single, comprehensive, overarching public'. This suggests that fora which *bring together* citizens and officials are not sufficient to ensure change – an argument that the case studies discussed in this chapter would support.

Other social movement researchers emphasize the importance of social networks in affecting individual decisions to get involved (Diani and McAdam 2003). Those coming from a socio-cultural perspective emphasize the significance of value systems, the way in which actors make sense of their own situations and their responses to dissatisfactions with institutional or broader social norms. For Melucci (1996: 66) networks represent the context in which interactions between individuals produce both the cognitive and the affective schemas that can connect individuals to collective action. Motivations for participation are produced within particular types of networks and this is linked to identities: 'what people choose to be'. Melucci describes an active process of making sense of oneself and one's connection to others and suggests that people become motivated to take part in collective action through a process of deciding that such action is worthwhile to achieve change, and that it makes sense in terms of how they see themselves and their relationship with the world.

Once they are engaged in action, a process of collective identity building is necessary for sustainability. This process is partly cognitive, relating to definition of the field within which change is sought, the means by which change is to be achieved and the meaning of the action in which actors are collectively engaged, but it also requires an affective investment. The rituals, practices and norms that develop among groups contribute to a process of distinguishing the collective 'we' of activists from other members of society.

Mansbridge has emphasized the significance of an 'oppositional consciousness' in determining the nature of the collective identity of social movement activists:

> We say that members of a group that others have traditionally treated as subordinate or deviant have an oppositional consciousness when they claim their previously subordinate identity as a positive identification, identify injustices done to their group, demand changes in the polity, economy or society to rectify those injustices, and see other members of their group as sharing an interest in rectifying those injustices. (2001: 1)

Those engaged in such struggle seek not only material change but also cultural change: they aim to convince people to see the world differently.

The significance of a collective identity which sets apart those engaged in social movements from the rest of society is problematic from the perspective of official policy that sees public participation as a route to social cohesion. So too is the notion of 'opposition'. It is this that can create difficulties when social movement activists are invited to take part in officially sponsored or sanctioned participation initiatives. But this can also cause problems for public officials who may also identify themselves with the groups or movements with whom they are engaged in dialogue during the course of their work (Barnes et al. forthcoming). I explore these issues through the two examples of participation described below.

A Community Health Forum

This forum was established in an area of a city which was the subject of a number of regeneration initiatives. The city had a troubled political history and local people were quite cynical about their local politicians. However, within the health service there were officials committed to community involvement and the city had been part of a number of public health initiatives which had prioritized such involvement. There was also a strong tradition of community activism, much of which was based around very local areas. This forum was unusual in covering two areas that had usually been the focus for separate action.

When residents in these areas discovered that the Health Authority (HA) was planning to close their local health centre, they decided to take action. The HA claimed that the centre was not sufficiently used, so residents decided to undertake research to examine this claim. They worked with a freelance researcher who trained them to carry out interviews and coordinated the research. One of the women who took part spoke of the enjoyment they experienced at being involved: 'it was brilliant doing the research, I really did enjoy it. It was a laugh a minute. Doing it on ourselves, teaching one another how to do it, role playing.'

The positive feelings were enhanced by the success of the campaign: the HA agreed to keep the health centre open and a new general practitioner was recruited to work there. Residents decided to continue working to improve health services in the area. Whilst they were pleased to have saved the centre, it was in poor condition. As one commented, the area was one in which there were significant health problems and action was required not only to improve health services, but to address the reasons for high levels of sickness: 'Our area where I live is the highest cancer rate in the country.... The mortality rate for our area is ridiculous. Now there has got to be a reason for that.... So, I started kicking in and becoming more and more active with the group.'

Our research took place six years after the success of the campaign to save the health centre. By this point the group was uncertain about its future and frustrated about the lack of support from health service officials. However, the establishment of the New Opportunities Fund (NOF) from the proceeds of the National Lottery offered a potential way forward. This fund was designed to enable community organizations to bid for money to establish Healthy Living Centres (HLCs) – centres which would not only provide services, but support action to improve health. In order to qualify to bid to NOF the group had to reconstitute themselves and they became a health forum, with some members taking on the role of trustees who would hold formal responsibility for financial affairs.

At the time of our research, members were preparing the NOF funding bid. They were also looking for other sources of funding, and trying to work with the health service to negotiate what services would be provided within the centre. Once the centre was established it would be owned and run by the forum trustees.

The group included people working for the NHS and other local agencies as well as local residents. Among the members were people who had direct experience of low incomes, joblessness, poor health and disability. Collectively, members could draw on a range of experience of activism, including within trade unions, service user and disabled people's organizations, religious groups, voluntary and direct action. Trustees spoke of long histories of active involvement in their local communities and some were identified by other local people as a source of information and advice about a range of issues including housing, benefit problems, health and transport. They demonstrated considerable concern and commitment to the local area and to the people living in it.

Members spoke of motivations coming from religious commitments, prompted by direct personal experience (for example, of poor treatment by health services), or by an awareness of health inequalities and service deficiencies that came through working in statutory agencies within the area. The 'citizen' members of the group demonstrated a strong belief in the importance of local people taking action on their own behalf and, at times, a healthy scepticism of statutory agencies and elected councillors: 'My only fear is that the medical staff, the so-called professionals, will take it over. They see it as a threat.'

In some cases it was unclear exactly how people's involvement in the health forum had started, because their community involvement was long-standing and one thing tended to lead to another. For example, one interviewee started the story of his involvement in the early 1980s in relation to the issue of council housing. Whilst members were not 'representing' other local groups, it was clear that these individuals provided an important means of connecting a range of activity taking place within the locality and brought to forum discussions substantial local knowledge of issues and concerns of people in the area.

Whilst the constitution required that trustees have formal responsibilities, the forum was open to anyone living in the area to take part. But there were few active members and it was not easy to encourage people to come to meetings. One interviewee estimated that there were about eight active members. There were twelve at the first meeting observed, ten at the second. The third meeting that was planned for observation did not take place because there were insufficient members to make a quorum – only six people turned up. People spoke about the reasons they saw for this difficulty in maintaining high levels of involvement:

- Historical competitiveness between the localities meant it was comparatively unusual for people from this broad area to be jointly involved in a community initiative.
- Inadequate public transport and difficult access within a hilly area meant that the location of meetings had a significant impact on who was able to attend.
- Frustration about lack of attendance of 'official' members of the group appeared to undermine the notion that the forum was a partnership.
- There was a suggestion that people might not return if they had made interventions that were challenging to the main focus of the group's work, or might themselves decide not to continue to attend because of differences within the group.

Observations of discussions suggested other reasons why few remained actively involved. The group was engaged in a complex task, which involved gathering substantial information in order to prepare funding bids that had to conform to criteria laid down by different funding bodies. At the same time, they were engaged in negotiations with the Primary Care Group (PCG) about the space required for a GP surgery within the centre, and the amount of rent that could be charged for this. They were also negotiating with the local authority about planning permission. They were aware that the owners of the site earmarked for the centre could sell, possibly at a higher price, to commercial bidders. There were continuing debates about the precise nature of the services and facilities to be provided within the centre, and about how they might be provided.

All this meant that the discussions were highly task-focused and the language often technical. Whilst one interviewee expressed some frustration at the way in which discussions tended to veer away from the point, observations indicated that the debate followed an agenda that was largely based on the need to update on action taken, and agree next steps in order to meet externally imposed deadlines.

The specific focus of the group at the time of the research influenced the way in which particular types of knowledge and expertise were prioritized. In particular, it demonstrated how rules emanating from within the 'official' sphere could downplay the value of experiential lay knowledge. Both meetings that were observed were attended by a consultant (paid for by the PCG) who had been brought in to advise and support forum members in the preparation of the NOF bid. He played an 'expert' role in discussions and his inputs were often couched in terms of information, proposals or advice-giving. But an exchange over the issue of how much rent the PCG would pay for consulting and office space demonstrated that group members were quite capable of engaging in detailed discussion of financial rules, as well as how these might be questioned. Interviews indicated that the core membership of the forum had developed skills and tactics necessary to ensure that they understood what was being discussed and that they had their say when they wanted. One described how she had developed confidence during previous meetings involving local authority councillors: 'I started saying, if one of the councillors was talking, "I don't know what's going on, I can't follow it. If you want to talk to the community, you've got to talk as if you're at the garden gate or your front door."'

Other exchanges demonstrated the considerable knowledge and expertise of group members. For example, one exchange about the type of information needed to support the bid led to an identification of a range of statistical data sources: not only from within health services, but also from welfare rights agencies, victim support, and credit union data. This, in turn, led into discussion about the significance of such advice services and how they were provided, which drew on the substantial experience of four women who had been involved in such services in different contexts.

A rather different example emerges from a report from one group member about a conference she had attended about farmers' markets. This led into an extensive exchange about the potential of such approaches in enabling people to buy healthy food, and how the group might incorporate ways of enabling such access through the HLC. In this instance, an attempt by the consultant to intervene in 'expert' mode was brushed aside by members who explicitly noted the amount of relevant expertise within the group. However, the need to focus on the immediate tasks eventually led to closure on this item with a suggestion that they should return to it later.

One member of the forum worked in a local Sure Start project,[2] but was a member of the forum because of her commitment to the project rather than because it was part of her job. She spoke of her ambivalence about the role she should play in the group:

> I've a level of expertise in health and I'm a Master of Public Health, so lots of networks and lots of expertise around that in community development, and I was there as a resource really.... I tried to be very, very explicit, saying 'I don't see myself as a key decision maker here, I'm here to support the community to make decisions.'

Whilst such 'insider' knowledge could be extremely useful to the group in its dealings with official agencies, this woman was concerned that too heavy a reliance on knowledge from official sources could undermine the objective of community members 'doing this for themselves'. This was partly an emotional issue – the level of commitment among community members could be damaged by too frequent a reference to sources of information to which most group members did not have access. The visibility of active members of the forum within their local communities meant that they were able to keep in touch with issues of direct concern to local people and they drew on these experiences not only in developing detailed plans for the centre, but in maintaining their commitment to this model of providing health care and a resource which could contribute to promoting health. This was evident in the following response to a question about why and how one member got involved: 'I always imagine faceless people sitting in offices in London deciding how many people are going to die in [our city] when they haven't got any idea of where it is.'

Although only a small number of people were centrally involved in the forum, many people in the area knew what was going on and regularly asked forum members how things were progressing. There was a view that the planned centre would have to be built – local people would not accept failure. The origin of the forum was in public opposition to proposed action by the HA. An oppositional consciousness motivated action in an area where there were strong networks among those engaged in community-based action – both citizens and officials. Within the forum there was evidence of a process of collective identity-building among the core group. One aspect of this was evidenced in the shared cynicism regarding local officials and politicians and hence the construction of a 'we' engaged in developing an alternative service. Beyond the core group, there was a wider sense of a collective 'we' within the community who shared the aspiration of a community-run health centre, although were not directly involved in its development. But as oppositional action developed into action to implement an alternative service, the official sphere had an impact on the way in which the group developed. This constituted the political opportunity structure which also framed the way in which collective action among community members developed in the context of the space created for 'partnership working' between community members and officials.

A number of issues emerge from this. First, the necessity to seek funding defined the group's activity and the content of their deliberations. Members had to learn different funding rules and develop skills to prepare and present bids. The task focus of the group was very different from an oppositional or campaigning focus, and left comparatively little space for exploration of personal interests or concerns. This may have limited the number and range of people wanting to be actively involved. Second, the group was one of many community organizations and partnerships competing for funding for regeneration projects. Whilst the health forum sought to work collaboratively with other initiatives, competitive funding processes produced a sense of uncertainty and some stress. Third, there was frequent reference to the barriers that appeared to be deliberately erected to frustrate progress, and to fears that public officials and elected members would arrive to claim the glory once the centre was opened.

Although the group remained community-led, the support of the PCG was recognized as essential to success. Official members of the forum were clear that they did not want to 'take over', but also acknowledged that they had access to knowledge which was valuable to the group, or could skew the group's deliberations, and that the creation of a new health centre might be achieved more quickly if this were done directly within the NHS. At the same time, there was frustration over the level of commitment being demonstrated by official partners and a degree of suspicion associated with this. From the PCG's perspective, there was no wish to define the membership of the forum, nor how they should go about their work. The decision to pay for a consultant to help prepare funding submissions demonstrated what they described as an 'arms length' approach to collaboration. The decision to support the forum to pursue their own HLC development was regarded as going beyond a historical commitment within the local health service to consult with the public. This decision was linked to an acknowledgement that a model that involved people as active participants in taking decisions about health services would be more likely to lead to health improvements. But there appeared to have been insufficient dialogue about the precise nature of the relationship between the PCG and the forum, resulting in the suspicion reported above.

Involving Young People in a Regeneration Initiative

The second case study was located in a different city, which had an ethnically diverse population. It took place in an area that was the subject of a regeneration project funded through the government's Single Regeneration Budget (SRB). It was a very deprived area and one in which the majority population was South Asian. The city council was Labour-controlled, but in this part of the city strong ethnic identities also affected the political landscape. The city council had recently instituted ward committees, which were intended to enable local people to become involved in planning and which controlled a small budget to support small-scale local projects.

A youth forum had been established by a young man who had an eight-year record of street work with youth. The forum was made up of Pakistani-Muslim young people – the dominant ethnic group in the area. All the officers and members of the forum were long-term residents of the area, and interviews indicated that they were motivated by a common concern to improve conditions for their own families and for others. One talked about worsening drug problems in the area: 'When I was sixteen/seventeen … I was 22 hours of the day out on the streets and parks and stuff and the only drug we ever heard of was cannabis; now there are so many drugs around.' The young men who established the forum saw it both as a route to getting young people involved in sport or leisure activities, getting them 'off the streets', and as an opportunity to represent their views and support young people to represent themselves. One member described the purpose as follows: 'basically: helping out, getting young people involved and giving them responsibilities, not only organizing trips but … when we do the *mela* [a Muslim festival] and that, we do stewards.'

The forum was supported by, but independent of, the local authority youth service. The youth service also ran a separate youth project. When the SRB project was set up, the youth service was given responsibility for securing young people's involvement. One way in which they sought to do this was by promoting a focus on young people's issues at the annual ward conference (part of the local authority's network of local involvement initiatives). Twelve members of the forum attended this event, as well as others from the youth project and from other local youth groups. It was decided that a further conference, dedicated solely to young people's issues, should be held later in the year, and that it should be organized by young people themselves, with the assistance of the youth service.

All youth organizations in the area were invited to join a planning group. Meetings were convened and chaired on local authority property by youth workers. On the instigation of the youth work manager, the meeting was divided into two: one section for the young people themselves, and another for workers, apart from those chairing the young people's meeting. An agenda for action was drawn up at the first meeting. The first part of this, produced primarily by young people, suggested various activities for the conference, as well as practical questions such as the date and venue. The second element concerned a drugs survey, proposed in the 'youth workers' group. The responsibility for this survey was to be split – on the strong suggestion of the district youth work manager. The youth workers would oversee the design, while the young people would advise on administration. It was planned that the presentation of findings should form a central feature of the Youth Conference. Subsequent meetings of the group focused on different aspects of this agenda, and sought to assign responsibility for organizing different elements to subgroups of young people. A sample questionnaire for the drugs survey was drawn up by the youth workers.

One of the youth workers involved in these meetings described their purpose as follows:

> we worked with young people to identify the areas of their concerns, and highlight them, and how we're going to deliver the conference. It was all part of a confidence-building process. Those meetings were about confidence processes for young people, to actually be part of a community, be active in it, but also give criticism, but it needs to be positive criticism...

Over the course of these meetings, friction between the forum and youth workers became increasingly evident. This focused on tension over the issue of recognition for the forum's contribution to the planning process. From the workers' perspective, this raised the question of the forum's dominance over conference arrangements among other youth groups in the area. Forum members were concerned that 'the youth workers wanted to take all the credit, but the young people said if we are not going to get the credit for it, why should we do it?' This perspective was exacerbated by forum members' perceptions that the workers were simply being paid to do a job: 'At the end of the day he's getting good pay to work here, and you know – basically he wants to show that he's actually doing something: they ARE doing the youth conference and we're some sidekick forum who are just going to help out.'

Matters came to a head at a planning meeting when forum members directly challenged workers over the perceived failure to recognize the forum's contribution on the letterhead of correspondence about the conference. There was no resolution of this and other areas of dissatisfaction, and the forum walked out. It was made clear to them that they were free to do this, and to continue organizing the conference themselves, and that the youth workers would provide support if requested.

It was clear that it was no longer possible for forum members and youth workers to work together. This was symbolized by the new venue for meetings that the forum had secured permission to use. It was also evidenced in a new spirit of enthusiasm, solidarity and purpose at the initial meetings of forum members to organize the conference after the split.

Yet this initial enthusiasm waned after the first couple of meetings, when it became clear that there was little funding available. The forum had written to a number of local banks and businesses, but at the time their meetings stopped had only secured £50 towards the conference. The educational institution that owned the premises where they met then claimed that it required the premises for classes and so the forum could no longer use it. There was an attempt to continue meetings in the local park, but this was dependent on the weather. The meetings that did take place seemed more to do with symbolically reaffirming the group's existence than debating issues or deciding on action:

> I mean we had something on, we went to the forum, or something and we met as a group. What did you do, oh, let's go and sort this out, use the telephone. It was nice and we had meetings as well in the evening. And all of us got together like a family.... Like what did you do, and we all got took seriously. And that's how it was, nice.

Members kept in touch by mobile phone, and through informal meetings. However, the first time that they all reassembled after having been deprived of their premises was at the second Ward Conference. Although that meeting took heed of their difficulties, when this study ended it remained to be seen whether they would secure alternative premises; what form the planning process for the Youth Conference would take; and what input the forum would have.

We can consider what happened in this case study in the light of issues relating to motivation, identity and the opportunities and constraints offered by the opportunity structure in which this took place. The forum had started off as a group of concerned local young people from the Pakistani community. Most had grown up together, although had not necessarily been friends before being involved in the forum. For example:

> I always wanted to get involved, but I didn't know where to go. I felt like there was no one ... I knew Mohammed then, but I didn't know he was into this.... And he was handing out leaflets and putting them in shop windows. And he goes 'You want to come to this?' ... So I went ... and then I thought, yeah, you know, Mohammed's someone who sees my way, you know. And then after that all the crew got together.

Membership and identity were key issues among the group convened to plan the conference and this became highly controversial. There was considerable pressure on groups in the area to establish themselves in order to receive funding. The forum felt that they were distinguished from other groups because they were run exclusively by young people who had grown up in the area. There was considerable resentment of groups run by youth workers who did not share this background, yet who were earning good wages, while the forum workers were all volunteers.

These factors seemed to lie behind the tensions in the original conference planning meetings. It was undoubtedly the case that the majority of young people attending these meetings were from the forum, and that they did put in a considerable amount of work. One forum member said:

> He wrote to the Sikh community, which didn't get involved; he wrote
> to the Hindu community, which didn't get involved. We had a drama
> group that attended the first or second meeting and that was it. We had
> a detached youth project, we had two youngsters from there and that
> was it.

However, their strong identity may have made others feel awkward
or even threatened. The sense that they were not receiving proper
recognition for their efforts seemed only to increase their attempts to
assert their presence and enhanced their oppositional consciousness.

There were also problems related to what was considered to be the
legitimate form of dialogue between young people and the officials
with whom they originally tried to work. Adults were very keen to
secure young people's views. However, the young people themselves
were reticent – partly from general shyness, and partly because they
had experiences of being let down in the past. Eventually they
would be coaxed into making some sort of statement of what they
wanted – for example, facilities for their local park, and a drugs
survey. These initial expressions would then be enthusiastically seized
on by the adults, without leaving space for the young people to
suggest other concerns, elaborate or prioritize. Speaking of the way
in which a 'wish list' had been generated at the original session at
the Ward Conference, one forum member described how this was
used subsequently by youth workers:

> And [a youth worker] was saying like, 'here's the list here', and I noticed
> he never said 'what do you want?' He only said, 'OK', for example, 'we'll
> have drugs', for example, and 'what would you want to do about drugs?'
> So he gave the main heading, and he let them do, you know what I
> mean? He's like a tree, and he's offering the branches.

While committed to the principle that young people should
have a say over policy, adults in these fora in practice constrained
their views. Another aspect of this concerned the deliberate attempt
on the part of youth workers to coach or train the young people
to put forward their views in an 'acceptable' manner. One forum
member described how he was perceived: 'I am just bringing out
the facts and they don't want to see the facts.... They think I am
a trouble-maker, that is how they portray me.' His perception was
confirmed by one of the youth workers, who said of him:

> when he's putting things across he's not seen as putting them across
> constructively. He needs to learn quite a lot. How to get people to do

things, how to get people to respond positively – he's not aware of these different politics.... I've worked damn hard with him to get him to the stage where he is now.... I'm trying to get him to understand that the best way to work around that is to always complement what other people are doing in the way.

The confrontational style adopted in meetings with council workers contrasted with the style of discussion between forum members following their split with the youth workers. This was more positive, with a focus on cooperation and constructive practical contributions, leavened with a considerable amount of 'in-humour'. Occasionally, joking threatened to get out of control, but this was always successfully checked by the chair or vice-chair, both of whom had considerable respect.

Dynamics and Tensions

In both case studies there was tension between collective action among community members with strong commitments to their area, and a genuine wish to act to improve local living circumstances, and official initiatives to open up spaces for public involvement and act to improve health and living conditions. But the ways in which these tensions were manifest were rather different.

In the context of the youth conference, the tensions focused around who were perceived to be legitimate members of the planning group, official perceptions of what constituted a 'representative' forum, and how the process of dialogue should be conducted. Two different sources of claims to act as legitimate representatives were evident: for members of the youth forum these claims were based in histories within and commitments to the area, whilst the youth workers were operating with a more formal notion of representativeness as requiring membership of the conference planning group to reflect the range of socio-cultural characteristics of young people in the area (Barnes et al. 2003). Youth workers were fulfilling what they saw as their responsibilities to their employers to deliver constructive input from young people, expressed in a way that would gain the support of officers and elected members in influential positions. In contrast, youth forum members saw the conference as an opportunity to 'tell it like it is' as they saw it – to achieve recognition not only for themselves but also for other young people. Their sense of justice incorporated both recognition and redistribution (Fraser 1997).

These tensions were exacerbated by the adult–young person power relations: youth workers felt it was their responsibility to train the young people and build their capacity, that without their guidance forum members might make foolish mistakes. This was at odds with the priorities of young people to achieve real change for their area, and their self-perception as competent individuals capable of taking responsibility and delivering change, provided they received the necessary resources. The experience of trying to work *with* local officials can be considered to have increased the oppositional consciousness among forum members. It highlights that citizens and officials may have different aspirations and priorities for participation and that they may not easily be reconciled. In this instance there was a tension between an official aspiration to create responsible citizens and the young people's aspirations for social justice.

In the case of the community health forum, the group retained its capacity to determine membership, but struggled to retain a *committed* membership once it moved from oppositional action to attempting to work in partnership with health organizations to secure funding for the Healthy Living Centre. The strong sense of a 'we' based in an oppositional consciousness became both more muted and diffuse at this stage. Dialogue tended to get bogged down in bureaucratic details and this constrained the potential for creativity as well as dampening the enthusiasm that had been generated by direct involvement in community-led research. Forum discussions demonstrated the considerable expertise of group members, but this was not prioritized in comparison with the tactical knowledge of how to put together a convincing funding bid. The necessity of retaining an effective working relationship with the PCG was recognized, but there was ambivalence among citizen participants in relation to this, as well as hostility about the role of local authority officers and members. For officials involved in the group, there were varying degrees of internal conflict about the position they should take and concerns about how to balance the contribution they could make through their expertise with a commitment to ensuring that the forum was genuinely community-led. They experienced tension between their identities as officials and as activists, or at least allies, of the public health movement.

Conclusion

These experiences suggest that it is hard to generate new policy discourses within invited spaces characterized by unequal power and in which official rules and norms predominate. They also suggest the importance of recognizing the difficulty of achieving the diverse and challenging aspirations which have been claimed for public participation – particularly when these may be implicit and un-negotiated. But they also demonstrate both the substantial commitment that exists among community members to act to improve collective well-being, and the goodwill among many public officials to enable participation in such projects. Hence such contested spaces contain significant potential as well as embodying substantial tensions.

From these and other experiences, it is possible to suggest what might be the conditions necessary to maximize such potential. First, officials need to develop skills for working with people who start from oppositional positions, and to work creatively with conflict rather than trying to deny it or close it down. This requires officials themselves to be supported and for such skills to be rewarded (Sullivan et al. 2005). Second, there needs to be space for affective as well as cognitive exchanges and for diverse forms of discourse to be valued. This can often be achieved through skilled facilitation (Barnes 2005), but may be 'squeezed out' in circumstances in which the imperative is to deliver in response to externally imposed agendas or criteria. Third, the rules of the game need to be negotiated and adhered to in order to ensure the development of reciprocal trust among officials and citizens. Barnes and Prior (1998) have suggested that this is easier to achieve when users and citizens have the opportunity to develop collective awareness than in circumstances in which people are encouraged to be competitive consumers. And, finally, autonomous organization or 'free spaces' (Groch 2001) are important to try out new ways of thinking and action, before engaging in dialogue with officials. Officials need to recognize the value of such spaces and offer support rather than control to enable them.

Notes

1. These cases are taken from a study carried out with Andrew Knops, Janet Newman and Helen Sullivan as part of the ESRC Democracy and Participation Programme, ref. no. L215252001. I acknowledge the work carried out in particular by Andrew Knops on the Youth Conference case study, and the cooperation of the project participants in making the research possible.

2. An initiative focused on children aged 0–5 and their families, intended to reduce the likelihood of social exclusion.

References

Barnes, M. (2005) 'Same old process? Older people, participation and delibera-tion', *Ageing and Society* 25(2): 245–59.

Barnes, M., and G. Bennett (1998) 'Frail bodies, courageous voices: older people and community care', *Health and Social Care in the Community* 6(2): 102–11.

Barnes, M., and R. Bowl (2001) *Taking over the Asylum: Empowerment and Mental Health*, London: Palgrave.

Barnes, M., and D. Prior (1998) 'Trust and the competence of the welfare con-sumer', in A. Coulson, ed., *Trust and Contracts,* Bristol: Policy Press.

Barnes, M., S. Harrison, M. Mort and P. Shardlow (1999) *Unequal Partners: User Groups and Community Care*, Bristol: Policy Press.

Barnes, M., J. Newman, A. Knops and H. Sullivan (2003) 'Constituting the public for public participation', *Public Administration* 81(2): 379–99.

Barnes, M., A. McCabe and E. Ross (2004a) 'Public participation in governance: the institutional context', in *Researching Civil Renewal: A Set of Scoping Papers Prepared for the Home Office Civil Renewal Unit*, Civil Renewal Research Centre, University of Birmingham.

Barnes, M., H. Sullivan, A. Knops and J. Newman (2004b) 'Power, participa-tion and political renewal: issues from a study of public participation in two English cities', in A. Cornwall and V.S. Coelho, *New Democratic Spaces*, *IDS Bulletin* 35(2): 58–66.

Barnes, M., J. Newman and H. Sullivan (forthcoming 2007) *Power, Participation and Political Renewal: Case Studies in Public Participation*, Bristol: Policy Press.

Bobbio, L. (2003) 'Building social capital through democratic deliberation: the rise of deliberative arenas', *Social Epistemology* 17(4): 343–57.

Diani, M., and D. McAdam, eds (2003) *Social Movements and Networks: Relational Approaches to Collective Action*, Oxford: Oxford University Press.

Fraser, N. (1997) *Justice Interruptus: Critical Reflections on the 'Postsocialist' Condition*, New York and London: Routledge.

Groch, S. (2001) 'Free spaces: creating oppositional consciousness in the dis-ability rights movement', in J. Mansbridge and A. Morris, eds, *Oppositional Consciousness: The Subjective Roots of Social Protest*, Chicago: University of Chicago Press.

Mansbridge, J. (2001) 'The making of oppositional consciousness', in J. Mans-bridge and A. Morris, eds, *Oppositional Consciousness: The Subjective Roots of Social Protest*, Chicago: University of Chicago Press.

Melucci, A. (1996) *Challenging Codes: Collective Action in the Information Age*, Cambridge: Cambridge University Press.

Sullivan, H., M. Barnes and E. Matka (2005) 'Building capacity for collaboration', in M. Barnes, L. Bauld, M. Benzeval, K. Judge, M. McKenzie and H. Sullivan, *Building Capacity for Health Equity*, London: Routledge.

Tarrow, S. (1994) *Power in Movement*, Cambridge: Cambridge University Press.

Young, I.M. (2000) *Inclusion and Democracy*, Oxford: Oxford University Press.

About the Contributors

Marian Barnes is Professor of Social Policy in the School of Applied Social Science, University of Brighton. She has researched user and carer movements, user involvement and public participation for over fifteen years and has published widely on this subject. She has also worked in a development capacity and carried out participatory research with user and carer groups. She led research on this area as part of the ESRC Democracy and Participation programme and was programme lead on the Participation and Citizenship research programme at the University of Birmingham. Contact: mb129@brighton.ac.uk

Graziela Castello is a Master's student in political science at the State University of Campinas (Unicamp), Brazil, and a research assistant at the Brazilian Centre of Analysis and Planning (CEBRAP) in São Paulo, Brazil. Her Masters' thesis is a study of the political construction of civil organizations in São Paulo. Contact: grazielacastello@yahoo.com.br.

Vera Schattan P. Coelho is a political scientist. She is a researcher and project coordinator at the Brazilian Center of Analysis and Planning (CEBRAP) in São Paulo, Brazil. Her interests centre on new forms of citizen participation, deliberation and consultation to improve social policies and democracy. She is the author of numerous articles on health policy, pension reform and participatory governance and is editor of *Pension Reform in Latin America* (FGV, 2003) and *Participation and Deliberation in Contemporary Brazil* (with Marcos Nobre, 34 Letras, 2004). Contact: vera@cebrap.org.br.

Andrea Cornwall is a social anthropologist. She is a Fellow at the Institute of Development Studies (IDS) at the University of Sussex, where her research interests include the politics of participation, sexuality and rights. She has published widely on participation and gender and is author of *Beneficiary, Consumer, Citizen: Perspectives on Participation for Poverty Reduction* (Sida, 2000) and co-editor of *Realizing Rights: Transforming Approaches to Sexual and Reproductive Wellbeing* (with Alice Welbourn, Zed, 2002). Contact: a.cornwall@ids.ac.uk.

Peter P. Houtzager is a Fellow at the Institute of Development Studies (IDS), University of Sussex. He is author of *Os Últimos Cidadãos: Conflito e Modernização no Brasil Rural (1964–1995)* (Editora Globo, 2004) and co-editor of *Changing Paths: International Development and the New Politics of Inclusion* (with Mick Moore, University of Michigan Press, 2003). Contact: p.houtzager@ids.ac.uk.

David Kahane is an Associate Professor of Philosophy at the University of Alberta. His research focuses on deliberative democratic theory and the inclusion of marginalized groups; and on questions of identity, privilege and obligation in the context of global injustice. Contact: david.kahane@ualberta.ca.

Adrián Gurza Lavalle is a Professor of Contemporary Political Theory at the Pontifical Catholic University São Paulo (PUC–SP), and researcher at the Brazilian Centre of Analysis and Planning (CEBRAP). He has published widely on political philosophy and cross-national studies on civil society. He is author of *Vida Pública e Identidade Nacional – Leituras Brasileiras* (Editora Globo, 2004), *Estado, Sociedad y Medios – Reivindicación de lo Público* (Plaza y Valdés/ UIA, 1998), and *La Reestructuración de lo Público – El Caso Conasupo.* (UNAM/ENEP-A, 1994). Contact: layda@usp.br.

Bettina von Lieres is a Senior Lecturer in the Political Studies Department at the University of the Western Cape in Cape Town, South Africa. She received her D.Phil. in the field of democratic theory from the University of Essex in 2002. She has written on issues of citizenship and participation in Africa. Her recent research is on the inclusion of marginalized groups in deliberative democratic spaces in Canada and South Africa. Contact: bvonlieres@sympatico.ca.

Simeen Mahmud studied Statistics at Dhaka University and Medical Demography at the London School of Hygiene and Tropical Medicine. She joined the Bangladesh Institute of Development Studies after completing her Master's and is currently Senior Research Fellow in the Population Studies Division. Her previous research has been on demographic estimation, the relationship between women's work, status and fertility, and demographic transition under poverty. Currently she is working on empowerment and development, citizenship and collective action, and social policy and exclusion. Contact: simeen@bids.sdnbd.org.

Ranjita Mohanty is a political sociologist and is Head of Research at the Society for Participatory Research in Asia (PRIA), New Delhi, India, where she runs the research and academic linkage programme. Her research covers various dimensions of collective action around natural resource management, peoples' movements as forms of resistance, mobilizing participation in state-created institutional spaces, interface and engagement between civil society and the state, citizenship issues of marginalized communities, and the complexities of participation and democratization. Contact: ranjita@pria.org.

Dennis Rodgers is Lecturer in Urban Development in the Department of Geography and Environment at the London School of Economics. He is a social anthropologist by training, and has conducted research in Nicaragua and Argentina, respectively on issues of urban violence and urban governance. In Argentina he focused specifically on local forms of post-crisis socio-political innovation, while in Nicaragua he underwent ritual initiation into a Nicaraguan youth gang, and lived in a poor slum for a year. His current research focuses comparatively on the urban transformations of late-nineteenth-century Paris and late-twentieth-century Managua. Contact: d.w.rodgers@lse.ac.uk.

Sandra Roque has worked in Angola, Mozambique and throughout Southern Africa. She is a senior consultant for *Austral Consultoria e Projectos*, a Mozambican company working on social and economic issues, and a member of the Angolan development NGO *Acção para o Desenvolvimento Rural e Ambiente* (ADRA). Her research has covered issues related to participation, development of local organizations and the relationship between state and society, in particular in urban areas.

She is currently working on a Ph.D. in social anthropology at the University of Cape Town on the integration of war-displaced people in Benguela, Angola. Contact: smroque@sortmoz.com.

Alex Shankland is a social scientist who has worked extensively in Brazil, Peru, Angola and Mozambique as a researcher, NGO manager and social development consultant. His research interests have centred on rights, participation and policy, particularly in the health sector. Formerly the Research Manager for the Development Research Centre on Citizenship, Participation and Accountability, he is currently engaged in fieldwork on the theme of representation and health policy in the Brazilian Amazon for a D.Phil. at the Institute of Development Studies, University of Sussex. Contact: a.shankland@ids.ac.uk.

John J. Williams is Chair of Research in the Faculty of Economic and Management Sciences at the University of the Western Cape, where he teaches in the School of Government. He has published widely on local economic development, geographical information systems, the World Bank, identity, human rights, culture, citizenship, epistemology, research methodology, community participation and social movements. His current research interests include social change, democratic governance, public policy analysis and development planning in local government. Contact: jjwilliams@uwc.ac.za.

Index